Contested Community

Contested Community

Indigenous Land Rights and Identity Politics in Eastern Bolivia

Veronika Groke

LEXINGTON BOOKS
Lanham • Boulder • New York • London

Published by Lexington Books
An imprint of The Rowman & Littlefield Publishing Group, Inc.
4501 Forbes Boulevard, Suite 200, Lanham, Maryland 20706
www.rowman.com

6 Tinworth Street, London SE11 5AL, United Kingdom

ISBN 9781793613738 (cloth)
ISBN 9781793613752 (pbk)

British Library Cataloguing in Publication Information Available

Library of Congress Cataloging-in-Publication Data

Library of Congress Control Number: 2020952130

To my mother, Ilse Groke.
In loving memory of my father, Karl Groke.

Contents

Contents

Acknowledgments

This book is the result of two years of ethnographic fieldwork carried out in the Guaraní community of Cañón de Segura and the nearby town of Camiri (both Bolivia) between 2006 and 2008. It is based on my PhD thesis, defended at the University of St. Andrews in 2012. Although many more people have—in one way or another—contributed to the completion of this book and I am thankful to them all, there are some to whom I am particularly indebted.

In St. Andrews, they include those members of staff and fellow postgraduates who, over the years, commented on project and chapter drafts in the PhD writing-up seminars. I am particularly grateful to Tristan Platt, Christina Toren, Adam Reed, Huon Wardle, Eileadh Swan, Giovanna Bacchiddu, Chris Hewlett, Juan Pablo Sarmiento Barletti, Phil Kao, Anthony Pickles, Moisés Lino e Silva, Máire Ní Mhórdha, Jan Grill, Jeanne Féaux de la Croix, Daniela Castellanos, Eleni Bizas, Ioannis Kallianos, Rosie Harrison, Fiona Hukula, Hsin-Chieh Kao, Giuseppe Ciancia, Nádia Heusi, Nina Holm Vohnsen, Qing Qing Yang, Huw Lloyd-Richards, Alexander McWhinnie, Cornelia Nell, Linda Scott, Conrad Feather, Jonathan Alderman, and Stacy Hope for sharing writings and insights, and for creating a feeling of community that made engaging in academic exchanges a pleasure. I would also like to thank Mark Harris, Rodrigo Villagra Carrón, Margherita Margiotti, Paolo Fortis, and Effie Pollatou for the advice and many encouraging words that made me feel that, just perhaps, it could really all be done.

A very special thank-you to Giovanna Bacchiddu, Chris Hewlett, Phil Kao, and Eileadh Swan for providing support of a nonacademic kind when it was much needed. The same goes for Linda Scott, Susan Massey, Kate Pattullo, Ann Slim, Joseph Tendler, 'Fluffy' John Dempsey, Martyna Mirecka, Zinaida Lewczuk, and Stan Frankland—I would have never made it without you all. Mhairi Aitkenhead, Lisa Neilson, and, temporarily, Lynne

Dalrymple, deserve a special mention for their administrative ingenuity and undefeated good-naturedness in running the anthropology department as efficiently as they did. They, along with Margaret Hutcheson, were a cheerful and down-to-earth presence emanating sanity in the midst of writing-up madness. I am grateful to Peter Gow for his suggestions and ever-present goodwill, and to Joanna Overing for being a constant source of inspiration and a wonderful friend. Thank you also to Napier Russell for brightening up many a dull evening with his humour and loveable dodginess!

In Bolivia, I am indebted to Isabelle Combès for taking me under her wing when I first arrived in Santa Cruz with very little Spanish and even less of an idea of how to get started, and for being a benevolent presence throughout the duration of my fieldwork. Thank you also to Chiaki Kinjo for the language exchange and initial encounters with the world of indigenous organisations. In Camiri, I would like to thank Doña Pocha, Cornelio Robles, Elio Ortiz, and Marcia Mandepora at Teko-Guaraní; at the Capitanía Kaami, Ramón Gómez, Marina Arroyo, Ernesto Arteaga, Josefina Segundo, Víctor Rodríguez, and the rest of the Kaami leadership, as well as Víctor Victoria and Elizabeth Arteaga; at the APG, Doña Nancy, Wilson Changaray, and Petrona Bruno; at the GTZ, Ángela Caballero and Marta Pello; and at CIPCA, Miguel Valdez and Nestor Cuellar for their support during my fieldwork. I am further indebted to the late Franz Michel of IDAC for granting me access to his organisation's archive, and for the many informative conversations we had in his office. Further, I am thankful to Chiny Mejía, Polaco Herrera, and their family (in particular their daughter, Mimi) for welcoming me into their home and into their lives during part of my fieldwork—life in Camiri wouldn't have been the same without you! I would also like to thank the Heredia Cruz family, as well as Claudia Saavedra and her family, Heydi Maldonado, and Don Pepe for their great kindness and friendship. Wakana Fukuda and Carol Martinez shared thoughts, gossip, and tea and provided an invaluable moral support base. In Isoso, a very special thank-you goes to my language teacher and guide Justino Arauz, as well as to Isabel Ortiz and their respective families, thanks to whom I got a fascinating glimpse of Isoso life and politics.

Of the fellow researchers I met along the way, I am particularly grateful to Kathleen Lowrey for sharing insights on Guaraní ethnography; to Sebastián Pardo for always pushing me to do better, and for sharing some of the magic of Argentina with me; to Isabelle Daillant, Vincent Hirtzel, and Mickaël Brohan for generously sharing information and knowledge; to the participants of the Primeiro Encontro Trilateral St. Andrews—Lisbon—Rio de Janeiro 2009, in particular Susana Matos Viegas, for their comments on an early chapter draft; to the guest speakers and staff and PhD students from St. Andrews, Aberdeen, and Edinburgh for the talks and academic and social exchanges during the STAR workshops in Kinloch Rannoch of 2009 and 2010; to the St. Andrews staff and students who commented on various papers during seminars and workshops; and, above all, to Bret Gustafson for providing advice and encouragement from my prefieldwork days onwards. To Bret as well as Mark Harris, thank you also for the interesting and useful feedback on the thesis given during my viva examination.

A very special thank you to my PhD supervisor, Tristan Platt, for sharing his vast knowledge with me and for the untiring support and kindness through difficult times. Being able to work with you has been a true privilege.

Revision of the thesis into its current form was initially made possible by a Leach-RAI postdoctoral research fellowship at Brunel University London (2015–2016). My sincere thanks to my wonderful colleagues from that time: Will Rollason, Peggy Froerer, Liana Chua, Eric Hirsch, Nicolas Argenti, Andrew Beatty, Maria Kastrinou, and especially my mentor, James Staples, for their friendship and their help in rethinking and improving my material. The fellowship also helped finance a translation of the thesis into Spanish for the *comunarios* of Cañón, expertly executed by Juan Rivera, and a follow-up visit to the fieldwork community in 2016. A special mention is due to David and Will Rollason for their invaluable help with the index and maps, respectively. Map 1 is based on map data from © OpenStreetMap contributors, available under the Open Database Licence (see www.openstreetmap.org/copyright). Map 2 is based on a hand drawing of Cañón de Segura by the *comunarios*.

I am indebted to the anonymous reviewers who commented on (and took to pieces) earlier drafts of some of the chapters as well as the finished manuscript. At Lexington Books, I am grateful to Kasey Beduhn for her patience and support throughout the publishing process.

My biggest debt by far—and one I am painfully aware I will likely never be able to repay—is to the people of Cañón de Segura, without whose incredible generosity, goodwill, and patience in the light of my initial cluelessness and enduring inquisitiveness this book would never have been written. My eternal gratitude goes out to them all, but a special mention is due to Ramón Gómez, Tomasa Bruno and their children Gloria, María Teresa, Daniel, and Reynaldo; Flora Bruno; Arsenio Bruno; Dionysia Gómez and her daughter Eusebia; Mariano Alvis; Marcelino Robles; and Francisco Álvarez. Thank you for sharing your knowledge of the beautiful Guaraní culture with me, as well as food, chicha, and a lot of laughter!

Finally, a big, huge thank-you to my mother, Ilse Groke, for supporting me throughout my studies, and for always being there for me and believing in me even when I did not. I am also immensely grateful to Lynda and David Rollason for their great kindness in taking care of my baby (and really us all) so I could finish writing my thesis. It couldn't have been done without any of you!

And last but not least, thank you, Will Rollason, for the invaluable suggestions and criticisms on many, many drafts of various chapters, the unfaltering moral support, and, more than anything, for adding a whole new dimension to my life that can only be described as 'happiness.' All my love to you and our two beautiful children—you are the sunshine in my life!

Acronyms and Abbreviations

ADN   *Acción Democrática Nacionalista* (Nationalist Democratic Action)

AGACAM   *Asociación de Ganaderos de Camiri* (Camiri Cattle Breeders' Association)

APCOB   *Apoyo Para el Campesino-Indígena del Oriente Boliviano* (Support for the Indigenous Peasant of the Bolivian East)

APDHC   *Asamblea Permanente de Derechos Humanos Cordillera* (Permanent Assembly of Human Rights of Cordillera)

APG   *Asamblea del Pueblo Guaraní* (Assembly of the Guaraní People)

CABI   *Capitanía del Alto y Bajo Isoso* (Capitanía of the Upper and Lower Isoso)

CD   Community Development

CIDH   *Comisión Interamericana de Derechos Humanos* (Interamerican Commission on Human Rights)

CIDOB   *Confederación de Pueblos Indígenas de Bolivia* (Confederation of Indigenous Peoples of Bolivia; formerly *Confederación de Pueblos Indígenas del Oriente Boliviano*)

CIPCA   *Centro de Investigación y Promoción del Campesinado* (Centre for the Investigation and Promotion of the Peasantry)

CNRA   *Consejo Nacional de Reforma Agraria* (National Council of the Agrarian Reform)

CONFEAGRO   *Confederación de Agropecuarios de Bolivia* (Bolivian Agriculturalists' Confederation)

CORDECRUZ   *Corporación de Desarrollo de Santa Cruz* (Santa Cruz Development Corporation)

CPE	*Constitución Política del Estado* (Political Constitution of the State)
CRE	*Cooperativa Rural de Electrificación* (Rural Electricity Cooperative)
DED	*Deutscher Entwicklungsdienst* (German Development Service)
DMI	*Distritos Municipales Indígenas* (Indigenous Municipal Districts)
EIB	*Educación Intercultural Bilingüe* (Intercultural Bilingual Education)
FIS	*Fondo de Inversión Social* (Social Investment Fund)
GDT	*Grupo de Trabajo* (Work Group)
GO	Governmental Organisation
GTZ	*Gesellschaft für Technische Zusammenarbeit* (Society for Technical Cooperation)
IDAC	*Instituto de Documentación y Apoyo al Campesinado* (Institute for the Documentation and Support of the Peasantry)
IDH	*Impuestos Directos a los Hidrocarburos* (Direct Hydrocarbons Tax)
ILO	International Labour Organisation
INC	*Instituto Nacional de Colonización* (National Institute for Colonisation)
INRA	*Instituto Nacional de Reforma Agraria* (National Institute of Agrarian Reform)
INSPOC	*Instituto Normalista Superior Pluriétnico del Oriente y Chaco* (Pluriethnic Superior Teacher's Institute of the *Oriente* and Chaco)
LDA	*Ley de Descentralización Administrativa* (Administrative Decentralisation Law)
LPP	*Ley de Participación Popular* (Popular Participation Law)
MAS	*Movimiento al Socialismo* (Movement toward Socialism)
MASRENA	*Proyecto de Manejo Sostenible de Recursos Naturales* (Project for Sustainable Management of Natural Resources)
MNR	*Movimento Nacionalista Revolucionario* (Revolutionary Nationalist Movement)
NGO	Non-fovernmental Organisation
OTB	*Organizaciones Territoriales de Base* (Territorial Grassroots Organisations)

PADEP	*Programa de Apoyo a la Gestión Pública Descentralizada y Lucha Contra La Pobreza* (Programme for the Support of Decentralised Governance and the Fight against Poverty)
PDA	*Programa de Desarrollo de Área* (Areal Development Programme)
PDCC	*Plan de Desarrollo del Campesinado de Cordillera* (Development Plan for the Peasantry of Cordillera)
PISET	*Producción, Infraestructura, Salud, Educación y Tierra/Territorio* (Production, Infrastructure, Health, Education and Land/Territory)
PISETRNGC	*Producción, Infraestructura, Salud, Educación, Tierra/Territorio, Recursos Naturales, Género y Comunicación* (Production, Infrastructure, Health, Education, Land/Territory, Natural Resources, Gender and Communication)
PND	*Plan Nacional de Desarrollo* (National Development Plan)
PODEMOS	*Poder Democrático Social* (Social Democratic Power)
SAN–TCO	*Saneamiento de Tierras Comunitarias de Origen* (Titling of Original Community Lands)
TCO	*Tierra Comunitaria de Origen* (Original Community Land)
Teko-Guaraní	*Taller de Educación y Comunicación Guaraní* (Guaraní Education and Communication Workshop)
TIOC	*Territorio Indígena Originario Campesino* (Indigenous Originary Peasant Territory)
UJC	*Unión Juvenil Cruceñista* (Santa Cruz Youth Union)
VAIPO	*Viceministerio de Asuntos Indígenas y Pueblos Originarios* (Viceministry for Indigenous Affairs and Originary Peoples)
YPFB	*Yacimientos Petrolíferos Bolivianos* (Bolivian Oil Company)

Introduction

When I left for Bolivia in June 2006, I had no very clear idea of where I was going to do my fieldwork. What I did know was that I wanted to work with Guaraní people, and that I didn't want to do my research in the *capitanías* of Isoso, an area that had been attracting anthropologists for a long time and was relatively well researched (e.g., Combès 2005a; Lowrey 2003; Riester 1984). Instead, my plan was to go to the Chaco region, where recent ethnographies on Guaraní people had been relatively scarce.

I arrived in Camiri, ungenerously described by my *Rough Guide* as a 'grim and functional oil producing town' (Read 2002: 311) in Cordillera Province of the Department of Santa Cruz in the southeastern lowlands of Bolivia, on a hot and dusty afternoon in July of 2006. At the time, all I had to go on was a couple of addresses and phone numbers a fellow anthropologist living in Santa Cruz had given me, some basic Spanish, and a lot of enthusiasm. Unimpressed with the town itself, which, on a first impression, didn't seem very interesting to me, I got myself a room in a hotel and started looking around in search of contacts that might prove useful.

I managed to locate the contacts provided by my friend, one of whom turned out to be an elderly gentleman with a white moustache running what was basically a one-man NGO in support of the local Guaraní population. His name was Franz Michel, and he seemed pleased to meet me and spent long afternoons chatting with me about Europe and Guaraní-related things. He also very kindly gave me access to the archival library he had put together in the office building of his organisation, the Institute for the Documentation and Support of the Peasantry (IDAC).[1] Asked about who might be able to help me in my endeavor to get access to a community, he suggested I approach the Assembly of the Guaraní People (APG), the Guaraní's political organisation about which I had already read a lot back in the UK. Alternatively, he said,

1

Camiri central market, August 2008.
Photo by the author.

I could ask at Teko Guaraní,[2] an NGO that also went out to the communities
a lot.

With Teko, an NGO dedicated to bringing education to the *comunidades*,
it was clear from the start that they wouldn't be able to help me in finding a
field site, but at least they pointed me toward a Guaraní language class that
was being held at the head office of the indigenous district, the Capitanía
Kaami. What followed were several months in which I spent a lot of time
hanging around the APG office, waiting for people who invariably either
turned out to have gone on a trip somewhere else ('*Ha viajado*' was a phrase
I heard a lot from the very friendly APG secretary) and would only be back
the following week, or who were busy in meetings and couldn't see me until
the next day—when I would come back only to be told that they had gone
away on a trip. When I did manage to talk to the people I was after, the result
was usually that, after introducing myself and my intended project (which at
the time I saw as dealing with different aspects of 'land' in the lives of *comunarios*), I was received with enthusiasm and told that I would certainly be
able to work in a community, and that the APG would support me as much
as they could. Only once, however, did I manage to pin someone down on
something more concrete: a trip to a *comunidad* further to the south, on which

the then-APG land officer promised he would take me. 'We'll let you know,' he said, but when I came back to the office sometime later to enquire about the trip, I was told that they had already gone.

Meanwhile, I spent the rest of my time studying Guaraní, reading old development reports in Franz Michel's office, and immersing myself in Camiri social life. One evening, when I was at a pub with some friends, I ended up sitting opposite a woman named Kati, to whom I started talking on account of her Germanic-sounding name. Having discovered that she had in fact spent some time in Germany years ago, we soon had a nice conversation going, in the course of which I bemoaned the fact that I hadn't been able to get anywhere in my dealings with the APG so far, which I had hoped would help me gain access to a community in which to carry out my fieldwork.

'Have you tried CIPCA?' Kati asked.

I told her that I had not.

'But you must go to CIPCA!' she insisted. 'They always go out to the *comunidades*; I used to work for them myself a while ago, and I'm telling you, they'll be able to help you.'

CIPCA, the Centre for Research and Promotion of the Peasantry,[3] is one of the largest and most influential NGOs in Bolivia. It was founded in 1970 by three Jesuits (Luís Alegre, Francisco Javier Santiago, and Xavier Albó, today one of the best-known Bolivian anthropologists), with the aim to promote peasants' and indigenous people's political, economic, and cultural positions, and has since then initiated countless projects and produced a significant body of literature relating to the various concerns of Bolivia's indigenous and peasant populations (see Gianotten 2006). While CIPCA's main office is located in La Paz, there are also branches in Camiri and Charagua, whose employees mainly work with the local Guaraní communities.

Having been too focused on the APG to consider looking for alternative options, it hadn't occurred to me to look them up. When I finally went to the Camiri office, I was told that I needed to talk to Marcelo Núñez,[4] who—miraculously—even was in his office and agreed to see me. Told about my research plans, he said it shouldn't be a problem to find a *comunidad* that was willing to take me in. He invited me on a trip to Charagua, a town close to Isoso some four hours' drive from Camiri, where some Guaraní leaders were having a meeting. The aim of the meeting, Don Marcelo said, was to induce the communal leaders of the Charagua Norte region to establish new *comunidades*, as they had recently been granted a large area of land, which they now needed to take possession of if they didn't want to forfeit their right to it. I happily agreed, and the next morning around 4 a.m. we embarked on the hot and dusty journey to Charagua in Marcelo's 1974 Toyota jeep, an adventurous vehicle largely powered by bottled gas.

After listening to Don Marcelo hold fiery speeches aimed at propelling the *capitanes* into action for most of the day, we had a quiet chat in the patio of the hotel where we were staying. Not only did Don Marcelo say that he would help me in getting access to a community, but he even had some specific suggestions. The *comunidades* he had in mind were Barracas, a 'captive community' (*comunidad cautiva*) in Alto Parapetí, and a *comunidad* close to Camiri called Cañón de Segura, which he said was a new *comunidad* only some ten years old. This latter one was located a short way outside of Camiri, and would thus make for a good place to start with, as it would be easily accessible and I would be able to go into town a lot more easily than from Barracas, which was more remote, and where access was therefore more problematic.

Things then moved very quickly: a few days after coming back to Camiri, I had permission from both the *capitán grande* of Kaami (who turned out to be a friend of Marcelo's) and the local *capitán* to conduct fieldwork in Cañón de Segura, and another week or so later I was happily established in my new home-for-a-while, a small but well-built adobe building just above the school compound that housed the community's medical supplies, and to which the *comunarios* referred as '*la posta*.'[5] Thus, the *posta* became my base for the time from December 2006 until August 2008.

The school compound with the shrine of the Virgen de Copacabana and the *posta* in the background (2006).
Photo by the author.

At the time of my fieldwork, Cañón de Segura was a small community of roughly 250 inhabitants (*comunarios*) distributed over some thirty houses, who mostly made a living from agriculture, although many families also kept animals, and people sometimes engaged in temporary labour outside the community. As the name implies, Cañón is situated in a canyon and is surrounded and permeated by the low, dry forest typical of the region, with a rainy season causing the landscape to burst into lush, green life between the months of November and January (which is when the sowing of crops takes place). Most of the *comunarios* were bilingual in Guaraní and Spanish, with almost monolingual individuals forming the exception.[6]

As could perhaps be expected, I went to Cañón harbouring various assumptions that had to be questioned, if not entirely discarded, at later points in time. When I had learned that Cañón was a 'new *comunidad*' whose foundation dated back only as far as the 1990s, the image that had automatically formed in my mind was that of a newly formed group of people, perhaps of migrants from different areas, who had got together to found a community on a piece of previously uninhabited land; a place without history, so to speak, or where 'history' had only recently begun, and the practice of life was therefore rooted only in a generalised notion of Guaraní culture shallow enough to be shared by everyone. Even though I was grateful to have finally found a place to do my fieldwork, and even though I kept asserting to those people in Camiri who would criticise me for not having gone for a more 'traditionally authentic' place such as Tëtayapɨ in Tarija Province that I was not interested in chasing authenticity as such,[7] but rather in finding out what people's lived realities were actually like, part of me was secretly disappointed. I felt like I was being presented with something that only vaguely resembled what I had really come for, that is, a 'proper' Guaraní *comunidad*, as if a new formation of the kind I was imagining would somehow be less 'real.'[8] In other words, I was neatly reproducing what Gupta and Ferguson have referred to as the '*hierarchy of purity of fieldsites*': 'All ethnographic research is . . . done "in the field," but some "fields" are more equal than others—specifically, those that are understood to be distant, exotic, and strange' (1997: 13).

My assumptions, however, turned out to be wrong, and my fears unfounded. Besides the fact that the kind of place I was envisioning would have been just as interesting, complex, and deserving of attention as any more supposedly 'authentic' one, the situation in Cañón was very different from what I had thought it would be. I soon found out that the *comunidad*'s newness to which Don Marcelo had referred consisted in its location rather than the makeup of the group of people who inhabited it, who had previously lived on the property of one of the big private landholders of the area. This situation, in Bolivia known as '*cautiverio*' ('captivity'), had remained little changed over various generations before a conflict broke out between *comunarios* and landowners that eventually resulted in the move to the *comunidad*'s current location in Cañón de Segura in 1994. It thus became clear that, rather than lacking its own history, Cañón had rather a lot of it, and not only that, it even turned out to be of great local importance.

Partly, this was due to the fact that in acquiring a piece of land and the legal title proving their ownership of it, the people of Cañón had officially entered into the status of '*comunarios*,' of inhabitants of a formally recognised *comunidad indígena*, rather than being the peons-by-default of a family that happened to have inherited the land on which their original home was located, and whose legal position was as a result precariously vague. Going back to my initial misgivings about Cañón, we can see that what I had thought of as the determining elements of a *comunidad* and what the law specified as such were two different things: whereas I had—perhaps by thinking about the *comunidades* in terms of the English 'community'—assumed that what was constitutive of a 'proper' *comunidad* as I imagined it was its people, the law specified the land title as the primary thing. In other words, I had not only been wrong about what Cañón was going to be like, but I had also started from the wrong premise altogether when I had taken the concept of '*comunidad*' for granted. By this, I am not suggesting that I was wrong and the law was correct; but rather, that it is worth examining the meaning of '*comunidad*' a little closer: if I had different assumptions about what a *comunidad* was than the Bolivian state did, what other interpretations were there? And what, indeed, was it the *comunarios* themselves thought? And what were the relationships, or even conflicts, that ensued as results of these different interpretations?

WHERE EVERYONE IS COMING FROM

Since anthropologists' takes on the role of history in anthropological writing can be very varied, it is necessary to situate this text within a wider context of discursive practices in order to clarify the role which I see history as playing in this book. This is particularly important in the case of Bolivia's Guaraní people, whose own situation keeps being impacted by the way they are—either through discourses of their own, or through those of outsiders—constructed as historical subjects in different ways (see chapters 1 and 2). In the early twenty-first century, with the advent of a new indigenist politics in Bolivia, the question of 'origins' became one of particular weight, as people started to appeal to the idea of 'originary peoples' (*pueblos originarios*) in order to claim certain rights for themselves (or, indeed, deny them to others;

see chapters 6 and 7). This section outlines the problem of 'origin' as it appears in the literature on Guaraní history and culture, and clarifies my own stance on the role of history within the context of this book.

At the time of the 2012 census, there were some 97,000 self-identifying Guaraní people in Bolivia (INE 2015), comprising three cultural-linguistic subgroups: the Ava (the most numerous), most of whom live in Cordillera Province; the Simba (formerly Tembeta), who live in the Department of Chuquisaca and are regarded as the most 'traditional'; and the Isoseño, situated in the Bajo Parapetí. All of them speak the same Guaraní language, but with slight variations between them (Combès 2005a: 20). Bolivia's Guaraní people (in the literature widely referred to as 'Chiriguano') are said to be the descendants of Guaraní migrants (and, according to some theories, a local Chané population; see discussion below), which has caused scholars to attempt to trace the migrants' origins by way of linguistic as well as archaeological studies. There is some consensus that their ancestors came from the Brazilian coastal region around Santa Catalina and subsequently mixed with Guaraní people from Paraguay (Gutiérrez 1965: 11–12; Dietrich 1986: 194–95). Some scholars favour a relatively recent date for these migrations, around the same time as the arrival of the Spanish conquerors (Nordenskiöld 1917; Métraux 1930) or even later, when migrations may have been sparked by their presence (Combès 2005a: 69). Others believe in a series of migrations starting from as early as the thirteenth or fourteenth centuries (Renard-Cassevitz, Saignes, and Taylor-Descola 1986; Combès 2005a; Melià 1988; Alconini 2002).[9] On the other hand, Xavier Albó lists several cases of small-scale Guaraní migrations taking place within Bolivia as late as the 1980s (Albó 1990: 38–43).

Concerning the reasons for these migrations, one hypothesis refers to the slash-and-burn agriculture that was traditionally practiced by Guaraní peoples, and which relied on expansion into new territories in order to relieve population pressures and saturation of cultivated soils (Melià 1988: 19). According to sixteenth-century Spanish records, on the other hand, their motivation was the search for precious metals for adornments and trade (Melià 1988: 21). The Guaraní tales of a land rich in metals lying to the west, in the documents sometimes referred to as 'Kandire,' has most famously been interpreted by Hélène Clastres in terms of the Brazilian Tupí-Guaraní myth of a 'Land without Evil' (see chapter 2), where humans can attain immortality 'without going through the ordeal of death' (H. Clastres 1995: 76). The idea that its pursuit also played an important role in the Guaraní migrations toward the Cordillera used to be widely accepted (cf. Pifarré 1989; Combès and Saignes 1991), but has more recently been challenged (Julien 2007).

According to Pierre Clastres (1977), the impetus for these often extensive migrations led by powerful shamans was the fact that Tupí-Guaraní society was undergoing changes toward the end of the fifteenth century that threatened to replace their egalitarian social structure with a system of centralised power reminiscent of the state. However, given that there were several Guaraní migrations toward the Cordillera over a long period, it seems unlikely that there can be a single explanation for these phenomena (Melià 1988; Combès 2005a). More contemporary migrations could, for example, be triggered by factors such as pressure exerted by *patrones* and other power groups (Healy 1982), unwelcome state attempts at integration of the region, or confusion caused by diverse agendas of different NGOs active in the same area (Albó 1990: 46–52; Lucero 2008: 67).

Apart from giving rise to different theories about origins and migration routes, the uncertain provenance of Bolivia's Guaraní population has also divided scholars on the question of their ancestry. The established position is today most famously advocated by Isabelle Combès, one of the leading experts on Bolivian Guaraní history. Combès and her followers maintain that Bolivia's Guaraní, to whom they refer as 'Chiriguano' in order to distinguish them from other Guaraní groups who do not share the same historical background, are a mestizo people that was formed from the synthesis of the Guaraní migrants with the local Chané, an Arawak group already settled in the Cordillera that was subdued by the newcomers (Combès and Saignes 1991; Renard-Cassevitz, Saignes, and Taylor-Descola 1986; Melià 1988). According to Combès and Saignes (1991: 53–54), Chiriguana, the spelling that appears in most early records, is the autodenomination adopted by the Guaraní migrants (Chiriones), who mixed with the Chané (Guana) and thus became mestizos with a distinct ethnic identity.

Combès's mission in pursuing the mestizo theory is the promotion of good scholarship. However, as she herself tells us, there is no mention of a mestizaje between Guaraní and Chané in Isoseño oral history (Combès 2005a: 75), and this idea is in fact outright rejected by many Guaraní people. More generally, Guaraní people also reject the name 'Chiriguano,' which carries derogatory connotations, as according to the most popular theory regarding its etymology, 'Chiriguano' is derived from the Quechua words for 'cold excrement' (Combès and Saignes 1991: 51–52). While it is not my intention to contradict Combès, who bases her theories on the careful study of primary historical sources and ethnographic materials, I concur with scholars like Bret Gustafson (2009: xix) that the use of a colonially derived ethnonym that is widely regarded as pejorative and therefore rejected by the people to whom it refers is unnecessary and problematic when talking about contemporary Guaraní people. I am here therefore using the term 'Chiriguano' only in instances where it appears in quoted texts; in all other cases, I am—in accordance with their own usage—referring to the people at the centre of this study (as well as their ancestors) as 'Guaraní.'

Rather than tracing particular features of Guaraní culture or society back through the centuries, this book provides a snapshot of a particular place at a particular time and the way it is embedded within a larger geographical and historical context. Accordingly, the following chapter presents a brief historical overview that is, due to the constraints of this study, selective rather than exhaustive. Its intention is to provide a narrative through which the themes and events described in the main part of the book can be situated within a wider context within Guaraní and Bolivian history. By this, I am not suggesting that every present-day situation can be seen as having been brought about by a particular and bounded number of events in the past, leading up to the present in neat succession. On the contrary: rather than the present being the logical outcome of a series of past phenomena, it is the needs of the present that impose their logic on the events of the past. As Marshall Sahlins (1985) reminded us, the recounting of historic events is never disinterested, in that what it presents as 'factual' already depends on the socially and historically shaped perspectives of those involved in the events and/or those recounting them (and, perhaps, an interaction between the two). This is a particularly good point to keep in mind when writing about Bolivia, whose history is not only convoluted and complex, but also particularly hard to grasp due to the abundance of ethnic groups, social classes, and political formations and the continuously shifting relations among them, which afford a diversity of different historical perspectives.

THE EVENT

On 12 December 2006, recently after I had arrived in Cañón de Segura for the first time, an event took place in the *comunidad* which not only marked the beginning of my own engagement with Cañón and its people, but, retrospectively, also provides a fitting point of departure for the present discussion. I will start by relating the event in full and then move on to drawing out the themes I am discussing in the course of this book.

In a couple of fleeting first encounters with some *comunarios*, I had been told two different versions of what the event was about: the *capitán's* wife had said that it was a literacy (Sp.: *alfabetización*) event, and the *capitán grande* of the indigenous district of Kaami in which Cañón was located that it had to do with the *comunidad* having acquired a new bull for their cattle project. It was to be held in the school, the centre of 'official' life in Cañón, at either 8:00 or 9:00 a.m. (this, too, my sources had disagreed on). When I went down to the school-yard in the morning of the indicated day, there were a few groups of people already assembled in front of the buildings. As I came down, Don Rogelio, the *comunidad*'s Education Officer,[10] approached me, radiating enthusiasm. He told me that the event was a celebration of the fact that Cañón de Segura was the only Guaraní community that had achieved full literacy of its inhabit-ants. He seemed proud of that fact, which he repeated several times. He said the vice-president of the literacy campaign was going to come from Camiri, as was the mayor, and the event was probably going to start around 10:00 a.m.

Having more time than I had assumed, I chatted with Rogelio a bit longer. He told me about the school and how it had been built little by little, with funding from different bodies (one, FIS, which he said was foreign,[11] the mu-nicipality, and the *comunidad*, which had contributed manual labour). They had started with the central building, which was also the simplest, basically four low walls and a roof with desks and a blackboard inside. There were five more buildings surrounding it by then, three of which were equipped with so-lar panels. One of those powered a TV and video, which, I was told, was used to show educational videos to the children. There were five to six teachers, all of whom came from Camiri to teach, except for one who stayed in one of the buildings in the schoolyard, but Rogelio said the *comunidad* was training some teachers of its own. Teaching was done bilingually, with the first couple of years or so purely in Guaraní.[12]

Rogelio asked about my house, and I praised it, expressing my surprise at finding that it had running water. Rogelio said that the water supply was quite recent, maybe five years old, and that before they had got it they had had to go quite far to fetch water at 4:00 a.m. in the morning, because later in the day there would already be cows occupying and muddying up the water hole, which belonged to private landowners (*patrones*).

Before me, there had been a nurse living in my house, but she had been ordered elsewhere by the municipality because the *comunidad* was deemed too small to merit a nurse of its own. I asked how the current system was working for them, with the nurse only coming in about once a month. He replied that it was far from ideal, because if there were any emergencies, or someone needed something in the middle of the night, there was no one to attend to them. While Rogelio and some others had learned about the most basic medicines, any more serious cases had to be referred to the hospital in Camiri. He said they were hoping to have a doctor or nurse from among their own people one day.

After talking with Rogelio, I sat with the women for a bit, who were busy preparing barbecued meat (*asado*) on a large grill behind the communal kitchen. Rogelio then came back to fetch me so I could join the children in the building next door, where they were watching a video. The video showed how the Guaraní used to be maltreated by the *patrones*, who only gave them coca instead of food and made them work all day and live in appalling conditions. It included a lot of shots of men ploughing the earth with picks, speaking about the people's desire to work their own land for themselves. Rogelio told me that the video was about a *comunidad* in the Ingre zone where there were no captive communities anymore, although they still existed in other zones. The video went on to talk about the importance of culture, showing people dancing in masks and drinking and preparing *chicha* during the *arete guasu*, the traditional 'grand fiesta' of the Guaraní.[13] The children came and went, talking among themselves, watching the video, watching me.

After the video had finished, I went outside, where the literacy lady Rogelio had told me about started talking to me, repeating Rogelio's claim that there were no illiterates in the *comunidad* anymore. She also mentioned that the particular programme they had come to 'evaluate' (which was the word she used for the event, whereas Rogelio had spoken about a 'celebration'), a literacy programme for adults, was mainly frequented by women. She spoke of how in some *comunidades* she'd seen old grandmothers who could barely see anymore attend these programmes, and how it had brought tears to her eyes to see them laboriously trace their own names like primary school children. The men, she said with evident disapproval, were very macho *'machistas'* and didn't want their women to participate in any decision-making processes.

The evaluation itself was to be held in the building opposite the video room, which filled up rapidly with women of all ages and a couple of men. The teacher who had been showing the video spoke a few words, then one of the evaluators, who had come from Cuba, spoke, making people laugh when her tongue slipped and she talked about 'Cuban history' where she had meant to say 'Bolivian history.'[14] Then Literacy Lady spoke, and a man with a video camera came to film her speech, so I left the room so as not to be in the way.

I was lurking in the entrance when I suddenly noticed someone standing behind me. Turning, I recognised Belén, the secretary of the Capitanía Kaami, whom I knew from attending Guaraní classes at the Kaami office. She greeted me and asked me to have a seat with her in front of the building where some chairs had been put out in a circle. Some five or six people were drinking maize beer (*chicha*) out of a bucket with the aid of *tutumas*.[15] They gave me some, as well as a little plastic bag of biscuits. I noticed a quiet young girl's T-shirt, which had the words 'Arakavi 2006' written on it. Seeing that another woman's shirt bore the same caption, I asked the girl what *arakavi* meant. She told me, *'tiempo bueno* [Sp. good time, good weather].' I only found out later that it was also the name of a project in support of schoolchildren implemented by Visión Mundial, the Bolivian branch of World Vision (see chapter 5).

The talking continued inside, interspersed with occasional clapping, then the people seated outside started to leave. After another cup of *chicha*, Belén and I got up to follow them. When I asked where we were going, they told me we were going to look at the cattle project. It was only then that I realised that both my informants had been correct in what they had told me: there were in fact two different events going on at the same time. It turned out that the mayor of Camiri, Gonzalo Moreno, had come to give a speech in the cattle corral and not for the literacy event, as Rogelio had suggested.

We walked down the *comunidad*'s main path for a bit, stopping once to rest in the shade, then we were offered a ride by two men in a pick-up truck. Another white truck overtook us, picking more people up along the way. To get to the corral, we had to get off the truck again and walk down a ravine. Belén told me that the ground there was made up of 'black earth,' which she said didn't hold the water very well but was good for agricultural purposes (as opposed to 'yellow earth,' which she said was the opposite in both respects).

Out there, where there were no more houses, the forest was almost un-spoiled by the otherwise ever-present rubbish that tended to accumulate by the side of paths and around the edges of the cleared spaces (Guaraní: *oka*) in front of people's houses, although people unconcernedly kept dropping their empty cookie wrappings. We passed a couple of water holes, then reached the corral, which consisted of a very neat fence, trough, and shed and was filled with cows and bulls and at least three little calves, all neatly branded with numbers. Four people spoke, among them Don Rogelio and the mayor, and the same man from the school filmed the speeches, which were all pleasantly short. I took a few pictures, then we all walked back and climbed onto the back of the white truck, where it was a source of amusement for people to try to keep the *chicha* bucket, which had been brought along, from spilling over. A few times the truck leaned toward the side so far that I thought it might tip over, but nothing happened, and even the *chicha* made it back to the school.

In the school compound, a feast of *asado*, potatoes, and salad was waiting for us. The mayor was already munching away when we got there, sitting at the only table with one of the few plates that had been put out in front of him. The food was sitting on the table in larger dishes for people to help themselves. I was given a piece of meat to gnaw on and sat down in between Belén and the quiet girl with the 'Arakavi' T-shirt. Some people were using knives to cut the meat, but only a privileged few had plates, and most were just holding the meat in their hands. The salad wasn't very popular, but an-other woman to whom I had been talking brought some in a plate, and we took turns to eat it, sharing one fork among the four of us.

After Literacy Lady and the mayor had left, a lot of people started drifting off, among them Belén and the quiet girl. I was ushered to a seat in between two men at the other side of the table. One of them turned out to be my new neighbour, Pedro Medina, a cousin of the *capitán grande*'s. They started asking me questions: where I was from, what my name was, what I was doing in Cañón, how long I was going to stay. I had to explain that Austria was not Australia; that it got hot there in the summer, although not as hot as in Bolivia, but very cold in the winter; and what the kind of anthropology I was doing involved, in particular that it had nothing to do with digging up bones. The two of them told me they had already had four or five researchers in Cañón before me, but none of them had stayed in the *comunidad*, they had all travelled back and forth from Camiri.

I then got talking with Don Danilo, one of the speakers from the corral. He told me that he had been wondering how his 'little sister' might be doing in her house all on her own while they were preparing the meat for the *asado* the night before. After all, he said, we were all human beings, no matter the skin colour and such things. I agreed, saying that it was only the cultures that were different, which was why it was interesting to study them. The fact that I had come to learn about their culture was generally received with a profession of pride and satisfaction by people, which came as a relief to me, as I had been very worried about making a nuisance of myself.

As I suggested above, besides being a good indicator of my cluelessness (and perhaps clumsiness in approaching the matter), my initial confusion about where best to start my investigation also reveals something about the situation of the indigenous *comunidades* in Bolivia themselves; namely, that it is by no means straightforward. All parties I had first consulted about whom best to approach had had a point, in that all the organisations they indicated to me—APG, Teko Guaraní, CIPCA—did (and do) deal with the *comunidades* in and around Kaami in some way or other. However, approaching the right authority (in my case, the *capitán grande* of Kaami) proved vital in getting me where I wanted to be.

The whole process would no doubt have been a lot smoother had I had funding to implement a particular project. *Proyectos* have become something of a currency among the Guaraní, and it happened more than once during my stay in Cañón that an already slightly inebriated *comunario* approached me at a fiesta, pleading, 'Doña Vero, can't we do a project? *One* project, Doña Vero!'; requests which, hardly having any money for my own fieldwork, I had to decline, merely being able to express the hope that something might be possible sometime in the future that would benefit the *comunarios* more than my own self-indulgent fieldwork. What struck me about these requests was their usually thoroughly general nature. Apart from Don Rogelio, who had some rather specific ideas for improvements that could be made to the school, people almost always talked about these *proyectos* in a non-specific way. When I asked them what kind of project they had in mind, they would tell me that it did not matter, anything was welcome. This tendency of people to accept any form of 'help' that gets thrown at them from the outside has become pervasive, and reflects the degree to which different NGOs and other organisations compete to implement their own agendas in the *comunidades*, to a great degree without any communication among them, resulting in a multitude of unrelated small-scale projects being put into practice in the same *comunidad*. I did hear representatives from different NGOs address this state of affairs in front of *comunarios* from different places a couple of times in the course of workshops. However, none of them suggested that the organisations themselves had any responsibility in coordinating their actions among themselves.

The event discussed above reflects this plurality of opinions about what a *comunidad* is or should be that are projected onto it by the various stakeholders investing in it. We can generally say that most *proyectos* are aimed at 'developing' a *comunidad* in one way or another, but the opinions about what kind of development is needed diverge. While one party in the above example stresses the need for education (in the form of literacy), the other is interested in advancing the *comunidad*'s economy (in this case, cattle breeding). What is more, however, the multiple and at times competing interpretations of what a *comunidad* is about that are generated by the various organisations according to their own interests and agendas can be seen in the *comunarios*' own interpretations as well. Not only is there disagreement about what the event represents (literacy or cattle programme?), but Rogelio's understanding of it as a 'celebration' of literacy as opposed to Literacy Lady's talk of an 'evaluation' further demonstrates that even the same interpretation can come with different meanings attached to it.

While these were interpretations generated by outside sources (which, as we have seen, could be as remote as Cuba) that were taken up and re-evaluated by the *comunarios*, there were also more specifically 'internal' meanings attached to the concept of *comunidad*. The video that was shown to the children during the event provides a glimpse of what people generally suggested life in a *comunidad* to be about: that is, to live in peace, *'tranquilo,'* as they were fond of saying, in particular meaning away from the dominance of the *patrones*, non-Guaraní landowners who often kept the people living in *comunidades* 'owned' by them in a state of semi-slavery. Whereas the video showed a generalised version of the Guaraní experience in such 'captive communities' (*comunidades cautivas*), Cañón had its own specific and recent history of escaping such a situation, which was still very much on people's minds at the time of my fieldwork. As Don Rogelio's remark about the water supply shows, the move away from the land of the *patrones* to the community's current location, which happened in 1994, was only one step in the ongoing process of gaining independence from them. Besides saying that they appreciated Cañón for being able to live *tranquilo*, people sometimes used the phrase, 'Here, we are able to do what we want,' which raises the question of what exactly that might be. Independence, from the *patrones'* influence as well as financially, was definitely high up on the agenda, as expressed in Rogelio's wish for more Guaraní professionals such as teachers and nurses, and the frequent talk about 'indigenous autonomy' (an idea that had been gaining momentum along with demands for departmental autonomy coming from the Cruceño capital) that occurred during regional meetings and other official events.

These desires tended to be voiced by people who either carried an official function in one of the Guaraní organisations, were working for or with one of the numerous NGOs in Camiri, or were otherwise much engaged in 'outside' activities. However, 'doing what we want' also meant other things for people whose lives were more centred on the *comunidad*. One important factor here was mobility: people appreciated the fact that they could come and go as they pleased, build their houses where they wanted, and work according to their own abilities and needs. Work, in fact, was one of the most frequently raised points: in Cañón, *comunarios* would say, it was possible to work *tranquilo*, without anyone interfering or telling one what to do. The fact that each family was able to own and work their own field (*chaco* in local Spanish, or *ko* in Guaraní)[16] and keep their own animals was also highly valued. A lot of the *comunidad*'s internal economy did not involve money, which gave people a sense of freedom that they missed in the towns. In reality, money represented a necessity even for *comunarios* (mostly, but not exclusively, in their involvement in the urban market), and something people were constantly short of and in pursuit of, but they often talked about it as a kind of necessary evil, something that was not—at least ideally—part of their own way of life. Guaraní people, I was told over and over again, did not need money to live together because they shared and helped each other out.

At this point, it is worth having a thought about the idea of culture. Not because I am here concerned with any anthropological debates about 'culture' in particular, but because the idea of *cultura* strongly informs many contemporary discourses about indigenous communities in Bolivia, whether 'external' or 'internal.' Celebrating their culture, or way of life (Guaraní: *teko, ñande reko*), was another theme that strongly featured among the things that *comunarios* 'wanted to do' in their own place. The epitome of this otherwise rather elusive concept is the fiesta, which again finds its traditional culmination in the *arete guasu*, a big joint celebration nowadays held during carnival time (around February). The *arete* involves the consumption of generous amounts of *chicha* (Guaraní: *kägui*; maize beer) and the performance of mythically inspired games. On the other hand, nonindigenous Bolivians regard the *comunidades* as something like a stronghold of cultural authenticity, for them represented by traditions such as dance, traditional dress, and indigenous arts and crafts, which they imitate, adopt, and use for their own purposes (whereby *comunidades* seen to possess more culture are deemed particularly authentic and, hence, valuable). Again, these two ideas of culture feed on and inform one another, but there are also discrepancies between them, so that it cannot be assumed that *cultura* necessarily means the same to non-Guaraní Bolivians as *ñande reko* means to Guaraní people.

In short, while the concept of '*comunidad*' is one that is familiar and firmly embedded in contemporary discourses throughout Bolivia, the meanings and purposes different people and interest groups attach to it are far from unanimous. Besides the physical and legal entity comprising a group of people, the land on which they live, and the legal title for its ownership, a *comunidad* is a multifaceted and multilayered complex of diverging and sometimes competing ideas, desires, and agendas.[17]

THE BOOK

My study of Cañón de Segura evolved into a case study of a Bolivian Guaraní *comunidad* in a more literal sense than initially intended. Originally, my aim had been to look at the importance of, and meanings attached to, land *within* the *comunidad*. However, while looking at life within the *comunidad* forms part of the current project, questioning the concept of *comunidad* itself has opened up new perspectives on what people are doing and why that could otherwise have easily been 'lost in translation,' that is, in continuing to assume—as most parties with an interest in the *comunidades* tend to do—that we know what we are talking about when talking about a '*comunidad indígena*' in Bolivia today.

In brief, the aim of this book is twofold: to bring the ethnography of Bolivia's rural Guaraní communities up to date to reflect the important changes in their legal and economic status that happened in the 1990s and early 2000s; and to provide a study of the institution of the Bolivian indigenous community from a lowland perspective. There are academic studies that deal with different aspects of *comunidad* within the Bolivian context, but those tend to focus on the Andean institution of the *ayllu,* which predates the *comunidad* as a form of indigenous social organisation (e.g., Platt 1982; Fundación TIERRA 2007), either conflating the two concepts altogether (cf. Rivera Cusicanqui 1987) or exploring the relationship between them (cf. Bonilla ed. 1991). This is most likely due to the fact that the idea of indigenous *comunidades* as it exists today has its roots in early colonial Andean history (see chapter 1). However, the historical trajectories of *comunidades* in the highlands since then have been quite different from those in the lowlands, and an in-depth ethnography of the institution of the *comunidad indígena* in the lowlands has been long overdue. While some excellent ethnographies on Bolivian Guaraní people have been published in recent years (Gustafson 2009; Postero 2007, 2017), their focus has been a lot more urban- and movement-centred.

As perhaps hinted at by the above discussion of the 'event,' my approach in this book is inspired by Marshall Sahlins and his notion of the 'structure of the conjuncture.' An event, Sahlins wrote,

> is not just a happening in the world; it is a *relation* between a certain happening and a given symbolic system. And although as a happening an event has its own 'objective' properties and reasons stemming from other worlds (systems), it is not these properties *as such* that give it effect but their significance as projected from some cultural scheme. The event is a happening interpreted—and interpretations vary. (1985: 153)

In this book, I am treating the concept of '*comunidad*' like an event in the Sahlinsean sense, in that I am interested in elucidating the relational aspects of the *comunidad*, rather than attempting to get at an ultimate definition or even Truth. The thing-in-itself—if such a thing exists—remains unknowable and is therefore of little interest in a study dealing with the daily lives of people, which are, on the other hand, greatly impacted by the variety of perspectives and interests that circulate alongside (and oftentimes in conflict with) their own. As Michael Taussig put it, 'my subject is not the truth of being but the social being of truth, not whether facts are real but what the politics of their interpretation and representation are' (1987: xiii).

The strategy of this book, then, is to establish the *comunidad* as a locus of conflict and negotiation. Given the breadth of the ground to be covered for this purpose, and the comparatively rather limited scope of the book, a certain degree of restrictedness and generalisation in the choice and elaboration of the themes discussed has been unavoidable. Where I am, for instance, talking about the opinions of 'the *comunarios*' or '*karai* (i.e., nonindigenous) people,' I am referring to general trends that could certainly be unpacked a lot further were one to investigate any of the topics raised here in more detail. Equally, certain issues that undoubtedly play important roles in the constitution of the *comunidad* (such as education, health, or questions about more specific trends that might be present among *comunarios* of different genders and/or ages, or *karai* people from different social and/or ethnic backgrounds) are only touched upon tangentially or omitted altogether. In this sense, the book is itself a self-consciously 'lopsided' take on the 'lopsided' takes of others. While acknowledging these shortcomings, I am, however, representing at least such general trends as can be identified with as much accuracy and discretion as possible.

This being said, it is also important to bear in mind the factor of change. Bolivia, as Bret Gustafson (borrowing from Anna Tsing) reminded us, is an 'unstable setting' in which 'the shifting strategies of movements and the fickle tactics of transnational aid and state actors'

> create networked relations, channels, and practices that may persist at one moment in time, only to delink and reconfigure in a different way later. This draws attention to the. . . prospects that these contingent articulations may or may not generate durable transformations, and the possibility that what we observe is inherently unstable, ephemeral, and fragmented. (2009: 24)

This instability inherent in the Bolivian political scene was acutely tangible during the entire time of my fieldwork, and has led me to develop an aversion against the ethnographic present: not only has the time of fieldwork passed, but with the end of writing, the book itself has passed on to become a closed history in itself and as such curiously unsuited to do justice to its dynamic subject matter. I am therefore recounting all events, encounters, and conjunctures to which I make reference in the ethnography-based main part of the book in the past tense. Present tense is used exclusively where I perceive a particular trend to be especially durable, or where its use is demanded by direct quotations. I am using present tense in the document-based reconstruction of events leading up to the founding of the *comunidad* as a legal entity in chapter 1 because it is, to my mind—in contrast with the constantly changing realities of the *comunarios*' lives—appropriate to the fixedness of the sources used.

The following chapters explore the case of Cañón de Segura by eliciting and bringing together the various claims and perspectives that impacted on the *comunarios*' lives at the time of my fieldwork. Part I provides a reconstruction of the history of Cañón leading to its birth as an official *comunidad* in relation to how this concept of a *comunidad indígena* as it exists in its current form has itself been shaped historically. Chapter 1 offers an overview of certain key events and developments in Guaraní and Bolivian history that will help situate the events and developments discussed in the following chapters. For reasons of space, I am here mostly referring to certain key trends and events, such as Toledo's reforms of the sixteenth century, the land reforms of the 1950s and 1990s, the founding of lowland indigenous organisations, and the changes in international development policy at the beginning of the 1990s. The general historical overview is interspersed with a reconstruction of the events that predated Cañón's founding as a *comunidad*, based for the main part on the legal documents that were produced in the process. From here, I move into a discussion of the *comunarios*' own understandings of their history as an object to be kept and used (chapter 2), which brings up questions about authorship, ownership, the end of history (in the sense that 'history' is seen as something belonging to the past), and the relation between history and memory that can be elicited from *comunarios*' own recollections of the 'historic' events.

Parts II and III are mainly ethnographic. Part II shows the *comunarios*' ideas about what a *comunidad* is about, and discusses how this was reflected in their daily lives, discourses, and actions. It deals with the idea of what is generally referred to in the ethnographic literature of South America as the 'good life,' as it is implicated in *comunarios*' talk about 'living *tranquilo*' and 'being able to do what one wants.' These ideas are manifested in the organisation of the *comunidad* and life within it, such as work, social reproduction, and commensality (chapter 3); spatial organisation and kinship; as well as in people's worries about, and aspirations for, the future (chapter 4). The aim of this part is to show that whereas 'history' may have finished with the establishment of Cañón as a legally recognised entity, the formation of Cañón as a *comunidad* remains an ongoing process.

Part III, finally, explores the ways in which this process is bound up with the actions of outside agents, and the ways in which those are interpreted by the *comunarios*. Chapter 5 discusses a particular vision of *comunidades* as similar to businesses to be developed, as it is often found in the approach of governmental and nongovernmental organisations. Chapter 6 explores non-indigenous Bolivians' ideas about Guaraní culture, and the way they relate to common racist beliefs about the nature of indigenous people. From there, I move on to the problematic positioning of the *comunidades* and their inhabitants within the shifting scene of local and regional politics in chapter 7. The distinction between 'inside' and 'outside' here is to be understood as a helpful convention rather than reflective of a fixed state of affairs. On the contrary, the overlap and entanglements between them should become clear throughout the course of the book.

The final discussion opens with the changes I encountered on a follow-up visit to Cañón and Camiri in 2016, and brings together all the elements explored in the previous sections in order to show how the different perspectives on the meaning and purpose of a Guaraní *comunidad* all contribute to shaping the actual realities of people's lives 'on the ground.'

NOTES

1. Also sometimes given as 'Institute for Guaraní Documentation and Support,' or IDAG.

2. 'Teko Guaraní' is the Guaranised acronym of *Taller de Educación y Comunicación Guaraní* (Guaraní Education and Communication Workshop). *Teko* in Guaraní means 'way of being,' or 'culture.'

3. See https://www.cipca.org.bo.

4. Because of the sensitive nature of some of the topics discussed, I am using pseudonyms to refer to informants throughout the book. Where names of informants appear in cited documents, I have left them out. While some insights into the workings of the community will possibly be lost by this approach, I feel that the privacy of my interlocutors is worth this small sacrifice.

5. Short for '*posta sanitaria*,' the *comunidad*'s medical centre.

6. There was, to my knowledge, no one in Cañón at the time who spoke no Spanish or no Guaraní at all. A few elderly people had a basic knowledge of Spanish and preferred to communicate in Guaraní whenever possible, whereas some of the children who had spent their earliest years away from the *comunidad* because of their parents' work commitments understood Guaraní but almost exclusively spoke Spanish.

7. Tëtayapɨ is famous throughout the region as one of the last strongholds of Guaraní cultural 'purity,' an image the Tëtayapɨ inhabitants themselves actively promote.

8. Cf. Gow (1991: 1): 'When discussing the organization of their communities, [Piro people] talk most about the village school and their legal title to land. No recourse is made by these people to what we might term "traditional" models of community organization, familiar to anthropologists through ethnographies of other Amazonian peoples. Indeed they contrast their current "civilized life" in legally recognized settlements with a school, called *Comunidades Nativas*, to their ancestors' lives in the forest, where they lacked "real villages."'

9. Some of the fortresses might even date back to pre-Inca times, when the Aymara federations already had to defend themselves against Guaraní attacks (Platt 1999), and some more recent excavations rendered a possible date of as early as AD 400 (Pärssinen 2003).

10. Since the founding of the APG and the subsequent reorganisation of Guaraní *comunidades* in *capitanías*, each of these levels of representation has a team of 'officers' (*responsables*) in charge of promoting the areas of production, infrastructure, health, education, and land/territory (PISET; see chapter 5).

11. Rogelio was mistaken in this assumption: The FIS is the Social Investment Fund of Bolivia, which the government founded in 1990 with the aim 'to develop basic social infrastructure and to provide financial and technical assistance in education, health, water supply, and sanitation projects' (IEG 2010). Since the government's increased move toward decentralisation in the 1990s, the FIS has been financing more and more projects on a municipal, institutional, and communal level (ibid.).

12. For a detailed study of the history of intercultural bilingual education (EIB) in Bolivia, see Gustafson (2009).

13. Educational videos like this were produced for use in the *comunidades* by Teko Guaraní. For a discussion of the *arete*, see chapter 3.

14. Shortly after coming into office, Evo Morales launched a literacy campaign for adults entitled '*Yo sí puedo*' ('Yes, I can'). Thanks to Evo's international socialist connections, the campaign was supported by Cuban personnel and finances from Venezuela (Gustafson 2009: 266–67).

15. Drinking vessels made out of the gourds of the calabash tree.

16. Due to the bilingual nature of my field site, most of my interactions with *comunarios* were conducted in Spanish, though I also picked up some rudimentary Guaraní that allowed me to largely follow the debates in the *asambleas*.

17. My argument in this book is in many respects similar to that of Peter Gow's *Of Mixed Blood* (1991). Gow explores the meaning of '*comunidad*' for the Piro people of Peruvian Amazonia, which he finds to be intimately tied to notions of kinship and history. In this book, I, like Gow, attend to the constitution of '*comunidad*' in a specific history. However, whereas conducting ethnography amongst the Piro led Gow to attend to kinship, working in Cañón directed my attention toward politics.

Part I

THE *COMUNIDAD* IN HISTORY— HISTORY IN THE *COMUNIDAD*

Chapter One

Cañón de Segura and Its Histories

> In the past year of 1991, between the months of April and June, the *comunarios* of Itakua requested and received permission from Señora Olga Vannuci Zabalaga to construct a chapel/meeting hall in the yard [Spanish: *patio*] of the hut [*rancho*] of one of the *comunarios*.
>
> Noticing that the building, of wattle-and-daub, was big (10m x 5m), Señora Vannuci ordered that it was not to be built where it had been started, but that it was to be made next to her own house instead. The *comunarios* objected, and this was when the conflict began. (IDAC: Michel 1992)[1]

Thus begins the 'history' of the captive Guaraní community of Itakua, as it was drafted in September 1992 by the Camiri lawyer and historian Franz Michel in his role as legal representative of the people who are today the *comunarios* of Cañón de Segura. This document was created during the course of the legal dispute between the *comunarios* and the Vannucci family, a family of landowners on whose property they were living, for presentation before the courts in support of the *comunarios*' case. In it, the author briefly summarises the history of Itakua over a period reaching back to the fourteenth century and provides an outline of the events that sparked the conflict between the two parties and the legal proceedings that had resulted from it up to the time of the writing of the document. However, hidden underneath this neat summary lie a multitude of opinions and perspectives which, at a closer look, reveal Michel's 'history' as just one among a variety of versions about 'what really happened.'

This chapter reconstructs some of these versions on the basis of the documentary evidence produced and utilised in the course of the legal conflict between the *comunarios* and the landowners that lasted from 1991 until 1995. The history of Cañón de Segura that emerges through this reconstruction is intimately bound up with the history of Bolivia, its indigenous communities, and its Guaraní populations, as well as with the more local history of Camiri, in whose foundation the Vannucci family had an integral part. In order to contextualise the voices arising from the documents, the text zooms in and out of different scales of historical development, starting in the colonial era and bringing us up to the time I started my fieldwork during Evo Morales's first term in office as president of Bolivia.

Although the story of Cañón de Segura and its people has its roots in colonial history, a point in time worth pinpointing is the year 1899, when the owner of Itakua, Victor Manuel Antezana, sells the property to Sinforoso Vedia, complete 'with all its usages, customs, and servitudes established either by previous conventions or by law' (IDAC: Montero 1899). Implicit in this formulation that makes no direct reference to the individuals concerned is the transfer of a whole group of people—the ancestors of the *comunarios* of Cañón—from one feudal master to another. More precisely, what is being sold, along with the land, buildings, and cattle belonging to the property, is the particular relationship in which these peasants stand with the landlords: that is, a relationship of servitude.

In order to understand how this situation came about, we need to go back to developments and events that took place in the early colonial era, which is also the time that marks the beginning of the entity of the 'indigenous community' (*comunidad indígena*) in Latin America.

COLONIAL ERA: ESTABLISHMENT OF COMMUNITIES IN THE HIGHLANDS AND 'IRREDUCIBLE SAVAGES' ON THE EASTERN FRONTIER

In the absence of earlier written sources, the history of the Guaraní begins to be accessible to us with the documents produced by the first Europeans to come into contact with them in the sixteenth century. If we recall, the Guaraní were settled along the eastern foothills of the Andean Cordillera at the time, where they had subjugated and mixed with the local Chané population (Combès and Saignes 1991; Melià 1988).[2] One of the most commented-upon features of Guaraní society at the time of these first contacts is their strong inclination toward warfare. Warfare among groups of their own ethnic background was commonplace for the Guaraní (Combès and Saignes 1991), and local groups would enter into 'circumstantial and temporary alliances' against other groups that could just as easily end up setting ally against ally (Saignes 1982: 90–1). However, the Guaraní also did not hesitate to attack even an 'external' enemy as powerful as the Inca Empire, which posed an obstacle to their advance to the west (Pärssinen 1992; Pärssinen, Siiriäinen, and Korpisaari 2003; Garcilaso 1966). Yet warfare was not the only option in the relations between Guaraní and Incas. As shown by relatively recent archaeological finds at the sites of Inca fortresses along the eastern frontier of the Inca Empire (Siiriäinen and Pärssinen 1997: 2; Alconini 2002), there also seem to have existed trading relations between the two groups, and the frontier between them was therefore not the impenetrable divide as which it has often been represented.

The same holds true for the Guaraní's relations with the Spanish, in which we can again see the pattern of changing alliances described by Thierry Saignes. In other words, the Europeans were (at least in the beginning) not regarded as 'other' or even important enough to enter into a lasting intra-ethnic alliance against them (Saignes 1982; see also MacCormack 1999; Schwartz and Salomon 1999; Guerrero and Platt 2000: 109).[3] Rather, the Guaraní tried to make sense of them in their own terms (Melià 1988: 61), while the Europeans were in turn busy setting up a divide between highland and lowland peoples that was largely based on the 'moralised topography' (Taussig 1987: 227) of the Spanish imperial perspective, in which the high and low of space were taken as an allegory for 'high' and 'low' human beings (MacCormack 1999; Platt 1999). The view of the Guaraní as savages is pervasive in the Spanish documents of the early colonial period (Garcilaso 1966; Pagden 1982; Oliveto 2010). Yet their very 'savageness' could serve as a justification for taking their women as spouses in order to 'civilise' them (Hennessy 1978: 20), and, as with the Incas, there also existed 'trade relations' between Spanish and Guaraní, namely, those of dealing in Chané slaves (Pifarré 1989; Saignes 1982).[4]

Despite these sporadic contacts, the Spaniards predominantly saw the Guaraní as a threat to their colonial enterprise, as their warriors (*kereimba*) kept attacking Spanish settlements on the frontier. Thus, the Spanish decided to 'pacify' the Guaraní (Oliveto 2010). To this purpose, King Felipe II of Spain in 1568 despatched Francisco de Toledo, fifth Viceroy of Peru, with the only formal declaration of war ever to be issued by a Spanish monarch against an American indigenous group (ibid.). Toledo's *entrada* (campaign; lit.: 'entry') against the Guaraní in 1574 was a spectacular failure, and similar expeditions undertaken in the following decades equally failed to definitively defeat the 'savages' (Pifarré 1989: 69–82).

Meanwhile, Toledo's undertakings in the Andean highlands were crowned by more success: besides introducing a system of tribute consisting of labour (*mita*) and tax (*tasa*) contributions, which were exacted from the indigenous population with the help of native authorities (*curacas*) (Gose 2008: 129),

Toledo resettled large parts of the Andean populations into so-called *reduccio-nes*, settlements administered by Crown-loyal Jesuit priests, in the interest of evangelising them (Gose 2008: 119–23) and making them more controllable, while at the same time checking the power of the *encomenderos* (Coello de la Rosa 2005). The *encomienda* was a system of indentured labour in which an *encomendero* appointed by the Spanish Crown, usually as reward for financial or military services rendered in the Conquest (see Platt, Bouysse-Cassagne, and Harris 2006: 240–41), 'took care of' an assigned number of indigenous people (the *encomendados*) in return for their labour (Heath and Carballo 1969: 32). Despite several attempts to dismantle it, this system survived until the mid-seventeenth century, when it was finally abolished because of the abuses committed under it and the *encomenderos'* unwillingness to comply with the rules set up for them (Salles and Noejovich 2008).

The Toledean resettlements were organised according to the contemporary Spanish ideal of 'a geometric order, with rectangular streets that converged in a square *plaza* situated at the centre' (Coello de la Rosa 2005: 5)—a setup that is still standard for towns and cities in Bolivia today. (A case in point here is Camiri, the 'gas capital of Bolivia' where my fieldwork endeavours began, whose foundation only dates back to the 1930s.) In other cases, in-digenous communities' landholdings as they had existed under the Incas were confirmed by royal patent as the Spaniards superimposed their admin-istrative apparatus on already existing structures (Heath and Carballo 1969: 31). Toledo's reforms are generally thought of as marking the beginning of '*comunidades indígenas*' in Bolivia (as opposed to more traditional forms of organisation such as the Andean *ayllu*, indigenous settlements without legal recognition, or haciendas).[5] While there is debate over how big a rupture of the spatial and social organisation of Inca times the imposition of these Spanish-style communities really represented (Guerrero and Platt 2000: 97; Platt, Bouysse-Cassagne, and Harris 2006: 515–27), Toledo's reforms helped consolidate the creation of the colonial personage of 'the Indian' by lumping together people from all kinds of different ethnic groups in the *reducciones* (Gotkowitz 2007: 13–14; Schwartz and Salomon 1999).

The situation looked somewhat different in 'Chiriguano territory,' where the fierce resistance of the Guaraní warriors ensured that by '1767, when the Jesuits were expelled from the Spanish Empire, they barely had one mission among the Chiriguanos, . . . in contrast to the tens of thousands contained in their mission systems among other ethnic groups' (Langer 2009: 16). Unable to either 'reduce' or conquer the Guaraní, the Spanish resorted to a politics of damage control in that they 'boxed in the Cordillera and the warlike Chi-riguanos' within a system of town-fortresses as the Incas had done (Langer 2009: 14). While the Guaraní were thus little affected by the Jesuitic resettlement endeavours, the continual mutual raiding that ensued between groups of Spaniards and Guaraní in the sixteenth and seventeenth centuries did result in a change in their settlement structure:

> The Chiriguanos evolved new military strategies after contact with the Spanish. Rather than living in huge longhouses that housed a whole lineage, they switched to smaller houses in which only the nuclear family and perhaps old parents or unattached individuals lived. Dispersed settlements made them less vulnerable to total devastation in a larger attack. They also made Chiriguano society less focused on larger kinship groups. (ibid.)

As the colonial frontier slowly encroached on Guaraní territory, the missions began to become a more attractive option. As a result, the Franciscans, who took over from the Jesuits after their expulsion, managed to rapidly found twenty-four missions throughout the Cordillera (Langer 2009: 16). However, this success was to a great extent due to the Franciscans' efforts to please the Guaraní rather than their ability to coerce or control them. Thus, while the friars did their best to convert the Guaraní and educate their children in the Christian ways, the Guaraní conversely 'forced the friars to give them clothes, food, and other such items with minimal work in what became essentially a one-sided exchange' (ibid.: 17).

To sum it up, the strong focus of the colonial sources on the bellicosity of the Guaraní at the expense of any other relations that existed between the two groups led them to be cast either as fearsome warriors or as savages, which are two stereotypes that still find themselves reproduced in certain discourses today (see chapters 3, 7). Further to note here is the much-commented-upon fact that the Guaraní at the arrival of the Spanish did not form a unified whole, which is interesting to bear in mind when considering present-day Guaraní people's approaches to history (see chapter 2). Thus, already in the sixteenth century we can see the emergence of trends that were to continue in changing guises throughout the following centuries. These further included, on the one hand, the reinvention of the indigenous populations of the *ayllus* as generic 'Indians' living in *reducciones*, or later *comunidades*; and, on the other hand, the use of this 'Indian' population by privileged Spaniards as cheap labour on their private estates (see chapter 2). Later developments, too, to a certain degree reverberate in the situation of Guaraní people in the twenty-first century. For example, the breakup of the longhouses of the past initiated a trend toward households that were reduced to the size of the nuclear family (see chapter 4). The situation that developed in the missions at the end of the eighteenth century, meanwhile, led to the emergence of another remarkably durable stereotype: that of the lazy Guaraní who only wants to take but does not want to work in return (see chapter 6).

EARLY YEARS OF THE REPUBLIC:
THE FRONTIER CLOSES IN

Around the beginning of the nineteenth century, political crises in Spain and the independence movements in Haiti and the United States created a new independence thinking in Upper Peru (the Spanish imperial name of the region that is today Bolivia). The result was a series of Independence Wars, beginning in 1809 and ending with the establishment of the Republic of Bolivia in 1825 (Klein 1982). There is little detailed information on the role of the Guaraní in these wars (Saignes 1990: 157). However, one conspicuous case is that of Cumbay, 'chief of seven communities of the Ingre' (Pifarré 1989: 274). Cumbay is an ambiguous figure: he goes from peaceful relations with the whites (1799) to attacks on their estancias (1804), to signing the peace again (1805), to further hostilities (1807), to yet another peace treaty (1809), to supporting the republican forces in their struggle against the royalists (1813) (Saignes 1982: 92–3). Thierry Saignes suspects this final decision to signify the expectation on Cumbay's part 'that the American emancipation would grant the Ava [Guaraní] a place in the new international order' (Saignes 1990: 161), and Combès speaks of his pursuit of a 'pact of coexistence (*convivencia*) [or] mutual respect' (Combès 2005a: 123) with the whites. Generally speaking, Guaraní settled in the largely royalist Franciscan missions chose the side of the Spanish during those conflicts, while the independent communities that had been involved in rivalries with the mission residents before (Pifarré 1989: 220) tended to ally themselves with the republicans (ibid.: 280). Once again, however, these alliances were of a fickle nature, and as the Franciscans, too, were expelled, 'the Indians themselves put the missions to flame and returned to their former villages without lamenting much the demise of the vast Franciscan mission system' (Langer 2009: 18).

As a result, 'by the early nineteenth century the mission system in the region had disappeared and most of the land that the Spaniards and the Franciscans had claimed had reverted to Chiriguano control by 1825' (ibid.). 'During the middle of the nineteenth century the balance of military power was clearly on the side of independent indigenous societies' (Langer 2002: 44) due to the state's economic and military weakness caused by the Independence Wars and continuing internal and external conflicts (Dunkerley 2007: chapter 6). The Guaraní even managed to extract 'tribute' from frontier landlords and government authorities during those years (Langer 2002: 48).

However, with the increasing demand in cattle that accompanied a revival of the silver-mining economy, the cattle breeders began to infiltrate Guaraní territories with increased persistence in the 1850s and soon pushed many off the most fertile lands (Langer 1989: 126–7; Pifarré 1989). In other cases, the indigenous population was conveniently regarded as 'part of the landscape' (Langer 2002: 54) due to their '"inferior" evolutionary status' (ibid.: 53), and Guaraní villages situated on land granted to colonists often passed into the possession of the new owner along with the land (Langer 1989: 135).[6]

The increasingly aggressive invasion of Guaraní territory brought about a renewed interest in the missions (Langer 1989: 125, 127), which had returned to the area, this time staffed mostly by Italian priests (Langer 2009: 63). While the Guaraní during this time often requested missions to serve as refuges from their enemies, the missions in the long run 'restricted Guaraní independence' by 'creat[ing] a system in which more and more of the Indian villages remained on the Creole side, whereas the independent villages kept fighting among themselves' (Langer 2009: 60). In 1874–1875, various *comunidades* coordinated a series of attacks on haciendas and missions but were defeated by the army. Following a massacre of Guaraní people in 1877 and their crushing defeat in the Battle of Kuruyuki of 1892 (Pifarré 1989), a wave of migrations to Argentina began, where the Guaraní provided a welcome workforce for the sugar plantations (Langer 1989: 142–43; Healy 1982: 20). The kinship links that were thereby established still cause frequent border crossings between Bolivia and Argentina today (Hirsch 2003a: 91).

Meanwhile, tensions between the state and indigenous populations were escalating in the highlands. The Disentailment Act of 1874, which recognised private property as the only form of landownership, provided an opportunity for estate owners to amass large landholdings and turn indigenous people into a free work force (Rivera Cusicanqui 1987: 14, 30), thereby strengthening the trend toward feudal landholding that had replaced the system of slavery at the birth of the new republic (Antezana 1969).[7] In response, indigenous leaders saw a resurgence in their influence as they tried to defend their communities' lands by recourse to colonial property deeds (Rivera Cusicanqui 1987; see also Platt 1992, 2014a). Fearing for their property, the landowners reacted with violence, which was met with more violence by the indigenous groups. As a result, the 'liberal' period of 1900–1920, whose official indigenous policies were marked by discourses of inclusion, was accompanied by a series of uprisings of Aymara and Quechua demanding the restitution of communal lands, the abolition of compulsory military service, the suppression of colonial forms of community schools, and free access to the market (Rivera Cusicanqui 1987: 37).

It is during this time, around the year 1920, that the couple Corina Zabalaga and David Vannucci acquire Itakua from the Vedia family (IDAC: Michel 1992). Zabalaga and Vannucci are first cousins (Guzmán 2012: 12–13) and their family already owns large tracts of land in the area, among others the

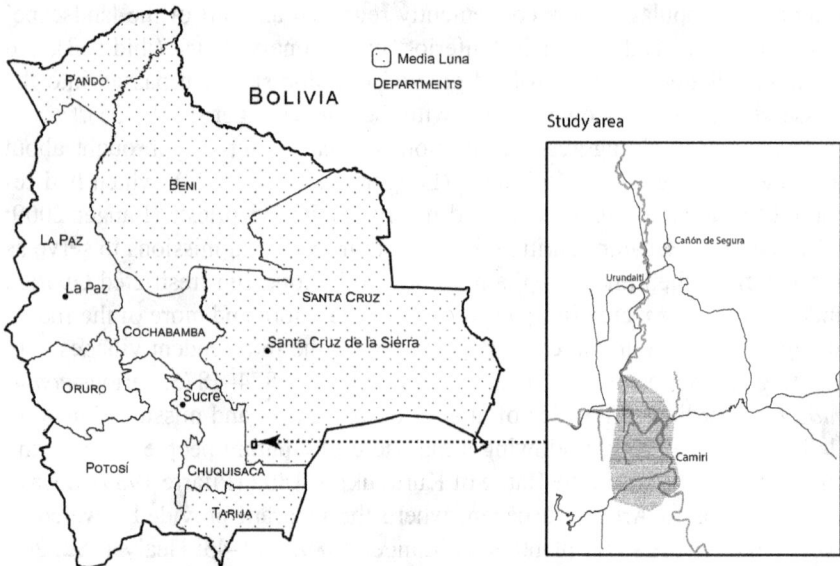

Map of Bolivia indicating Camiri and an approximate location of Cañón de Segura.
Map by the author.

farm 'Ka'amiri' (Guaraní: 'low forest') and the cattle ranch 'Isipoty' (Guaraní: 'white liana'). Both were established by their Italian immigrant grandfather (also called David Vannucci) in the nineteenth century, again on the land of local Guaraní communities (Peña 1999: 264).

About the contradictions of this period, during which the announced aim to integrate the indigenous population into the state became mixed up with strategies of their political exclusion, Nancy Postero writes:

> [T]he transformations of the liberal republican period cannot be understood merely by an analysis of the political sphere. Rather, the process of nation making was carried out through complex linkages between political reforms promising universal inclusion and cultural understandings about race that produced profoundly exclusionary effects. (2007: 35)

Consequently, indigenous people ended up being effectively excluded from state practices while local *patrones*, conjuring up colonial power relations, took over the task of controlling them on behalf of the state (ibid.: 36; see also Albó 2008b: 15; Healy 1982).

In short, in the eastern lowlands, Bolivia's republican era started much like the colonial one had ended; that is, with groups of Guaraní people engaging in sporadic warfare with each other and the European-descended *criollos*. However, although the power balance at the frontier ebbed back and forth for a while, by the late nineteenth century *criollo* presence in the Cordillera had become strong enough to either push Guaraní villages off their lands or take possession of them together with their land. This, then, marks the beginning of the phenomenon of the 'captive communities' as it is known today (see further on, this chapter). Further contributing to the advance of the fragmentation of Guaraní communities were the massive defeats of 1877 and 1892, which basically marked the end of the Guaraní's warrior culture. Especially Kuruyuki came to be perceived as a turning point in Guaraní history, which has come to be interpreted in different ways by different interest groups over time (see chapter 2). In addition, the early twentieth century saw an aggravation in indigenous people's legal position, as their communal lands were declared illegal and large tracts of them sold off to private landowners.

In the year 1959, after the death of their father David Vannucci, the siblings Manuel, Alfredo, Olga, Carmen, Elsa, and Amelia Vannucci Zabalaga request the registration of 691.50 hectares of 'workable land' each from the Agrarian Court in Camiri. Additionally, 400 hectares are to be titled to the 'peasants' living on their land after some of them denounce their *patrones* of 'violent despoliation.' The name of the property being divided is given as 'the former estate Urundaiti or Itacua'[8] (IDAC: Michel 1992).

Like many toponyms in Cordillera Province, Urundaiti and Itakua are Guaraní-derived names referring to features of the landscape: Urundaiti is a Hispanicisation of Urundeiti, composed of the words urundei *(name of a tree growing in the Gran Chaco called* soto *or* quebracho colorado *in Spanish) and* ti *('much, abundant'), and translates as 'place of the sotos, or soto wood' (Ortiz 2004: 249). Itakua is a combination of* ita *('stone') with* kua *('hole'), thus 'stone with a hole in it' (ibid.: 93). To avoid confusion, it is worth keeping in mind that 'Itakua' (or Itacua, Ytacua, Itaca; various spellings) is used in the documents to refer to the property as well as the community of peasant workers living on it at the time, whereas 'Urundaiti' (also: Urundaity, Urundayti) refers to either the same property or the legally titled* comunidad *of the same name. The latter was created from a piece of land subtracted from the property at the time the Vannucci siblings obtained their land titles as a 'gift' to the Guaraní people who had until then been living 'in captivity' (*en cautiverio*) on their estate.*

The finalised titles are issued on behalf of the Vannucci Zabalaga siblings on 11 February 1965, consolidating on behalf of each one an area of 691.50 hectares as requested. The titles for the peasants are issued on the same date as 'community property in the former estate Urundaiti or Itakua.' However, their share of the land has, by this point, decreased to 268 hectares (IDAC: Michel 1992).

The landowners' making concessions to their Guaraní peons alerts us to the fact that, by the late 1950s, their situation had—at least on paper—changed in significant ways. This change began with their re-emergence into the public consciousness as political agents of sorts (albeit in a primarily nega-tive sense) during the Chaco War of the 1930s, replacing their status as sim-ply features of nature ('part of the landscape'). More importantly, perhaps, the Vannuccis' land grant is a nod to a new and 'revolutionary' legislation introduced in 1953: the Agrarian Reform of the Revolutionary Nationalist Movement party (MNR).

THE TWENTIETH CENTURY: THE NEW NATION AND THE RISE OF INDIGENISM

In June 1932, a minor dispute between Bolivian and Paraguayan armed forces became the pretext for the Chaco War which ended in Bolivia's defeat in 1935 (Klein 1982: 182–85). The reason both countries had such an interest in the inhospitable Chaco region was that natural gas deposits were suspected to lie under its surface. Such deposits had been discovered in the eastern Boliv-ian departments of Tarija, Chuquisaca, and Santa Cruz toward the end of the nineteenth century (Klein 1964: 48–49), which suddenly threw the eastern region into the spotlight of the national and international extractive industries. Unable to begin serious extraction without the assistance of foreign capital, the Bolivian State in 1922 signed a contract with the US-American Standard Oil Company, granting it a massive one-million-hectare concession (ibid.: 53). This concession included a particularly rich site deep within cowboy country close to what is today the town of Camiri.

Having started as a camp for oil workers in the 1920s, Camiri was formally created in 1935. The Vannucci family, by then the owners of Itakua, had an important part in the town's founding: it was on the property of Ysypoty, then owned by the widow Carmen González de Vannucci, that the first oil camps had been built (Peña 1999: 23), and it was the expropriation of 300 hectares of said property by Supreme Decree that provided the land for the establish-ment of a more formally planned town in 1935 (ibid.: 71). This measure was deemed necessary due to the increased influx of people that was caused by two different yet related factors: while some were drawn to the area by the new opportunities presented by the presence of the oil company, others came seeking refuge from the Chaco War (ibid.), fought over natural resources and even by some suspected to have been instigated by Standard Oil and the competing British Royal Dutch Shell drilling in Paraguay (Klein 1964: 57), which raged to the south and east of Camiri.

The war brought about the 'nationalisation' of the Bolivian conscious-ness to a degree to which it had not previously existed by bringing to-gether people from all kinds of backgrounds to fight side by side (Rivera Cusicanqui 1987: 43; Antezana 1969: 272; Toranzo Roca 2008: 42–44). However, Bolivia's Guaraní people were affected particularly negatively, and not only because their territory provided the setting in which the war raged: as a form of Guaraní is spoken by the majority of Paraguayans, '[t]he Bolivians, their own countrymen, considered them potential traitors, and the Paraguayans considered them potential spies' (Maybury-Lewis 1999: 926). Given the ever-growing trend toward migrations to Argentina, which was seen by the Guaraní as a 'land of (freer and better-paid) work,' but also a 'land of knowledge' and 'refuge' (Combès 2005a: 260), many hacienda owners resorted to involving their workers in a system of debt peonage that practically enslaved them (Langer 1989: 148–49; Healy 1982), or procuring a work force by assuming guardianship of impoverished or 'orphaned' Guaraní children under the pretext of wanting to teach them 'the ways of "civilization"' (Langer 1989: 150).

The postwar years saw the increased mobilisation of marginalised sectors of the population in trade and peasants' unions and the emergence of new political actors such as the Revolutionary Nationalist Movement (MNR), a reformist party founded in 1941, which appealed to the political currents of the time:

> In 1945, highland Indians held their first national congress to articulate objec-tions to ongoing Indian labor abuses, and Indians began organizing unions and militias to take over the large latifundios. Particularly in the Cochabamba val-leys, peasants began to raise the possibility of destroying the hacienda system, employing the slogan 'land to those who work it.' . . . In 1952, the MNR brought together the fragmented segments—labor, the miners, the middle class, and the Indian peasants—to institute a revolutionary republic under MNR leadership that promised to develop a national political economy based on economic de-velopment and modernization.[9] (Postero 2007: 37)

The 1952 'social revolution' introduced universal suffrage, thus marking indigenous people's emergence as citizens (and, in a way, paving the way for Evo Morales's election as president in 2005) (Toranzo Roca 2008: 45). However, this breakthrough of the indigenous sector into national politics came at a price: in the interest of ending ethnic discrimination, Bolivia's in-digenous population—up to this point referred to as '*indios*'—was renamed '*campesinos*' (peasants), recasting issues of ethnicity in terms of class.[10] The way to more equality promoted by the MNR was basically one of 'educating' their indigeneity out of people, thereby 'depriv[ing] people of their *originario* identity. . . . The means to this end was the state school system . . . , the peasant unions supported by the *comandos* of the MNR, and the system of military service which rested essentially on recruiting young people of rural origin' (Albó 2008b: 21).

The tensions inherent in the MNR's reforms were also felt in their Agrarian Reform of 1953, which gave indigenous people the right to apply for individual land titles: while some parts of the highland's indigenous sector benefitted through the strength of their unions, others resented the imposition of union representation, which they saw as conflicting with the more traditional representative institution of the *ayllu* (Postero 2007: 39).[11] While, however, the dissolution of the large landholdings (*latifundios*), in which large proportions of the land tended to lie idle, did go ahead in the highlands, the same did not happen in the eastern lowlands, generally referred to as the *oriente* (cf. Healy 1982; Rivera Cusicanqui 1987; Urioste 2003; Toranzo Roca 2008: 44; Healy and Paulson 2000: 7–8):

> The MNR party had a tenuous hold on power at the state center and little capacity to impose radical change in the peripheries. There it relied on landowner support. Thus the land reform that swept the Andes did not liberate the Guarani from peonage. In fact, it stimulated a renewed rush on Guarani lands by outsiders [such as Quechua and mestizo settlers]. (Gustafson 2009: 53)

In the face of this increasing pressure on land in the *oriente*, 'the counter-revolutionary face of the MNR began to gestate in the eastern lowlands, with the development of a new landowning and agroindustrial oligarchy, the beginnings of what would become one of the country's most important structural conflicts' (Albó 2008b: 19). As settlers from the highlands (where land was getting scarce due to the increased division of smallholdings into so-called '*minifundios*' [Healy and Paulson 2000: 8]) streamed into the eastern lowlands in search of land,[12] the increase in industrial growth in the *oriente* during this period also caused another wave of migrations as thousands of Guaraní were drawn to the city of Santa Cruz in search of work in the sugarcane and cattle industries, which provided a 'closer to home' alternative to working in Argentina (Postero 2007: 47).

In 1964, the coup d'état of René Barrientos ushered in a series of military regimes while at the same time maintaining the structure of the 1952 state (Gianotten 2006: 41–46). The military leaders of this regime and those to follow were largely regarded by the *campesinos* as the successors of the MNR (despite the fact that they had removed it from power) and had the *campesinos*' support (Albó 2008b: 20). Widely lacking popular support otherwise and pitted against the labour unions, Barrientos's government entered into a pact with the peasantry—the so-called Military-Peasant Pact—which worked 'by securing the continuance of land distribution under the 1953 Agrarian Reform and giving assurances to the peasants that their land titles would not be reversed' (Roca 2008: 75) in return for their cooperation. However, in the 1970s, a resurgence in indigenist ideologies in the highlands brought about a rupture between the peasants and the government (Mallon 1992: 47; Healy and Paulson 2000: 9; Gianotten 2006: 44–46), and the 'failed' land reform of 1953 was abandoned (Urioste 2003; Rivera Cusicanqui 1987).

In summary, the Chaco War of the 1930s brought with it both a reconfiguration of Bolivia's borders and the awakening of a national consciousness among its populations. At the same time, it resulted in the Guaraní being branded traitors on the one hand (see chapters 6 and 7), and engaged in forms of debt peonage meant to control their movements on the other. Meanwhile, increasing indigenous mobilisation and organisation in the highlands ushered in the social revolution of 1952, in the course of which 'Indians' were renamed 'peasants' in an attempt to make society more equitable by removing the issue of ethnicity. A land reform in 1953 broke up the *latifundios* in the highlands but left those of the lowlands largely untouched. The migration of highland peasants to the *oriente* that resulted from the increasing division of lands in the Andes put further pressure on Guaraní lands. In the 1970s, a resurgence of indigenist ideology put an end to the indigenous peasants' alliance with the government, and any attempts at further land reform were halted.

Some thirty years after the Vannuccis' gift of land to their peons, the situation between them and the remaining Guaraní people living on their land suddenly blows up. At the request of a lawyer acting on behalf of the inhabitants of Itakua, the Departmental Inspectorate of Agrarian Work and Peasant Justice orders an inspection of the property to take place on 23 August 1991. The lawyer's letter paints a bleak picture of the *campesinos'* situation. It talks about over ninety Guaraní people who live in Itakua, where their ancestors lived for 500 years until the Spanish came and usurped their land and then got themselves Agrarian Reform titles, bringing about an unconstitutional state of servitude and creating a *latifundio*. They exploit the people settled on the land, who are definitely the ones cultivating it and thus giving it the 'social function of agrarian property.' The people, he says, are being threatened and attacked by the supposed owner, Olga Vannucci, who is about to expel them from their territory at any moment. Thus, an 'intervention and reversion' of the property should be held, so that the land can be measured properly (IDAC: Montero 1991a).

One of the concepts introduced by the agrarian reform of 1953 was that of 'the land to those who work it,' so that the right to landownership depends on its continuous productivity (Colque et al. 2016: 70–71). This is what the comunarios' *lawyer meant by 'social function': land left lying fallow ceases to fulfil such a function, and thus its owner forfeits all legal rights to it. However, in the case of large landholdings like the Vannuccis,' determining who exactly was 'working' any particular piece of land in a legal sense was not always straightforward, since despite the formal abolition of slavery with the passing of the first Constitution of the new republic in 1831, the exploitation of indigenous people continued long thereafter in the form of feudal-type work relations (Rivera 2005: 199) and debt peonage (Langer 1989: 148–49). As we shall see further on, Olga Vannucci herself is quite happy to claim the* comunarios' *labour for herself when she writes to Padre Iván about her 'right to work honourably for a living' on the land that is legally hers.*

That such large landholdings still existed in the first place was due to the fact that the National Council of the Agrarian Reform (CNRA), which had officially been in charge of the dismantling of the *latifundios* since 1955, in reality approved vast illegal land grants in the lowlands that had been handed out by the military governments of the 1960s and 1970s (Colque et al. 2016: 78). Requests for the titling of *campesino* lands, meanwhile, piled up in the CNRA offices unattended (ibid.: 17–18).

THE LATE TWENTIETH CENTURY: INDIGENOUS MOBILISATION IN THE LOWLANDS AND NEOLIBERAL REFORM

The 1980s saw the return of democracy to Bolivia, and that of the MNR to power. They also, however, saw Latin America shaken by an international economic crisis, in the course of which the tin mining industry collapsed in Bolivia (Klein 2011). As a result, many former miners ended up in the (illegal) coca industry, taking with them their more 'modern' forms of organisation and market rationality (Dunkerley 2007: 40). In order to boost the economy, the government adopted the kind of aggressive neoliberal policies that were being advocated by the World Bank at the time (Easterly 2005; Kohl 2002). With major economic support coming from the United States, the government found itself in the paradoxical situation of having to adopt coca eradication measures in return for funding while at the same time trying to get as much as possible of the coca-derived profits reinvested into the national economy (Klein 2011: 52).

In the resulting 'rapidly deteriorating socio-political climate [in which] workers and peasants vigorously opposed International Monetary Fund-inspired attempts at economic stabilization' (Sanabria 1999: 537), indigenous groups began to mobilise in the eastern regions (Roper 2003). The result was the establishment of several indigenous organisations. The most overarching of these, the Indigenous Confederation of the Bolivian East (CIDOB), was founded in 1982 with the support of the local NGO APCOB with the aim of representing the interests of Bolivia's lowland indigenous groups (Hirsch 2003b). Since its establishment, CIDOB's main concern has been the fight for the recognition of indigenous territories. In 1987, the Assembly of the Guaraní People (APG) was founded with the help of CIPCA, another Bolivian NGO, representing all Guaraní groups, which had by then cast off the label 'Chiriguano' that had so long been used by non-Guaraní (*karai*) people as almost synonymous with 'savage' (ibid.).[13] The Isoseño have, since the early 1990s, further been represented by their own organisation, the Capitanía of the Upper and Lower Isoso (CABI).[14] The APG maintains close links with other Guaraní Assemblies in Paraguay and, more recently, Argentina, where it has been involved in initiating the set-up of similar organisations (Hirsch 2003a). Predating the foundation of the APG by three years, the Capitanía Kaami was founded in 1984, at the time representing nine Guaraní communities with the aim to liberate Camiri's municipal Guaraní population from their condition of servitude and reconstitute the ancestral Guaraní territory (Caballero et al. 2010: 3).

It is perhaps no coincidence that the story of Cañón de Segura's coming-into-being as an official *comunidad* has its beginnings in this period of increased Guaraní political empowerment. As far as can be made out from the documentation, relations between landowners and *campesinos* had turned sour by 24 April 1991,[15] when a letter signed by Olga, Carmen, and Amelia Vannucci Zabalaga, but written as though from a single point of view, is sent to Padre Iván Nasini, an Italian priest working with the NGO 'Teko Guaraní' in Camiri. The letter identifies the writer as the owner of 'Itacua,' where the *peón* Rubén Bruno lives, and says that, unexpectedly, the Catholic Church has erected a shed (*galpón*) there for the purpose of reading mass to the *campesinos*. The author declares herself perplexed at the fact that 'men full of Christian holiness' would attack 'Christian women who have carried the faith in their soul for generations.' As a Christian, she says, she was very prepared to have the shed built next to her house, but the Padre should have consulted her first. She states that the place is not a *comunidad*, and the *campesinos* are workers of the house. The property itself is very small, and all the surrounding large areas belong to her siblings, who (like her) hold legal titles to their land. The *campesinos* live there for free and keep their animals, and they work for her whenever there is work, for which they are paid the legal fee. In line with the Agrarian Reform of 1953, the Vannucci family gave all the *campesinos* land in Urundaiti when being granted their titles, but some did not want to settle in the place that was assigned to them and voluntarily stayed in Itakua (IDAC: O. Vannucci, C. Vannucci and A. Vannucci 1991).

A startlingly rude reply letter from Padre Iván to Olga Vannucci dated 06 May accuses the family of having usurped the land from its rightful owners, the Guaraní, adding, 'Therefore, when you say that Itacua is your property, you are lying.' The state, he says, is racist and has always favoured a privileged few, and its land titles therefore mean nothing. Doña Olga is acting in an un-Christian way, and the shed will be built where the people want it, not she. In the end, 2x1m [the size of a grave] is enough space for everyone, which she would do well to keep in mind before quarrelling over a piece of land (IDAC: Nasini 1991a).

At the same time, first attempts are being made by both the Vannuccis and the *campesinos* to ground their positions in a legal framework. A letter from 20 May by the public prosecutor (*Fiscal de Partido*) of Cordillera Province instructs Olga Vannucci, her brother-in-law Eloy Palenque, and the latter's son 'Sadoc' to let the building of the chapel go ahead, and to further guarantee the *campesinos'* free access to their houses and stop all threats and intimidations against them so that peace (*tranquilidad*) may return to the *comunidad*. This is the first mention in the documents of Sadoth Palenque, the nephew of the legal owner of Itakua, Olga Vannucci (IDAC: Pozo Vedia 1991).

It is worth noting the prosecutor's choice of words here in that it acknowledges Itakua's status as a comunidad. *This is contrary to the Vannucci sisters' letter that draws an active distinction between property (*propiedad*) and* comunidad, *implying their mutual exclusiveness. This latter interpretation of course by extension implies the impossibility of the existence of anything like a 'captive community'; rather, the* comunarios' *presence on the Vannuccis' land is framed in terms stressing the benevolence of the* patrones *who let 'the campesinos live there for free.'*

The next thing we know, Olga Vannucci and Eloy and Sadoth Palenque have trumped the *campesinos'* effort by getting a higher authority (the district attorney; Sp.: *Fiscal de Distrito*) to annul the ruling of the public prosecutor on the grounds that intervening in private property is beyond his authority and therefore represents an 'assault on the state-protected right to property.' A letter to this effect reaches the chief of the provincial police guard on 15 June, in addition alerting him to the fact that the *campesino* Rubén Bruno and one of his brothers have publicly announced their intention to enter the property 'Urundaiti-Ytacua' and build the chapel on 17 June (IDAC: Peñaranda 1991).[16]

On this very date, Padre Iván sends a letter to the police chief to clarify the circumstances of the *comunarios'* fight with the Vannuccis. According to him, the *comunarios* asked permission to build a 'chapel' of Olga Vannucci, which she first gave but then withdrew again after seeing how big the building was going to be. Sadoth Palenque destroyed it almost completely and threatened and insulted the *comunarios*. The *comunarios* did not go to the public prosecutor to ask for land, but to denounce those abuses, which is why the public prosecutor was in fact the correct authority to approach. They went to see the public prosecutor three times as ordered, but the other party refused to show up on the last occasion, announcing that they were not going to humour the *comunarios* in any way. The public prosecutor judged in favour of the *comunarios* because they are the original inhabitants of Itakua, which is proven by the cemetery that exists on the land, and they wanted to build the chapel on the patio of a *comunario*, so they would not have taken up any of the owner's land since a house's patio is private property, meaning that Sadoth Palenque committed an offence in intruding there. In addition, the *comunarios* denounce Eloy Palenque for accusing Rubén Bruno and his brother of cattle theft in the presence of a policeman, which they regard as slanderous (IDAC: Nasini 1991b).

Apart from spelling out the event that sparked the conflict (that is, the destruction of the comunarios' *building by Sadoth Palenque), this letter provides the first mention of the cattle theft issue, which was later to add a whole new dimension to the case. Nasini's glossing of what is otherwise generally referred to as a 'shed' (*galpón*) in terms of a 'chapel' here is interesting for the way it prioritises one aspect of what to the* comunarios *was a multipurpose building, recalling the Padre's previous denunciation of the* patrones' *'un-Christian' behaviour, which—judging from Olga Vannucci's letter in which she stresses her Christian values—was a topic of some importance to them.*

The minutes of an 'extraordinary interzonal meeting' of Guaraní authorities on 20 July 1991 show the concern raised by the Itakua case within the APG. In 'Ytakua,' somebody explains, they say that the whites are the only defenders of the territory when really it is the Guaraní who defend the country, like they did in the Chaco War. A testimony by a *comunaria* says that since her early childhood, the Guaraní have been enslaved and mistreated by the *patrones*. Now, the *patrones* are saying that the Guaraní are not from this place, when really 'this *patrón*' [likely Eloy Palenque] is not from here and does not know the local history. The Guaraní, on the other hand, know the history of their ancestors, and they have always been and always will be there and therefore have to keep going forward (*seguir adelante*) (IDAC: APG 1991).

In order to be able to 'analyse the problem of their situation,' various authorities are instated in representation of Itakua: Rubén Bruno is officially named leader (*capitán*), with his brother taking the role of 'magistrate' (*corregidor*) and one of their nephews being appointed secretary. They also vote for a 'mayor' (*alcalde*), a treasurer, and two '*vocales*' (i.e., board members without specified function) (ibid.).

It doesn't take long before the conflict is dragged into the public arena. A week after the APG meeting, on 27 July, an article entitled 'Guaraní from Codillera Province Denounce Various Abuses' appears in the Catholic newspaper *Presencia*. Among others, the article mentions Eloy Palenque, owner of the property (*finca*) Itakua, who does not let Guaraní people hold meetings and denies them any land rights. Allegedly, he also threatened Rubén Bruno and his brother with death and with taking them to court. The rationale he gives for his conduct is that 'only the whites defended the territory during the Chaco War.' The APG demands that he be held responsible for his actions, including the refusal to let 'the natives' build a chapel (*Presencia* 1991).

On 31 July Olga Vannucci, after taking time to gather her thoughts, authors a response to Padre Iván's accusations from 06 May in which she warns him of his dangerous lack of knowledge of the Bolivian 'legal reality' and addresses his accusations one by one, in the process providing some snippets of family history. The world, she says, is a 'changeable society' in constant flux, in which ethnic groups move about constantly. Her grandparents arrived in Camiri in 1890, and her parents bought Itacua in 1920 from the Vedia family. Since then, they have always contributed to regional development 'in a Christian way.' Her father died in 1946, and in 1959 she and her siblings asked the Agrarian Reform [i.e., CNRA] for titles for the lands which by then already belonged to them 'by tradition.' She herself has never invaded anyone's land; in fact, the Vannucci siblings left 500 hectares to the 'native population' to work when they got their land title, allowing four families to stay on their land because they did not want to go with the others. Saying that the land was not really hers would be like saying that the Christian religion was also an 'invasive doctrine' that was replacing the 'natives' cult.' There is no difference between the Guaraní and her, apart from their different origins. According to the historians,[17] the Guaraní only came to the area shortly before the Spanish; they came as invaders and enslaved the local population. She has the same right to occupy the land as Nasini has to teach the catechism (IDAC: O. Vannucci 1991).

The fact that she has land titles and pays taxes means that the state of Bolivia has given her rights and obligations——trying to negate them is simply an 'inadequate idea' and not even worth analysing. In answer to Nasini's allegations that the Bolivian State is racist, she replies that it is true that the state always favours a privileged few and that the indigenous peoples are always being persecuted, she herself and her neighbours being victims of these injustices, as evidenced by the 'deficiencies' in the local infrastructure (ibid.).

She herself is a Christian just like her ancestors, and as such not to be judged by the Padre; she, too, has the right to work honourably for a living. She is only defending 'that which costs [her] so much work,' and she asks Nasini and his 'followers' to respect her rights just as she respects theirs. Nasini should remember the commandment that says, 'Thou shalt NOT STEAL,' and should teach people to respect private property just as the Messiah did (ibid.; emphasis in original).

On a public level, the quarrel continues in the media: In an article from 01 August in the right-wing newspaper *El Deber* entitled 'Priest Denounced for Inciting Indigenous People,' Eloy Palenque accuses Padre Iván of encouraging the Guaraní to take over lands 'that are being worked' and hints at 'subversive elements' inside CIPCA, CIDOB, and the APG that are permanently pursuing the ethnic struggle (*El Deber* 1991a).

The article is followed by an open letter to the people of Camiri published in the same paper on 06 August, in which Eloy Palenque defends himself against the accusations made against him by the 'known agitator' Silvio Aramayo, then the president of the APG. He never, he says, destroyed a chapel, since there was never one built, and besides, his Christian faith would have prohibited him from doing such a thing anyway. The *comunarios* did try to build a chapel, but permission was not granted because his sister-in-law [Olga Vannucci, the owner of Itakua] knew that they would use this as a pretext for claiming land rights to part of Itacua. The Guaraní held a meeting inside the property, so he asked them to go and do it in their own *comunidad* [Urundaiti], since they did not have the owner's permission. No threats were uttered; he only suggested to them that with their actions, they were risking clashes with the landowners. Aramayo is a liar, and serious problems will arise for the landowners if he is not stopped. Palenque calls on the public opinion to 'decide the agitator's character' and judge who is 'on the side of Truth and God' (E. Palenque 1991).

What is striking in the accounts presented by both sides in this conflict is the conflation of different categories of people to further their respective arguments for their superior rights to the land. Olga Vannucci, in her letter to Padre Iván, identifies with the local Guaraní people, claiming equal rights to land and positioning herself as a victim of government discrimination, at the same time as she acknowledges her Italian heritage. The comunarios' *lawyer conflates the Spanish conquerors of the sixteenth century with the*

*Bolivian landowners of the twentieth century. This exemplifies the fluidity
of ethnic identities in Bolivia (cf. Zavaleta Reyles 2008), the manipulation
of which has become a popular political tool on all sides of the many di-
vides running through Bolivian society (Canessa 2007; Fabricant 2009; see
also chapter 6 this volume).*[18]

In another *El Deber* article from 13 August, Olga Vannucci and Eloy
Palenque denounce Padre Iván for inciting 'the natives' to invade private
properties, ignoring their legitimate owners. Olga Vannucci says that some
of her workers have been incited by Padre Iván to build a chapel inside her
property without permission. She mentions the letter in which Nasini accuses
her family of having usurped the Guaraní's land and adds that he did not take
into account the fact that her family had been adding to the region's development for almost a century, and that they help the natives (*El Deber* 1991b).

*Likely a remnant of medieval Spanish monarchical and patriarchal extended-
family organisation (Karst and Rosenn 1975: 60), the idea that the Guaraní
are a type of 'natives' who are in need of the 'paternalist supervision and
protection' of* patrones *is (or at least has been until fairly recently) deeply ingrained in the attitudes of the landowning classes of the* oriente *(Healy 1982:
75–76; see also chapter 6). We also find this idea reproduced in the rhetoric
of highland indigenous settlers to the lowlands, who talk about 'civilising' the
local groups whom they see as backward and lazy (Canessa 2014: 162–64;
Healy 1982: 52–53).*

At this point in time, another key player starts to appear in the documents:
Franz Michel, a lawyer and historian from Camiri who runs the Institute for
Peasant Documentation and Support (IDAC) that works with and publishes
literature on the Guaraní people of the region, has joined forces with Padre
Iván in support of the *comunarios* (IDAC: Montero 1991b).

After a gap in the documentation, where the most exciting thing we find
is various *comunarios* registering their respective branding irons with a
lawyer in Camiri (IDAC: Paredes and Bruno 1991; Paredes and F. Gómez
1991; Paredes and M. Gómez 1991; Paredes, M. Romero, and A. Romero
1991; Paredes and Segundo 1991), some mysterious letters surface that
were allegedly written by members of the Bruno family from Itakua. They
are addressed to a married couple employed by the Palenque-Vannuccis,
and in them the authors announce having stolen various of the Vannuccis'
cows and ask for the couple's collaboration in butchering and selling them.
The letters further hint at the *comunarios'* intention to take over the Van-

nuccis' land, along with threats should the employees tell them anything about it (IDAC: P. Bruno and family 1991).

After this, a two-month silence ensues (coinciding with the festive period of Christmas and New Year), which is broken on 17 February 1992 by a joint letter from Franz Michel and Padre Iván to the public prosecutor denouncing Sadoth Palenque's attempt to prevent the *comunarios* from holding any meetings or gatherings in Itakua. The Constitution, they say, protects people's right to hold meetings, and Palenque should be asked to adhere to it. Their request is supported by a representative of the Permanent Assembly of Human Rights of Cordillera (APDHC) because, they say, Palenque is further violating the Universal Declaration of Human Rights (IDAC: Michel, Nassini, and Leyton 1992). The letter is followed by a note on 18 February, signed by the public prosecutor, in which she tells Palenque to leave the *comunarios* alone (IDAC: Rioja 1992).

Shortly afterward, on 23 February, one of the Vannucci sisters, Amelia, dies. In a 'testimony' from 25 March, her remaining siblings Alfredo, Carmen, and Olga state the legitimacy of their succession to her property, for which purpose they tell us some further details of their family background: their parents, David Vannucci and Corina Zabalaga, were married in Lagunillas on 27 December 1909. Of this marriage were born the children Amelia, Alfredo, Carmen, and Olga Vannucci Zabalaga (IDAC: Claure 1992).[19]

March passes quietly, but in April we suddenly find that Sadoth Palenque, Olga Vannucci's young nephew, has put in a request for a land title. 'For many years,' the document reads, 'I have been settled on and in possession of the rustic estate (*fundo*) referred to as "Cañón de Segura"' comprising some 1,000 hectares. An outline of its limits, improvements made, and livestock grazing on the land is added to the letter. There are, he adds, no *campesinos* living in the place (IDAC: S. Palenque 1992).

In response to this letter, a viewing of the place is ordered for 28 April, which the claimant, owners of neighbouring properties, judges, and witnesses are ordered to attend. A topographer is put in charge of gathering relevant information. The resulting report, dated 11 May, gives the measurements of Cañón (1,744.93 hectares) together with a map. The document insists that the land is to be used purely for cattle farming, with no 'cultivable surfaces' indicated (IDAC: Centellas 1992).

In light of the vast fields that were being cultivated by the comunarios *of Cañón at the time of my fieldwork, this assessment is, of course, an interested interpretation. Similar tactics used by large estate owners in southeastern Chuquisaca to circumvent the regulations set out by the Agrarian Reform*

*have been described by Healy (1982). Palenque's claim that he had been
working the land in Cañón 'for many years' is also not to be taken too literally, given that, according to the* comunarios, *he was barely an adult at the
time the conflict began.*

A judgment of 15 May 1992 confirms Sadoth Palenque as the new owner of
Cañón de Segura on the basis of the assumption that he has been in Cañón
for 'several years,' and that he has made 'improvements' to the place and is
keeping animals there. Cañón is 'vacant land' (*tierras baldías*), and therefore
no one has more right to claim it than Sadoth, who has privileged rights due
to the time he has been there. The document refers to the Agrarian Law and
the Constitution, which 'establish work as the fundamental source for the
acquisition and holding of property' (IDAC: Montalvo 1992).

On 08 June, the Palenque-Vannuccis approach the police to accuse Rubén
Bruno, his brother, and their nephew of cattle theft (IDAC: C. Vannucci and O.
Vannucci 1992). As a result, over the next month and a half various witnesses
are summoned by the police to give their statements on the matter, including
the accused, who denounce all allegations. It soon becomes clear that the Vannuccis' witnesses' accounts do not really add up (IDAC: Chilo 1992; IDAC:
V. Guzman 1992; IDAC: Plata 1992; IDAC: M. Justiniano and Torrez 1992).

In the meantime, Eloy Palenque is campaigning publicly again. In a
statement broadcast by Radio Sararenda, one of the local radio stations
in Camiri, on 08 July, he denounces the APG for having denounced him
on another radio station, Radio Santa Cruz, the day before. His defence
consists of a counter-attack, presented point by point: First, Itacua is not a
comunidad, it is a *propiedad* whose rightful owner is Olga Vannucci. Second, he has never threatened anyone, that is just the invention of two lying
campesinos. Third, Olga Vannucci is the absolute owner of the property,
so she can act as such; besides, she is affiliated to AGACAM, the Association of Camiri Cattle Farmers. Fourth, a year ago, the *campesinos* started a
court case against the Vannuccis, which they lost on the grounds that they
had already got their land from the Agrarian Reform [referring to the 268
hectares in Urundaiti], so that is where they should build their *comunidad*
instead of violently interfering in private property. Fifth, there is a current
court case against the *campesinos* for the theft of 'more than 100 heads of
cattle.' Sixth, the cattle farmers of Camiri are not afraid of the APG—they,
too, have power to defend themselves from the usurpers (*avasalladores*) of
land; they are organised in defence associations (*grupos de choque*) and will
defend themselves to the last. Palenque ends with a warning to the authorities that 'lamentable events' might occur as a result of the conflict with the
campesinos (IDAC: E. Palenque 1992).

At the same time, Carmen and Olga Vannucci and Eloy Palenque are also publicly crusading against Padre Iván. In a letter to the public of 08 July, they write about how Iván Nasini is misinforming the Camireños when he should really stick to preaching. He speaks vulgarly on the radio. He is a 'vagabonding foreign personage' (*personaje extranjeril de vida trashumante*) who forgets that people who defame public functionaries get locked up. Nasini says that the accusations of cattle theft 'ARE A STUPIDITY' and has publicly insulted Eloy Palenque by referring to him as 'el Palenque.' Nasini as a priest has no authority to interfere with Palenque's private property. They add a list of the times Nasini has been told to back off before by various authorities, yet still he keeps making fun of the legal system, even though he is 'nothing but a foreigner.' The Camireños must judge who is to be scrutinised, 'he or us' (IDAC: O. Vannucci, C. Vannucci and E. Palenque 1992; emphasis in original).

The final judgment in the cattle theft case is passed on 23 July, in which the accused are found guilty of all charges (IDAC: M. Justiniano and Torrez 1992).

The mixed-up registers present in these accounts are evidence of different morality systems that are combined or played out against each other, depending on the needs of the time: the law (right to private property), public opinion, physical strength (defence associations), and so on. Further demonstrating the moral dimension of the conflict, even issues that are not directly related to the question of land rights are brought into the argumentation, like Olga Vannucci's AGACAM affiliation or the comunarios' *presumed cattle theft. Palenque's final threat puts all responsibility for the resolution of the conflict on the authorities, suggesting a violent response as the inevitable (and legitimate) consequence should they not decide in the Vannucci family's favour.*

Carmen and Olga Vannucci and Eloy Palenque's letter to Padre Iván, in which they stress their local status, again shows the strategic use of identity present also in their earlier exchanges, which brings certain double standards to the fore: instructing Padre Iván that he has no right to speak because he is a foreigner, the Vannucci sisters conveniently forget that their not-so-distant ancestor came from the same country as the Padre himself, Italy. What is particularly interesting here is the way in which the Palenque-Vannuccis are suddenly claiming superior rights due to their longer presence in the area, whereas the Vannucci sisters' letter from 31 July 1991 denied any such claims on the part of the Guaraní on the basis of the inherently changeable nature of society involving constant movements of people. Itself containing various insults to Padre Iván, the later letter criticises him for insulting Palenque, going so far as to suggest that Padre Iván should be locked up for defaming the Vannuccis, at the same time as they themselves feel free to publicly accuse the Itakua comunarios *of cattle theft. Nasini, they say, should honour the law and leave them alone, forgetting that they have also been told to leave the* comunarios *alone but nonetheless still publicly threaten them and the APG with violence. The last part of the letter is illuminating in that it exposes one of the prejudices ingrained in Camireño society: that the law is only for certain kinds of people; or rather, that certain people's actions are automatically to be seen as being within the law, even when they are not. Or, to put it another way still: that some people are lawful* by convention.

Fortunately for the *comunarios*, these prejudices are not shared by all the agents of the law who are involved in this case. On 09 November, Franz Michel pens a letter to the sectional judge (*Juez de Partido*) on behalf of the *comunarios* of Itakua, in which he asks for constitutional protection (*amparo constitucional*) for them. They are, he makes clear, not questioning the *patrones'* ownership of the land; they just want their right to life and work to be respected. For more than sixty or seventy years, their families occupied small pieces of land within Itakua not surpassing two hectares per person, and they had never had any problems before the past year, when they were suddenly denied their lands because they had put in a demand to get them titled for themselves. He adds how Eloy Palenque, 'using the old Roman property concept of "use and abuse"' (IDAC: Michel and Comunarios 1992), cut down all the trees around the *campesinos'* houses and destroyed the fences around the fields (*chacos*) so the cattle could 'circulate.' Even though Palenque has told the people to leave his property, he has never suggested paying them for the improvements they have made to the land. They just want to be allowed to sow their fields and protect them from the cattle with new fences (ibid.).

Finally, on 17 November, a request is phrased by one of the lawyers of the *comunarios* accused of cattle theft, in which the sentence against them is questioned on the basis of the incoherence of the 'evidence.' A whole list of such incoherences is followed by the conclusion that the accused are being incriminated not for what they have done, but for what is *said* they have done, and that the verdict is therefore illegal and unconstitutional (IDAC: H. Justiniano 1992).

Simultaneously to these events, on a national level the corroded remnants of the Agrarian Reform of 1953 were crumbling. While the failings of the Agrarian Reform were many—the multiplication of unsustainable *minifundios* in the Andean regions, corrupt handouts of land grants in the lowlands, overlapping of land titles, fraudulent reversions, conflicting institutional competencies, and uncertainties over the legal ownership of reverted properties, to name but a few that have been identified (Colque et al. 2016: 78–80)—it was the publication of the alleged illegal titling of almost 100,000 hectares in favour of the then-education minister Hedim Céspedes Cossío in October 1992 that dealt the final blow to the National Council of the Agrarian Reform (CNRA) (ibid.: 78, 205). In November of the same year, the government ordered the takeover (*intervención*) of the CNRA and the associated National Institute for Colonisation (INC). 'The audit commission (*comisión interventora*) [in charge of the investigation] paralysed the operation of these two agrarian institutions, intending to put the chaotic situation in order, but after a few months opted for the generation of the conditions necessary for the formulation and adoption of a new land law' (ibid.: 18). As a result, the commission spent the next three years modifying the law of 1953, with the support of consultants and funding from the World Bank (ibid.: 81).

The 1990s also brought further political advances for Bolivia's indigenous populations. In 1990 and 1996, the lowland indigenous organisations held two marches for 'Territory and Dignity' and 'Territory, Dignity, and Natural Resources' respectively, which were joined by *campesinos* from the highlands (Padwe 2001; Postero 2007: 49). These first two marches, mobilising thousands of people and setting a precedent for further similar mobilisations within Bolivia and beyond,[20] did not fail to make an impact on the government: in 1991, the government ratified Convention 169 of the UN's International Labour Organization (ILO), which recognised indigenous peoples' rights to socio-cultural, economic, and legal self-determination (including rights to ancestral lands) and outlined states' responsibilities toward them (ILO 1989), and an amendment to the political Constitution passed in 1994 officially declared Bolivia a 'multi-ethnic and pluricultural State' (Klein 2011: 57). The Popular Participation Law (LPP) passed the same year as part of President Gonzalo 'Goni' Sánchez de Lozada's 'Plan of All' (*Plan de Todos*) gave more autonomy to the municipalities and recognised indigenous peoples (along with peasant communities and neighbourhood groups [*juntas vecinales*]) as Territorial Grassroots Organisations (OTBs) with juridical personality, which were to function as 'territorially based popular representatives able to participate at the municipal level' (Postero 2000: 2). The LPP also legally recognised indigenous peoples' customary laws (*usos y costumbres*), thereby 'magnif[ying] the importance of cultural heritage as a basis to advance political and legal claims' (Albro 2006: 393).

In the face of increasing—often conflicting—internal and international pressures, the *Plan de Todos* constituted the government's attempt to improve the Bolivian economy in a way that would please everybody:

> The important innovation of the Bolivian *Plan de Todos* was that it simultaneously attempted to reconcile the demands of subnational regions for greater autonomy with those of international institutions for open markets. The *Plan* allowed regions to gain some degree of autonomy and financial resources to

embark on local projects through the Law of Popular Participation, while multinational firms would gain access to Bolivia's natural resources through the Law
of Capitalization and related economic policies. (Kohl 2002: 453)

To these factors were added the World Bank's official endorsement of grassroots approaches of development (Binswanger-Mkhize, Regt, and Spector
2009) and the increased international interest in indigenous rights on the part
of human rights organisations and transnational development agencies alike
(cf. Anaya 2004), which promoted a combination of political decentralisation, popular participation, and indigenous autonomy as the winning formula
in the empowerment of indigenous peoples worldwide (ibid.; Davis 2002).

Meanwhile, in the Itakua case, a letter by a lawyer acting for the APG from
15 March 1994 tells of their request for the annulment of Sadoth Palenque's
land grant of Cañón de Segura. It states that the *comunarios*, 'members of
the Guaraní Nation and affiliated to the APG,' had 'always' lived on the land
but had had no titles, apart from the 268 hectares that had been given to the
comunarios of Urundaiti in 1961 (IDAC: Avilés 1994). The *patrones* are
accused of committing various human rights violations and unconstitutional
acts, such as the destruction of *comunarios*' fields, killing of their animals,
fencing *comunarios* in with barbed wire, and preventing them from accessing
water. Since the *comunarios*' original lands (*tierras originarias*) had been
granted to the Vannuccis by the state, the *comunarios* decided to leave the
lands where their ancestors were buried and their children had been born.
The *comunarios* were threatened by Sadoth Palenque, who claims a title to
Cañón de Segura, which in reality is still under revision. There was no official notification of the neighbours (which include the Guaraní communities
of Urundaiti and Guazuigua), and the land Sadoth is claiming overlaps with
that of a neighbouring landowner. Sadoth cannot have been working the land
from Sucre, where he was studying, which is a disregard of the agrarian law.
He has lied about all his 'improvement works' and has never kept any cattle
there. Further, according to the Agrarian Reform Law, the 'accumulation of
land in few hands' is illegal (ibid.).

*According to Healy, restriction of access (to vital resources, local markets,
and information) constituted, along with debt peonage, the landowners'
strategy for bringing Guaraní* comunidades *under their control by ensuring
their 'total dependence' on the* patrones *(1982: 126–27). It is this attitude of
complete ownership of their land that Franz Michel referred to as 'Roman
property concept' in the earlier letter quoted above. Often attributed to Roman law,[21] this kind of ownership (*dominium*) is characterised by the owner's
rights to 'use, enjoyment, and abuse' (*usus, fructus, abusus*) of their property:*

Usus *denotes the right of the owner to use the thing personally according to its destination.* Fructus *denotes the right to take the fruits of the land, and to keep them or consume them. . . .* Abusus *refers to the right to perform material acts of destruction and legal acts of disposition in relation to the land. Material acts of destruction refers to, for example, demolishing, or burning. (Pierre 1997: 253–54)*

Roman-derived law had a great influence on the lawmaking processes of the New World through medieval Spanish (and later French) legal codes (Karst and Rosenn 1975). Likewise, the tendency to dispute the moral rightness or even 'legality' of any piece of legislation that we find repeated in the exchanges between comunarios *and* patrones *and their respective representatives can be traced to the same antecedents: a Romanesque idealism in which the only true law was one that reflected eternal truths of morality and justice on the one hand, and, on the other, early modern Hispanic-Catholic legal and political theories that encouraged people to question seemingly unjust laws on the grounds that they might be failing those requirements (ibid.: 58–60). These theories found their application in the colonies, where Spanish royal decrees often failed to reflect the realities encountered by the colonial authorities, in the motto of 'I obey but I do not comply/execute' (*'obedezco pero no cumplo'*). According to Karst and Rosenn (1975), this tradition has left as its legacy in Latin America a curious legalism in which the letter of the law is fetishised at the same time as it is also frequently put into question.*

The APG lawyer's letter continues with an appeal to President Sánchez de Lozada to annul the land grant to Sadoth Palenque because of its legal defects. Alternatively, the title to the property 'Urundaiti' should be annulled. A viewing of Cañón and Itakua should be held to establish the situation of the *comunarios* and the situation in Cañón (where no work has been carried out yet). The *comunarios* should be officially told to move to Cañón, and the Vannuccis notified of this decision (IDAC: Avilés 1994).

A receipt dated 28 April, in which a contractor hired by Sadoth Palenque to carry out various improvements in Cañón confirms having received payment for them, alerts us to the fact that Sadoth has had these improvements done only recently—the contract was signed on 28 January 1994 (IDAC: Medrano 1994).

From a letter of 09 May addressed to 'the public opinion' and co-authored by the same contractor, we can infer that what happens next is the *comunarios'* occupation of Cañón: the contractor talks about how '*comunarios* from Urundaiti' damaged property of the Palenque-Vannuccis and threatened him and some forty other 'small cattle breeders and agriculturalists of the zone' with axes and machetes when they went to see what was going on (IDAC: Medrano and Verazain 1994). In response, the cattle breeders joined the Vannuccis to set up the 'Committee for the Defence of Private Property of Cordillera Province' and appeal to the cattle breeders' and farmers' associations and the authorities to protect other 'productive properties' supplying the Camiri market. They denounce 'foreign elements' that provide capital and logistic help to destroy their properties and demand that institutions getting money from abroad should be closed. Otherwise, 'there might soon be bloodshed' (ibid.).

After this, things happen rapidly. On 11 May, Eloy Palenque is still up in arms against the *comunarios*' 'invasion' of his son's property, which is preventing any work from being carried out there (IDAC: Suárez 1994). However, on 23 May, a letter by Franz Michel to the APG informs them of an agreement with Eloy Palenque, which he has reached with the mediation of the Camiri Cattle Breeders' Association (AGACAM): Palenque will give the *comunarios* Cañón if they leave Itakua; all seven court cases between the two parties will be closed; the *comunarios* will pay for the improvements carried out by Palenque on the land of Cañón de Segura (IDAC: Michel 1994a).

In the following month of June, there is a busy exchange of letters between Franz Michel, AGACAM, the APG, and a representative of the Development Plan for the Peasantry of Cordillera (PDCC),[22] in the course of which the APG accepts the deal offered to them, and the cost of the 'improvements' in Cañón is established (IDAC: Michel 1994b; IDAC: Pinto and Del Río 1994; IDAC: Córdova 1994; IDAC: Cuéllar, Vaca, and Antenor 1994; IDAC: von Oven and Zarzycki 1994). After some bickering about the details (such as the exact length of the fence built by Sadoth Palenque's contractor [IDAC: Michel 1994c, 1994d]), an estimate is fixed at US$5,000.

A report of a viewing of Cañón by INRA and CORDECRUZ from 02 July mentions that there are twenty-two families working to build houses and fields.[23] They have also cleared a road. There are six court cases going on between the Vannuccis and the *comunarios*, one of which—the cattle theft one—has seen two *comunarios* imprisoned for two years. The deal now is: Sadoth relinquishes his title to the *comunarios*; the *comunarios* leave Itakua to the Vannuccis; all legal action is stopped; the *comunarios* pay Palenque US$5,000 for improvements; the *comunarios* take care of the legal registration of their new title themselves. Cañón has been established to measure 1,744.93 hectares and borders on Yatiguigua (north), Guasuigua (south), Tobatiqua (east), and Calvimontes (Itakua) (west); boundary stones will be set up to avoid any future trouble (IDAC: Martinez 1994).

Possibly slowed down by Franz Michel's withdrawal from the negotiations between APG and AGACAM in November 1994 (IDAC: Michel 1994e, 1994f), the 'sale' of Cañón is finally formalised on 17 February 1995. On 12 March, the new official inhabitants of Cañón de Segura sign a formal agreement with the neighbouring *comunarios* of Urundaiti, in which they 'grant' them twenty-five hectares of their newly acquired land, on the condition that they must only use them for agriculture, and only on flat land; a work party (*grupo de trabajo*, or GDT) must be formed, and no individual work is to be carried out; no trees must be felled for firewood or charcoal; the Urundaiti *comunarios* can keep the land as long as they work it; if it is not worked for one year, Itakua can take it back. The respective communal authorities are responsible for upholding the deal, but Itakua reserves the right to take legal action if necessary (IDAC: Romero, Demetrio and Altamirano et al. 1995).

In 1996, a year after the sale of Cañón, mounting internal and international pressure resulted in the passing of a new agrarian reform law (the INRA Act), which for the first time made it possible for indigenous communities in Bolivia to apply for communal legal ownership of lands:

> The state can expropriate land previously titled to private parties that has been abandoned without indemnization and can also expropriate land that does not meet a socioeconomic function with indemnization. . . . Land expropriated by the state as well as remaining public land is to be either distributed collectively and free of charge in favor of indigenous or peasant communities or sold at market value at a public auction. The former process has priority over the latter. (Deere and Leon 2001: 37)

The titling of such 'Original Community Lands' (TCOs)[24] involved the prior completion of a Spatial Needs Identification Study, carried out by the government, which used an algorithmic formula to determine the amounts of land considered necessary for a community's 'economic, socio-cultural and conservation needs' (Padwe 2001).[25] However, some authors have noted that these approaches are not sensitive to the cultural specificities of indigenous land use. Rather, the Spatial Needs study 'posits cultural identity as an epiphenomenal byproduct of a certain set of material variables' (ibid.: 4). It further provides a 'scientific' cover for political decisions through the 'directionality of legibility' caused by its complexity that obscures its processes to the indigenous people while enshrining them in a discourse of 'unassailable rationality' (ibid.: 15–16). The kinds of developments the study foresees rest on the assumption that indigenous people will continue in their 'indigenous ways' in the foreseeable future, which sets up and serves to maintain a distinction between 'indigenous' and 'nonindigenous' Bolivian citizens (ibid.:19). The INRA Act's general approach to land titling caused problems for highland peoples, too, in that it did not take into account the highland valleys' heterogeneity in terms of 'soil types, production systems and ways of accessing and owning land' (Urioste 2003). A particular point of criticism here is the fact that the INRA Act did not allow for any forms of individual or mixed tenure, which would be more appropriate in certain cases (ibid.).

Similar criticisms have been expressed of the LPP: for one, the LPP was based on an erroneous assumption of homogeneous social participation and conditions of municipal management of the entire indigenous population (Hoyos and Blanes 1998).[26] In fact, as Ana María Lema found in a study published in 2001, it was often not even entirely clear to people what exactly this 'participation' was meant to entail. In other cases, the increased autonomy of the municipalities failed to change previous power relations due to local elites' firm grip on influential positions:

> In Huacareta the *hacendados* continue to dominate local government . . . with one of them holding the office of mayor. Another interesting feature is that in Huacareta, the *hacendados* very quickly adopted the LPP by registering their property, including the Guaraní people who work on it, as an OTB, thus securing access to resources and projects. . . . This resulted in projects that favoured particular communities. (Nijenhuis 2002: 156)

Even where this was not the case, the political 'decentralisation' brought by the LPP in fact increased the reach of the state's structures and influence into the lives of rural people to a level unknown before, and the new rights given to them could even function as a distraction from other questions (Postero 2000). This also applied to the mechanisms of the market economy, in which newly established TIOCs found themselves immersed: after the titling of their lands, indigenous groups were required to come up with a management plan that detailed their intended use of the available natural resources (such as, for example, timber and wildlife). The result was often 'big-time commercial logging' of local forests, carried out under such NGO-inspired headings as 'sustainable development, participation and equal distribution of profits' (Postero 2000: 9). Given the slowness of the land titling process, indigenous leaders often even resorted to illegally selling off large tracts of forest to logging companies before they could be exploited by third parties still present in the area (ibid.).

Besides these complications that impeded the LPP from living up to the hopes of those who had seen it as a potent means for indigenous empowerment, Goni's 'Plan of All' also failed to please the wealthy elites in the *oriente*. By focusing decentralisation measures on the municipalities, the government had gone against the desires of the civic committees, which had been promoting more departmental autonomy since their establishment by counterrevolutionary forces in the 1950s. Among them, the Civic Committee of Santa Cruz (or Pro-Santa Cruz Committee) had grown particularly powerful (Eaton 2007; Nijenhuis 2002: 47).[27] At the same time, however, the

LPP's empowerment of the newly recognised OTBs facilitated the rise of a new set of political actors in the highlands: the *cocalero* movement, headed by Evo Morales and represented by a new, peasant-union-based party, was taking advantage of the new possibilities for participation in formal politics 'to capture municipal governments not only in the coca zones but throughout the department of Cochabamba' (Klein 2011: 59).

In short, Bolivia's economic and political situation was radically rearranged by the effects of an international financial crisis in the 1980s. The focus of its economic activity shifted from the highlands (mining) to the lowlands (farming and livestock activities), with the illegal sector of coca production also gaining in importance. A similar thing happened with indigenous mobilisation, which had previously been concentrated in the Andean highlands. Responding to these new internal demands as well as international pressures, a series of reforms in the 1990s aimed to transform Bolivia into a decentralised showcase of Indian-friendly neoliberalism. However, while the Popular Participation Law sought to empower indigenous communities in their move toward 'development' (see chapter 5), and the INRA Act of 1996 finally granted them communal land rights, the fact remained that communities were treated as if they were a) all the same, and b) internally homogeneous. At the same time, the LPP's stress on decentralisation to the local level intensified the opposition between the national government and prefectures and civic movements in the east of the country (see chapters 6 and 7) while empowering the coca growers' movements in the west.

In Cañón, the couple of years or so following the *comunarios'* legal acquisition of their lands pass with the *comunarios* getting their new land title formalised and registered with various institutions. A letter by a lawyer dated 13 May 1997 providing information about the buildings, crops, and animals in Cañón says that the objectives for the Titling of Original Community Lands (SAN–TCO) have been fulfilled. At that time, the *comunidad* is made up of some 126 people who have been 'settled there for various decades.' They are said to be living off agriculture, cattle breeding, hunting, and fishing. All agreements concerning limits have now been signed with the neighbours and there are no conflicts, therefore the *comunarios* should be granted a communal title to Cañón (IDAC: Rengel 1997).

The case of Cañón de Segura here described had its beginning in 1991, at a time before the INRA Act, when Guaraní mobilisation was still gaining momentum. It thus constitutes a case of a community's liberation from 'captivity' that was achieved through the collaboration of various local actors at a time when there was no generalised legal formula for the resolution of such conflicts. As

*such, it provides us with an insight into the various interest groups with invest-
ments in the* comunidades *and their agendas, such as local landowners, NGOs,
state authorities, and—not least—the* comunarios *themselves.*

    *Having acquired the land in Cañón in a transaction described as a 'sale'
before the passing of the INRA Act, the* comunarios *lost no time in having
their community titled as official 'Original Community Land' (TCO) once
INRA took effect in 1996. The letter's author's assertion that the* comunarios
*had been settled in Cañón 'for various decades' is an interesting sleight of
hand, since it conflates the fact of the* comunarios' *longstanding residence
in one place with their newly established presence in another one, which is
perhaps a response to the INRA Act's definition of TCOs as spaces to which
indigenous and originary peoples have 'traditionally had access, and where
they maintain and develop their own forms of economic, social, and cultural
organisation' (INRA, article 41). Likewise, considering that there is no river
with the capacity for fishing nearby, the description of the* comunarios' *livelihoods (agriculture, cattle breeding, hunting, and fishing) seems to be a convention for writing about indigenous people rather than an entirely realistic
description. All this points to the way Bolivia's indigenous people's newly
gained rights brought with them new expectations of how to be indigenous
that were also to have an impact on the lives of the* comunarios *of Cañón.*

The formal registration of Cañón on 13 August 1997 (IDAC: P. Gómez 1997)
marks the official end of the *comunarios*' troubles—from here on, everything
that happens is meant to be in their own hands.

TWENTY-FIRST CENTURY:
THE RISE OF EVO AND THE MAS

By the early twenty-first century, indigenous groups had gained enough
political impact to contribute to the resignation of two Bolivian presidents:
Sánchez de Lozada in 2003, after a massacre of Aymara and neighbourhood
group protesters in El Alto; and his successor Carlos Mesa in 2005, after renewed massive protests by the same sector. These protests were related to the
government's policies on the exploitation of natural gas (which had replaced
mining as the country's main extractive industry), which were seen to be ben-
efitting foreign businesses at the expense of the Bolivian people (Eaton 2007:
73; Webber 2008a). Groups representing indigenist and class interests united
in a common struggle against the government's ever more aggressive attempts to privatise natural resources, and for the demand 'to refound Bolivia
through a revolutionary Constituent Assembly which would see the organic

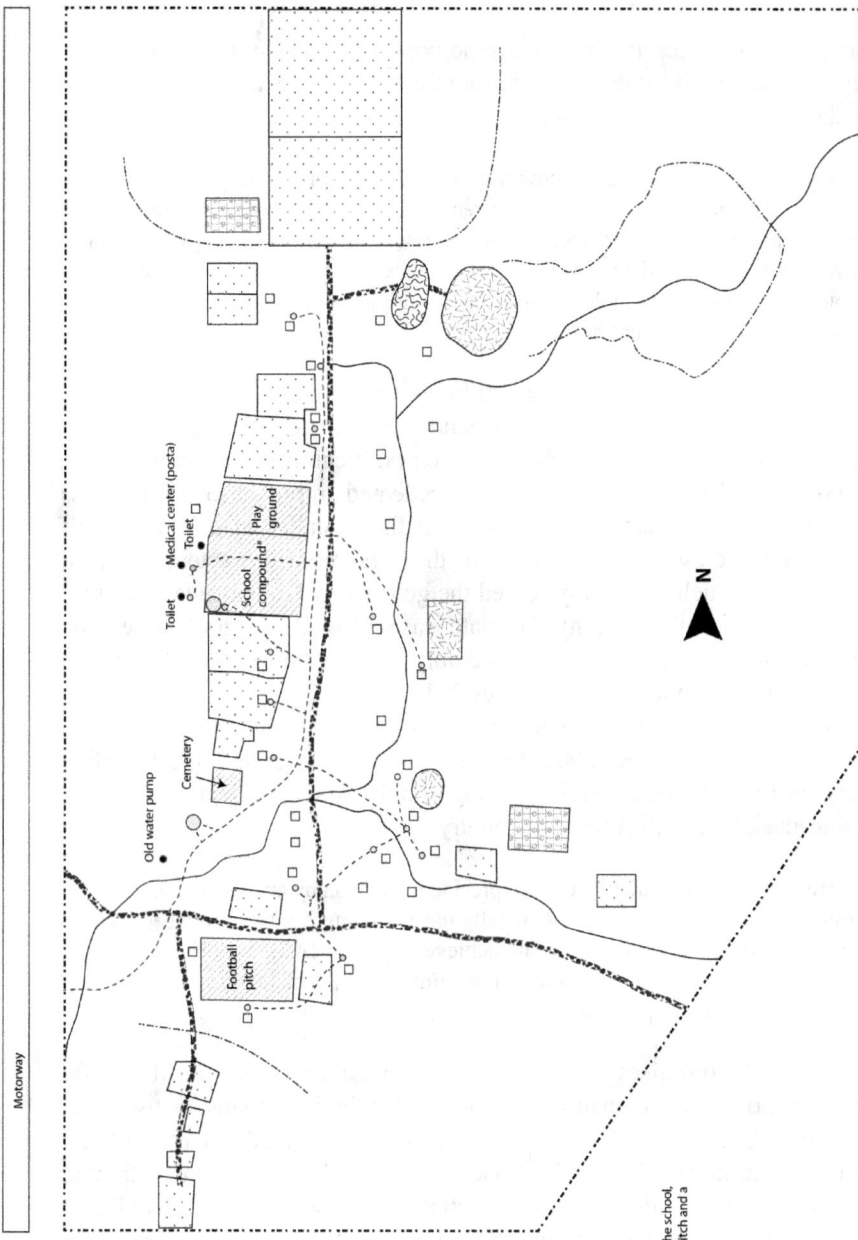

Approximate map of Cañón de Segura, showing the *comunidad*'s layout and main features in 2006–8.
Map by the author.

Legend

▢	Fields
▨	Beehives
▨	Communal areas
▢	Houses
∘	Standpipes
○	Water tanks
⬭	Reservoir
⬭	Animal enclosures
—	Minor paths
⋯	Water pipes
⋯	Major paths
⌇	Fences
⌁	Coummunity boundary

ᵃ The school compound comprises the school, teachers' accomodation, a football pitch and a shrine to the Virgin of Copacabana

Motorway

Old water pump

Cemetery

Toilet   Medical center (posta)
Toilet
"School Toilet
compound" Play
ground

Football
pitch

N

participation of representatives of all the popular sectors in the country, and
reverse the internally colonial racial domination by the white-*mestizo* élite
over the majority indigenous population' (Webber 2008a: 61).

> Notably absent from the scene, however, was a revolutionary party with roots in
> the key movements and a broad, cross-regional social base capable of unifying
> the multiplicity of popular struggles on the rise. Rather, the MAS [Movement
> toward Socialism], led by *cocalero* union leader Evo Morales, was the only
> popular party able to articulate some of the sentiments of the organised masses
> beyond a local or regional basis. (ibid.)[28]

In this highly charged climate, the rift between the largely indigenous highlands and conservative elites in the lowlands began to deepen as the latter saw
their economic positions threatened and their political influence dwindle (Eaton 2007: 73). The response was an unprecedented amplification of demands
for autonomy in the eastern departments of the so-called *media luna* ('half
moon,' for the crescent shape in which they encircle the western highland
departments), which eventually forced the government to concede a referendum on departmental autonomy. The date was set for 02 July 2006—the same
day as elections for a Constituent Assembly that was to rewrite the national
Constitution were to take place (Assies 2011: 106).

By that date, however, Bolivia's political scene had undergone dramatic
changes. On 18 December 2005, presidential elections ended in a landslide
victory for Evo Morales, thereby making him the first self-identifying indigenous leader of a South American country.

> No previously democratically elected president had won by an absolute majority
> on the first round, and no democratically elected Congress had produced such
> a majority for a single party [as that achieved by the MAS]. . . . The scale of
> Morales's victory therefore conferred on him a mantle of legitimacy that his
> predecessors had conspicuously lacked. (Crabtree 2008: 1)

In line with the promises made in his election campaign, on 01 May 2006
Morales announced the 'nationalisation' of the hydrocarbons industry via
Presidential Decree 28701.[29] The decree was nicknamed 'Heroes of the
Chaco' decree in allusion to the Chaco War, which had become reframed
in terms of 'a gallant defense' of the nation's patrimony (that is, its oil and
gas fields) against capitalist foreign exploiters in the course of which many
indigenous people had sacrificed their lives (Perreault and Valdivia 2010:
696). The formulation employed here is illustrative of the political line the
MAS has been claiming since its coming into power: that is, the promotion
of a nationalism strongly tinted by populist-indigenist interests and the desire

to go against the (national and international) status quo in the endeavour to right past wrongs and improve conditions for a larger part of the population.[30]

In summary, in the 2000s, both indigenous movements in the highlands and civic movements in the lowlands gained strength, the former demanding the 'refounding' of the nation according to more equitable rules, and the latter calling for autonomy from La Paz. Reflecting the impact of the indigenous movements on other sectors of the population, in 2005, Evo Morales was elected Bolivia's first indigenous president. In 2006, Morales officially brought the hydrocarbons industry under state control. It was these recent developments that shaped the social and political climate in Cañón and Camiri during the time of my fieldwork.

COMUNIDADES CAUTIVAS AND THE QUESTION OF 'TWENTY-FIRST-CENTURY SLAVERY'

While the MAS's programme to 'decolonise' Bolivia's political and legal system made it popular with popular movements and a large sector of the indigenous population, it continued to antagonise the elite opposition in the *oriente*. On the same day that Evo gained his historical victory, new prefects were elected in the nine departments. This, too, was a historical moment in that the prefects (who had until then been nominated by the executive) were for the first time elected by popular vote (Assies 2011: 106). In Santa Cruz, the winner was Rubén Costas, the former leader of the Civic Committee and one of the most fervent promoters of the autonomy movement.

On top of the ever-present issue of departmental autonomy—a proposition that gained a majority of the popular vote in the referendum of 02 July in the *media luna* departments but was rejected by a majority of Bolivians on the national level (Assies 2011: 106–7)—several of Evo's policies upset political and civic leaders in the *oriente*. One point of conflict was the above-mentioned nationalisation of the gas industry, whose profits *media luna* leaders would rather have seen returned to their own treasuries than redistributed among all the departments and various national-scale projects. Another particularly unpopular policy was Evo's increased targeting of the land issue, complete with an updated legislation (Law 3545 of 28 November 2006) meant to facilitate and speed up the process of assessment and titling of lands in the lowlands that had been dragging along way behind schedule since the ratification of the INRA Act in 1996 (cf. Guzmán ed. 2008).[31,32]

Besides the failure of many *latifundios* to fulfil the 'socio-economic function' set out as mandatory by the Bolivian Constitution (CPE 2009; see chapter 6), the continued existence of 'captive' Guaraní families on various haciendas in the Department of Santa Cruz made the inspection of land-holdings even more pressing in this region.[33] Legally, all forms of servitude had been abolished in 1938 (Gotkowitz 2007: 127), but forms of debt peonage that persisted in the Cruceño lowlands, and which tied Guaraní people to haciendas in a state akin to slavery, had thus far proved immune to any state attempts at land reform. This phenomenon, since the 1990s known under the term 'captive communities' (*comunidades cautivas*) (Castañón Pinto 2011), increasingly attracted the attention and criticism of scholars (cf. Healy 1982; Kidd 1997; Gustafson 2010; Castañón Pinto 2011), the press (*Presencia* 1991; *El Deber* 2005), and national and international institutions.[34] In 2008, the Inter-American Commission on Human Rights (CIDH) published a report in which it denounced the existence of 'conditions of debt servitude and forced labour' on some haciendas and concluded that 'this phenomenon, which affects approximately 600 families, [and which] is known as "*comunidades cautivas*," . . . undoubtedly represents contemporary forms of slavery that must be eradicated immediately' (CIDH 2009). The report also deplores other violations of the Guaraní's human rights, such as their continuing lack of access to their 'ancestral lands' and to 'legal justice,' and urges the government to increase its efforts toward the speedy resolution of these issues (ibid.).

A report by the United Nations Permanent Forum on Indigenous Issues published the following year came to similar conclusions: it denounces such abuses as 'forced labour, child labour, poor working conditions, sexual abuse, the loss of—and consequent lack of access to—lands, the non-existence of social services, restrictions on the right to freedom of association, discrimination, and judicial bias' (Ortiz 2009: 15), which stand in violation of nineteen 'international treaties ratified by Bolivia' (Ortiz 2009: 4). This latter report was the result of an enquiry that was requested by the Bolivian government itself in response to a series of violent confrontations in 2008 between landowners in the contested Guaraní TCO of Alto Parapetí and officials of the National Institute of Agrarian Reform (INRA) and the APG. These incidents occurred in the context of the planned titling of a TCO in Alto Parapetí, which the ranchers sought to impede until after 04 May, when a public vote would be cast on the 'autonomic statutes' the Prefecture of Santa Cruz had drawn up in defiance of the national government. The confrontations of 2008, which were initiated by the landowners, involved the takeover of the Camiri INRA office by cattle ranchers and members of the Santa Cruz Youth Union (UJC; a youth organisation tied to the Santa Cruz Civic Committee) and the subsequent expulsion of INRA officials; the armed ambush of an INRA-APG delegation en route to Alto Parapetí; and the seizure and public whipping of a Guaraní lawyer in the central square of Cuevo (Gustafson 2010).

The incidents of 2008 demonstrate some of the problems attached to the land titling process in the Cruceño lowlands: for one, the involvement of civic movements from the capital shows the strong links that existed between local cattle breeders and the elites at the head of the Prefecture (see chapter 7). Given the continually weak grasp of the national government on the eastern regions, this alliance constituted a considerable complication for the practical execution of the letter of the law.[35] Further, the confrontations were the violent manifestation of a clash of opinions between Guaraní and landowners that hinged on their different conceptions of their respective 'rights.' While the APG was phrasing their demands for the titling of the captive communities' lands in terms of a 'liberation from slavery' (Gustafson 2010: 54–57), the ranchers phrased theirs in terms of a 'defence of land' (ibid.: 57–8), with both parties stressing the 'illegality' of the other's position.[36]

According to a CIPCA report looking at the first eleven years following the passing of the INRA Act, its implementation was complicated by the fact that the law combines 'communitarian as well as liberal components' (Guzmán ed. 2008: 43), which means that 'the law gives arguments to both social sectors (farming and livestock businessmen, and *campesinos*/indigenous people) to legally back up their right to lands, which in many cases overlap' (ibid.: 44). Thus, despite the fact that the INRA Act and its amendments were specifically designed to sort out issues of landownership, who is 'right' in the eyes of the law may in fact not always be clear. However, the subjection of the Guaraní lawyer to colonial-style 'racialized public punishment' (Gustafson 2010: 51) reveals that there is a moral dimension underlying the legal one in the landowners' ideas about their 'rights' that presupposes race-based social inequality, not as a problem to be solved, but as a natural given.

After initial problems in the drafting process (see Assies 2011), the new Constitution was finally approved by popular referendum on 25 January 2009. It recognised departmental, regional, municipal, and 'indigenous originary peasant autonomy.'

NOTES

1. Where foreign-language texts are quoted in this book, the translations are my own.

2. Contrary to P. Clastres's vision of Tupí-Guaraní egalitarianism (Saignes 1990: 12), Combès suggests that the 'integration' of the Chané was achieved through enslaving, marrying, and even occasionally eating them (Combès and Saignes 1991; Combès 1992; Melià 1988) and was thus not one on equal terms. Combès laments the fact that most studies prior to Combès and Saignes's of 1991 have ignored the Chané component of 'Chiriguano' society in favor of its Guaraní elements (Combès 2005a: 314, 331). That the Chané can nonetheless not be overlooked is, in her

opinion, demonstrated by the case of the Isoseños, whose political structure follows an Arawak model that, for the longest time, functioned to protect and legitimate the interests of the powerful Iyambae family (Combès and Villar 2004; Combès 2005a).

3. For a contrasting view of the conquest, see Wachtel (1977). According to him, 'a series of societies, hitherto completely self-contained, experienced with the arrival of the white man the impact of an event originating quite outside their world' (ibid.: 2), in the course of which '[t]he Indians seem to have been struck numb, unable to make sense of events, as if their mental universe had suddenly been shattered' (ibid.: 13).

4. The Spanish generally accused the Guaraní of 'maltreating, killing and even eating the Chané,' while they themselves took them to work as slaves in the mines, and sometimes eradicated entire groups they had conquered (Pifarré 1989: 54). Toward the end of the sixteenth century, Guaraní raids of neighbouring peoples, which had taken place since before the conquest, even increased as a result of the Spanish demand for slaves (Saignes 1982: 83, ft 18).

5. For a useful summary of Toledo's relocation policies, see Spalding (1975).

6. Pifarré (1989: 315) also mentions in passing that various *comunidades* 'disappeared' by being converted into *karai* towns (in Cordillera, these include Charagua and Saipurú). In contrast, in the first half of the twentieth century some new *comunidades* were created by the secularisation of former missions in Cordillera (Pifarré 1989: 406).

7. For a critical in-depth analysis of the complex relationships between *hacendados*, free *ayllus*, and landless peasants in the Bolivian highlands in the eighteenth and nineteenth centuries, see Klein (1993). For the impact of foreign markets on *ayllus* and haciendas in the eighteenth to nineteenth centuries, see Spalding (1975).

8. Spanish: *fundo*; a large rural estate.

9. For more detailed discussions of the 1952 revolution and its advent and aftermath, see Gotkowitz (2007), Kohl (1978), and Heath and Carballo (1969).

10. Following this logic, the political Constitution of 1967 only talks of 'peasant communities' but does not mention 'indigenous communities' (Roper 2003: 140). An identical reframing of indigenous people as '*campesinos*' happened in the Peruvian agrarian reform of 1969 (Campanera Reig 2012: 12).

11. For a discussion of the relation between *ayllu* and state, see Platt (1982).

12. As Kevin Healy has shown, relations with these new settlers, who often worked on the big haciendas alongside Guaraní peons, were often tense: 'In effect, the Colla from the highlands, encountering the Chiriguano in an inferior social position, rapidly adopted the prejudice and the myth that the Chiriguanos were "nomads" rather than agriculturalists, intrinsically inferior, infantile, and incapable of managing their own affairs without the paternalist protection of their "Christian" *patrón*' (Healy 1982: 52). For this reason, Guaraní people tended to be excluded from the unions which the newcomers set up in order to better defend their interests (ibid.: 53).

13. The form this representation '*karai*-style' has taken as a consequence of the APG's collaboration with CIPCA has not remained without criticism. See, e.g., Ledezma (2007: 25): 'When contemporary Guaraní organisation is reconfigured in 1987 with the emergence of the Assembly of the Guaraní People (APG), on the one hand a functional organisational structure is established for the currents of development of this era, and on the other hand an instrument that will allow to retake, little by little,

"access to the spaces of power," a focus which is, to this date, driven by the majority of the leadership and institutional political activists. That is, we have converted ourselves into "fishers of established power," the power that is part of the structure of the state created in the image and semblance of those who control, manage, and dominate via this machine of homogenisation and subordination that is the nation-state.'

14. Since 1993, the CABI has also had its own NGO, the Fundación Ivi Iyambae (Land without Masters Foundation) (Combès 2005a).

15. As we shall see further on, the beginning of the conflict actually goes back to the end of the previous year (see chapter 2).

16. This could mean that they said it in front of a group of people in Itakua, or even on one of the radio stations in Camiri, as there are other instances of either party using the radio as a medium to broadcast their own perspective to a wider audience in seek of public support.

17. She mentions Hernando Sanabria, Enrique Finot, Germán Coimbra Sanz 'and others.'

18. In the words of Nicole Fabricant, 'whereas expeditions and conquests in the late 1800s depended on assertions of pure Spanish blood to acquire material assets, in this new racial politics of the Andes, it is suddenly necessary for Europeans to claim a shared identity with the very people they previously attempted to eradicate' (2009: 773).

19. Curiously, no mention is made here of Manuel or Elsa Vannucci; see IDAC: Michel (1992).

20. There have been eight more indigenous marches organised by CIDOB so far: for territory and natural resources with autonomous management (2000); for the announcement of a Constituent Assembly to reform the national Constitution (2002); for the support of indigenous participation in the Constituent Assembly and communitarian redirection (*reconducción comunitaria*) of the agrarian reform (2006); for greater indigenous rights and autonomy to be included in the new Constitution (2007); for the titling of new indigenous territories and increased indigenous autonomy (2010); the 2011 and 2012 marches in defence of the Indigenous Territory and National Park Isiboro-Sécure (TIPNIS), which protested government plans of the construction of a motorway connecting Villa Tunari in the Department of Cochabamba with San Ignacio de Moxos in Beni Department that would cut through the park; and a march to protest land grabs and deforestation in the Bolivian Amazon on the occasion of the Amazonian forest fires of 2019. There have been several marches demanding 'land and dignity' in other Latin American countries since 1990, such as Paraguay 1998 (Guaraní and Toba) and Mexico 2001 (Zapatista Army of National Liberation).

21. According to Federico Escobar Córdoba (2006), the tripartite division of *usus*, *fructus*, and *abusus* was not actually used by Roman writers but was introduced in later legal texts. Álvarez Moreno mentions the inclusion of the concept of *abusus* in the definition of *dominium* as an addition made by late medieval scholars (2011: 18).

22. A development programme for the Guaraní *comunidades* of Cordillera suggested by CIPCA and CORDECRUZ on the basis of a 1986 assessment. The programme was to be implemented via the newly created PISET teams of APG and *capitanías* (see chapter 5).

23. The Regional Corporation for the Development of Santa Cruz, which was one of nine departmental development organisations (CORDES) established in 1979. The CORDES were dissolved again with the Administrative Decentralisation Law (LDA) in 1995 because of their increasing bureaucratisation and inefficiency (Nijenhuis 2002: 47).

24. The TCOs were renamed 'Indigenous Originary Peasant Territories' (TIOCs) via Supreme Decree 0727 on 06 December 2010.

25. The full titling process of a TCO is described by Jonathan Padwe as follows (2001: 8–9): First, an indigenous organization has to present their claims to INRA (the National Institute of Agrarian Reform). VAIPO (the Viceministry for Indigenous Affairs and Originary Peoples) then prepares an official document of characterisation of the group making the claim, identifying its customs and traditions. Next, INRA conducts a 'geo-referencing' phase, measuring the demanded area and dividing it into 'polygons.' The Spatial Needs study is then carried out by VAIPO, after which INRA clears one measured polygon after the other, identifying third-party claims to the land. By the time the first polygon is designated for the indigenous group, it 'will look somewhat like "swiss cheese," with the third-party inholdings as the "holes"' (Padwe 2001: 9). In the case of Kaami, which gained its TCO status in 2002, this process translated into the roughly 30,600 ha titled to the Capitanía being divided into thirteen smaller zones, each of whose coordinates had to be meticulously circumscribed so as not to interfere with other properties in the same area (INRA 2002).

26. In a comparative study of the two Guaraní zones of Iupaguasu and Isoso, Hoyos and Blanes show that while the municipality plays an important part in such things as the elaboration of education projects and participation in elections in Iupaguasu (Hoyos and Blanes 1998: 27), it is less important in the Isoso (ibid.: 28). This is explained by the different historical background of the two zones: Iupaguasu has been reconstructed as an indigenous zone with the help of NGOs and the Church after the dispersal of its original population. This has brought with it a change in the zone's internal structure, such as the abolition of the *capitanías* and representation via assemblies on the regional and communal levels, whose members are elected by general vote (ibid.: 1998: 21–22). The internal organisation of the Isoso, on the other hand, follows a pattern of consanguineal succession of *capitanes grandes* that can be traced back to at least the early colonial period (Hoyos and Blanes 1998: 18–19; Combès 2005a). Here, interactions with the municipal level are mediated through the *capitanes*, and 'popular participation' is thus a lot more limited than in the case of Iupaguasu.

27. Kent Eaton maintains that 'throughout the political volatility of the 1960s, 1970s, and 1980s, support for either a change of government or change of regime in La Paz—rather than demands for autonomy from La Paz—was the consistent response by Santa Cruz elites to national governments they did not like' (2007: 78). The Cruceño demand for departmental autonomy was thus not an uninterrupted phenomenon but rather disappeared and resurfaced according to the political realities of the time.

28. For a more detailed study of the history and election of Evo and the MAS, see Webber (2008a, b).

29. As Kohl and Farthing have pointed out, 'Despite vociferous protests from multinational corporations, northern governments, and particularly northern media, Bolivia's new gas law was not in fact a classic nationalisation—there was no expropriation of assets and all the foreign companies negotiated new agreements. . . . In Bolivia private multinational firms still extract the majority of the country's natural gas and minerals, although the share going to the state has changed dramatically' (2012: 230).

30. This is not to suggest that the MAS as a party does not harbor its internal contradictions. For an analysis of the tensions that have developed in the MAS's leadership structure and policies over time, see Harten (2011) and Postero (2017).

31. Spanish: *saneamiento*; this includes the potential expropriation of properties which are not in fulfilment of the 'socio-economic function' (see Law 1715, 18 October 1996, Articles 64–75).

32. The slowness of INRA's land titling process was notorious. Ten years after the passing of the INRA Act, of 28,935,178 hectares requested on behalf of indigenous lowland communities by CIDOB, only 4,657,443 hectares had been titled, with another 4,000,000 or so still awaiting *saneamiento* (Guzmán ed. 2008: 33). I once heard a member of the APG suggest that the communities would in fact be better off buying land for the *comunarios* to live on and cultivate than hoping for help from INRA, which was not only hopelessly slow but also really favored the landowners over the *comunidades*.

33. More exactly, the latter condition legally implicates the former: according to Article 157 of Supreme Decree 29215 of 02 August 2007, 'where there exists a system of servitude, forced labour, debt peonage and/or slavery of families or captive persons in the rural area, . . . they are contrary to the benefit of society and collective interest, which consequently implicates a non-fulfilment of the socio-economic function, even if effectively used areas should exist on the premises.'

34. Besides the ones here mentioned, those included the International Labour Organisation (ILO) and the German Development Service (DED) (Gustafson 2010: 56).

35. In Bret Gustafson's words, 'The battle over authority and law-making was . . . reduced to a quite physical struggle over the presence of certain kinds of state actors in the region' (2010: 58).

36. Cf. Viceministerio de Tierras (2008a): '[Various municipalities and cattle ranchers' organisations in the Departments of Chuquisaca, Tarija, and Santa Cruz] have created an interinstitutional coordination committee to avoid the titling of lands in the entire Chaco and the creation of a Guaraní Original Community Land (TCO) in the locality of Alto Parapetí. The . . . committee announced that it would make use of their constitutional rights to defend the natural resources of the region and promote cattle breeding activity. . . . The committee . . . demanded the immediate derogation of the "illegal Law 3545 for being contrary to collective interest, outside the constitutional framework, an outrage against sustainable development, and for not adequately valuing the Socio-Economic Function, especially with reference to the animal load, the valuing of investments and social aspects."' The formation of this committee was only one among various pacts signed between municipal authorities, cattle ranchers, the Santa Cruz Civic Committee, and—perhaps more surprisingly—elements of the leadership of the Upper and Lower Isoso (CABI) (ibid.).

Chapter Two

'Tenemos Nuestra Historia'

A Case of History Objectified

Guaraní people's relationship with history is a tricky one. The Guaraní's lack of interest in past events too remote to concern people they themselves were familiar with has been documented in the writings of anthropologists and missionaries from the late nineteenth century onward (Combès 2005b: 228).[1] Likewise, the people of Cañón de Segura did not show much of an interest in the history of their local 'ancestors'[2] whose mortal remains, stored away in earthenware burial urns, were occasionally unearthed on the community's land. Yet one thing I heard frequently during my stay in Cañón de Segura was the *comunarios'* assertion that *they themselves* 'had history': *'Tenemos nuestra historia'*—'We have our history!' people would tell me proudly. When asked about this history, they would refer me to a document of a dozen typed pages, written by the lawyer-come-historian Franz Michel from Camiri who at one point represented them in their legal struggle with the *patrones* (IDAC: Michel 1992). A copy of this history existed in the community, which the *mburuvicha* (chief) kept in his house. This document roughly outlined the history of the old 'captive' community of Itakua, along with an account of the fight with the *patrones* that had prompted the *comunarios* to move and a summary of the court cases between *patrones* and *comunarios*, which were still ongoing at the time at which the document was written. In brief, the conflict had been sparked by the destruction of a meeting hall the *comunarios* had built by the property owner's nephew, Sadoth Palenque (see chapter 1). In the aftermath of this event, the *capitán* of Itakua, Rubén Bruno, was killed in an accident. The *comunarios* attributed his death to the use of witchcraft by the *patrones* and therefore regarded it as a case of murder. As a result, they often referred to Rubén Bruno as a victim of 'war,' a word they frequently used to describe their struggle with the *patrones*.

This chapter discusses the role played by history in Cañón and its relationship with memory and myth. It starts out with an exploration of Guaraní
people's relationship with history more generally, then moves into the *comunarios'* own understandings of 'their' history as an object to be kept and used
to ensure the legitimacy of their landownership, and an exploration of how
the different registers of 'history' present in Cañón functioned to transform a
legal document into a kind of 'founding myth.'

FROM THE TRENCHES OF KURUYUKI:
MYTHICAL HISTORY AND THE 'DEATH' AND
'RESURRECTION' OF THE 'GUARANÍ NATION'

In order to better understand the *comunarios'* enthusiasm for this document
which they called 'their history,' let us go back for a moment to the event
that was to become regarded as the defining moment in the history of the
Guaraní people of Bolivia (then referred to as 'Chiriguano'), that is, the
battle of Kuruyuki of 1892.[3] The confrontation of 1892 is said to have been
sparked by the rape and assassination of a Guaraní girl by the magistrate
(*corregidor*) of the town of Cuevo (called Ñuumbyte at the time) that went
unpunished by the authorities. It was instigated by a young messianic leader
(*tüpa*), Apiaguaiki, who had promised the Guaraní invulnerability against
the weapons of the whites (Saignes 1982: 98). Although only supported by
one of the *capitanías* (Guaraní chiefdoms, today more like districts) (Combès 2005b: 226), Apiaguaiki managed to gain a large enough number of warriors for his cause to hazard an attack. Cuevo was razed to the ground, but
the rebels were finally subdued by republican forces in the hills of Kuruyuki,
leaving some 800 Guaraní dead (Pifarré 1989: chapter 24; Saignes 1982:
96). The overall number of those killed in the various skirmishes between
December 1891 and March 1892 is estimated by Isabelle Combès to exceed
6,000 (Combès 2005a: 39–40).

    The reaction of historians concerned with Guaraní history to this crush-
ing defeat virtually amounted to a proclamation of death: the Guaraní
had come to the end of their celebrated history as warriors and thereby,
it was largely agreed, had ceased to exist as a people in any meaningful
sense (Sanabria 1972; Saignes 1990). If one adheres to the stereotypes of
the fierce Chiriguano warrior and 'savage' that had first been established
by Spanish chroniclers bearing witness to the confrontations of the early
colonial period (see chapter 1), the assumption that Bolivian Guaraní culture and society were indeed dead makes sense, and from there it follows
naturally to agree with those who would interpret the recent emergence of a

strong political Guaraní presence and unified self-representation in Bolivia as a 'resurrection' (Pifarré 1992).

Notwithstanding the supposed death of their society and culture, self-identifying Guaraní people in Bolivia today are a force to be reckoned with: not only do they represent (after Quechua and Aymara) the third-largest indigenous population in the country, but their political organisation, the Assembly of the Guaraní People (APG), which was founded in 1987, is also one of the politically strongest of Bolivia's indigenous organisations. Casting off the name of 'Chiriguano,' which by then was regarded as a derogatory term, the APG for the first time united all the *capitanías* under the common objectives of reclamation of lands and promotion of development in all the communities. The openly visible confirmation of the Guaraní's 'resurrection' as a unified people came with the APG's participation in the first commemorative event of the Battle of Kuruyuki in 1992, which had been organised as a celebration of a hundred years of Guaraní unity by local development organisations assisting the APG (Combès 2005b: 229). The event was a huge success: it united thousands of Guaraní from Bolivia, as well as Paraguay and Argentina, sporting banners with slogans such as 'Dead of Kuruyuki, rise from your trenches, march with us to the Land-without-Evil' (Pifarré 1992: 8).

Somewhat ironically, the bases for this presentation of a unified Guaraní people were provided by the very literature that purports to reflect the past and present realities of Guaraní culture—that is, the theories elaborated by ethnographers and historians (Combès 2005a: 2, 14; Combès 2005b: 230). Isabelle Combès demonstrates this on the basis of the 'Kandire' myth, which, in its Clastrean 'Land-without-Evil' sense (see Introduction), has been adopted into present-day Guaraní culture, even though 'before the 1980s, no explicit references to Kandire, nor to the Land without Evil, were ever recorded among the Chiriguano of the Bolivian Chaco' (Combès 2006: 138). While the coinciding of the emergence of the term in the usage of Guaraní leaders with the 'birth of the indigenous organisations and an accelerated process of the (re)valuation of their culture' (ibid.) indicates a political motive, the fact that, until very recently, the term was only known among indigenous elites, scholars, and lawyers suggests that it has been adopted from ethnographic and ethnohistorical texts. However, as Combès recognises, these 'lies' or 'historical errors' nonetheless

> succeed[ ] in creating—or at least consolidating—a current reality (or truth?), which is the organisation of the Assembly of the Guaraní [People]. With the APG, the 'Guaraní nation' is born as nation, on the basis of a historical and ethnic discourse. In this case, then, the 'lie' turns into reality through its own force . . . and thereby ceases to be a lie. (Combès 2005b: 230–31)

Land is often presented as linked to Guaraní culture and identity, as is exemplified by the APG's usage of the concept of the 'Land without Evil.' In recent APG discourses, the Land without Evil has taken on a political and ecological dimension in addition to the cultural one. It now also signifies Bolivia, and in particular the Chaco region that is home to the majority of Bolivia's Guaraní populations, as the Guaraní's 'native land,' in which the notion of a place of origin blends with the vision of an idealised wealthy, egalitarian, and ecologically intact state of the future that is to be attained through the economic development of Guaraní communities (Equipo Nizkor 2003). The Land without Evil in its current usage by the APG thus combines ideas about culture and nature, legitimate ownership, past, present, and future in one evocative concept that has become popular among Guaraní and non-Guaraní people within and without Bolivia.[4]

There can be little doubt that the present-day portrayal of the battle of 1892, too, is in fact an elaborate ideological construction. Although Guaraní resistance to the advance of the colonial, and later the republican, forces, colonists, and missionaries was continuously fierce, there was never a point in time when this resistance was organised in the unified form in which contemporary Guaraní discourses would have us believe. At the Battle of Kuruyuki itself, only a fraction of Guaraní warriors (*kereimba*) actually went to fight in support of Apiaguaiki:

> Of the six '*capitanes grandes*' of the time, only one decidedly supported the *tumpa*: the chief Güiracota. Others, like Tengua, held a very ambiguous attitude; others, like Mandepora in Macharetí, guarded a 'neutrality' that was dangerous to the success of the movement. Others, like Chituri in Gran Parapetí, supported the Whites. The neophytes of the missions, the Chiriguano peons of the Ingre, and others from the zone of the Isoso also marched, sometimes out of obligation, sometimes not, against the *tumpa*. (Combès 2005b: 226)

The point of this historical reinvention is obvious: to provide a foundation for the APG on which to build its claims of a united Guaraní 'nation' that can function as such for outsiders and Guaraní alike,[5] a kind of 'invented tradition' (Hobsbawm and Ranger eds. 1983) that will—at least for representational purposes—bind people together in the name of a united struggle, and that will do so in a striking and visible way. As Combès notes on the subject, 'in order to mitigate the forgetting [of one's own history], history has to be reinvented, appealing this time not to the historical sources, but to the present one wishes to shape and to the future one desires' (2005b: 228).

However, at the same time as Kuruyuki is thus of considerable importance as a powerful symbol of Guaraní identity and unity, the enthusiasm people genuinely seem to feel for the commemorative event has not spread to Guar-

Participants of the 2007 commemorative event at Kuruyuki dancing the *'arete guasu.'*
Photo by the author.

aní history in general. The sympathy displayed toward the battle's victims is the projection of a very current political outrage rather than a feeling of nostalgia; such feelings continue to be reserved for people's own beloved dead. Talking with some friends from the APG one night about the significance of having Kuruyuki as the place where Bolivia's first Guaraní University was to be established,[6] they all agreed that it was important for its location in the 'heart' of Guaraní country as well as its historical meaning, since 'our grandfathers died there.' At this point one of them cut in, chuckling, 'Ah well, there are those who say, the grandfathers are dead anyway, so who cares!'

In light of the above, today's representations of the events of 1892 as endorsed by the APG and its supporters have the character of a myth rather than of 'history' in the conventional sense: they describe a bounded episode rather than constituting an ongoing, open-ended narrative, in which the protagonists and antagonists (that is, Guaraní and *karai*) stand firm, resisting any scholarly endeavour to 'set right' the facts. The way in which all history ultimately retains a mythic element was famously explored by the historian William McNeill in an address to the American Historical Association in 1985. As he put it, 'the same words that constitute truth for some [historians] are, and always will be, myth for others, who inherit or embrace different assumptions and organizing concepts about the world' (McNeill 1986: 8–9). To McNeill, this organising of data into meaningful narratives is essential for the production of historiography:

> Facts that [can] be established beyond all reasonable doubt remain[ ] trivial in the sense that they [do] not, in and of themselves, give meaning or intelligibility to the record of the past. A catalogue of undoubted and indubitable information, even if arranged chronologically, remains a catalogue. To become a history, facts have to be put together into a pattern that is understandable and credible; and when that has been achieved, the resulting portrait of the past may become useful as well. (ibid.: 2)

Consequently, history is never entirely separable from myth, but is really a kind of 'mythistory' that can only deal in truths rather than universal Truth with a capital 'T,' the latter of which McNeill sees as an 'eschatological hope' rather than an achievable goal (ibid.: 10). This becomes especially apparent in a case such as Kuruyuki, where the project is a political more than an intellectual one and as such is interested in function rather than truth.

Much as Kuruyuki has thus become a kind of founding myth of the 'Guaraní nation,' the 'history' of Cañón as it appeared enshrined in its document functioned as the founding myth of the newly established *comunidad*. Here, too, a particular event, complete with its own villains and heroes, had been isolated and elevated as foundational to a particular group of people. What is different in this case, however, is the fact that of the many versions of this 'myth' that circulated among the *comunarios*, most were based on particular individuals' firsthand experiences. The document, which so often became conflated with its content in the way people talked about it, in reality only constituted one version of the events it described, namely, that of a *karai* outsider from Camiri.

THE CASE OF ITAKUA IN THE MEMORY OF THE *COMUNARIOS*

Over the course of my fieldwork, I had various conversations about what they remembered from the time of the land struggle with *comunarios* whose personal circumstances differed greatly from one another. Rogelio Torres, for one, was a man in his mid-forties who originated from Muyupampa, an area largely inhabited by Quechua people. Despite feeling a little like an outsider at times, he strongly identified with the *comunarios* and was passionate about the *comunidad*'s history, occasionally even referring to remoter Guaraní ancestors as 'we.' He had held various official roles in Cañón over time, and at the time of my fieldwork occupied that of Education Officer (*responsable para la educación*). Rogelio was happily married to Doña Filomena, with whom he had five children. Filomena's mother, Doña Apolonia, was the oldest person I asked about the Itakua case. She claimed to have forgotten most of the events of the time of the move, whereby I suspect this 'amnesia' to have been motivated by the vulnerability of the *comunarios'* position at the time, which was felt not only in their dealings with outsiders but also in their relationships with each other and the inhabitants of the neighbouring communities. In the end, however, I was still glad that she told me more than the 'three words' she had initially promised me. A widow living next door to her only son and his wife accompanied by a granddaughter, Doña Apolonia ran a little business in Cañón, selling odds and ends such as cigarettes, sweets, and little plastic bottles of the ever-present sugarcane alcohol nicknamed '*trago*' (booze). During my stay in Cañón, I came to greatly admire her wicked sense of humor, and making pottery with her and Doña Filomena is one of my dearest memories of that time.

The youngest person I spoke to about the Itakua case was Luz Medina, the daughter of a high-ranking Kaami functionary, who had been a child during the time of the conflict. She had three young children and lived with them in the same house as her parents, since her husband lived in another *comunidad*. Luz was one of the best cooks in Cañón, and (together with her mother Doña Estefanía and younger sister) became my 'cooking instructor' for the duration of my fieldwork, as well as one of my closest friends in Cañón. Their nearest neighbour was Luz's cousin Don Elías, who also told me at length about his experience of the conflict. At the time of my fieldwork, he was working for Caritas and took pride in the fact that he had been involved in the project that finally gave the *comunidad* its own water supply. Possessed by an often restless energy, Don Elías was greatly invested in the idea of continuously improving and developing Cañón as a *comunidad*. He also happened to be one of the original three implicated in the case of cattle theft that was initiated by the Palenque-Vannucci family (see chapter 1), as was his uncle, Don Aurelio. A kind and thoughtful man in his fifties, Aurelio often took time to talk to me when I approached him with questions (which I did often because, apart from being knowledgeable on a lot of topics that interested me, he also showed an interest in finding out about life in Europe, and talking to him was always a pleasure). Besides his political involvement in the events surrounding the move, Aurelio was also profoundly affected by them personally, as he had close kin ties with the *mburuvicha* Rubén Bruno who died during the time of the conflict.

What transpired from these conversations was that, on the one hand, different people put different foci on the events, reflecting their personal involvements in them as well as their status within (and outside of) the community. On the other hand, however, there were certain recurrent elements in the accounts that suggested that they were of more general importance to the people of Cañón. The following is a selection from these conversations, arranged in the form of a dialogue so as to draw out the discrepancies and overlaps between them.[7] The account of 'Skinny Guy' that follows those of the *comunarios* differs from the rest in that it not only provides the opinion of an outsider to the *comunidad*, but of an outsider who had not been directly involved in the events. For lack of any statements from the party opposed to the *comunarios*,[8] I am including this account because it gives us an example of a radically different view that was informed by, if not necessarily identical to, the perspective of one of the driving forces behind the eruption of the conflict, Sadoth Palenque Vannucci.

Elías Rocca: The *patrones* somehow managed to get documents to say that they were the owners of Itakua, even though the people who lived on the land had lived there for a very long time, as had their grandparents. There used to be more families in Itakua than there are now in Cañón, between thirty and forty. Some left earlier and moved to Urundaiti, which used to be part of the same property, but the land there was scarce, so soon there was no space left for people to move to and the rest of the *comunarios* stayed in Itakua.

Luz Medina: The *patrones'* house in Itakua was close to the *comunarios'* houses, so they would frequently come to harass us (*venían a molestar cualquier rato*).

Apolonia Medina: The owner of Itakua, Doña Vannucci, was good, but her nephew was trouble. Sadoth Palenque didn't want us to keep animals; he would tell us, 'This is not a *comunidad* (*aquí no hay comunidad*).' He wanted us all to move to Urundaiti, but there were about eighteen families in Itakua, so there was no space for us all in Urundaiti.

Aurelio Rocca: There used to be a school, but the *patrones* closed it down. The people used to celebrate mass in the school, and when it was closed down, they went on to doing it at my house, underneath a tree. Padre Iván was the priest coming to celebrate mass in the *comunidad* in those days, and we spoke to him about the possibility of building a shed (*galpón*) where we could celebrate mass instead of having to do it out in the open. Padre Iván spoke to the owner, Olga Vannucci, to ask her permission to build the shed, and she agreed that we could. So Padre Iván suggested to take it upon himself to get corrugated metal sheets (*calamina*) for the roof, while the rest of the *comunarios* would construct the rest of the building from wood. Padre Iván managed to get twenty-two sheets of corrugated metal.

When the building had already been put up, Olga Vannucci suddenly changed her mind and said that we couldn't make the building after all. That had been Sadoth Palenque's idea, who lived with Olga Vannucci who was his aunt, and whom he called mother. He told her that if the *comunarios* constructed the shed, they would then want to set up a *comunidad* and take the land away from her.

Elías Rocca: On the 25th of December of 1990, the owner (*dueña*) of the property, Olga Vannucci, requested the *comunarios* to build a chapel. We started work on it in April of 1991, but the *dueña's* brother-in-law, Eloy Palenque, didn't want us to build it because he thought that we'd take the land away from the family if we did. Because of him, the *dueña* then changed her mind and denied that she ever gave her authorisation for the building of the chapel, and both sides took lawyers to defend their rights in the matter.

As becomes apparent from the juxtaposition of these accounts, the foci which different witnesses' versions put on the events surrounding the *comunarios'* falling-out with the *patrones* diverge significantly from one another: while Elías Rocca's account stresses the legal and bureaucratic aspects of the conflict, those of Apolonia and Luz Medina abound in more personal accounts of the fear and hardship endured during this period. In some instances, the *comunarios'* accounts even directly contradict each other. Were there, for instance, forty or eighteen families in Cañón at the time of the beginning of the conflict? Did the *comunarios* request permission for building the shed, or did the request come from Olga Vannucci? And was it Eloy or Sadoth Palenque who persuaded Olga Vannucci to withdraw her permission? Of course, in some of these cases (such as the latter two), the discrepancies between the *comunarios'* accounts will be the result of simple misrememberings. Some others may be due to variations in the time frame people were talking about (e.g., there may have been around forty houses in Itakua before some of the *comunarios* moved to Urundaiti, and eighteen that were left afterward). In some cases, however, the 'truth value' of people's statements almost certainly depends on what aspects of the events they want to put the emphasis on—recall the different renderings of the purpose of the famous 'shed' in the documents (chapel or school building? See chapter 1), which is echoed in the *comunarios'* accounts above, of what would most likely have been a multi-purpose building similar to the current school buildings in Cañón.

The question of whether the land in Cañón was won in court or bought (see Elías Rocca below) is another such case: while those insisting that the land was won might be stressing the legality and rightfulness of their case against the *patrones*, those who say that it was bought might want to emphasise the sacrifices the *comunarios* had to make in order to gain ownership of Cañón. These framings of events work to construct reality in different ways, whereby trying to determine which version is 'truest' is a moot undertaking.

Aurelio Rocca: Sadoth Palenque went to tell the *comunarios* to destroy the shed, or else he would come back the next day to do it himself. However, we did not, so at 10:00 the next morning Sadoth returned on horseback and with a gun and again told us to destroy the shed or he would, and blood would flow. We told him that the shed was a house of God, and that we had built it for the future of our children, but Sadoth Palenque wouldn't listen. He tore down all the wooden beams holding the corrugated metal roof, which had not been nailed together yet. One beam almost fell on his head, which made him even more furious, and he went on to tear down the whole building. The next day, we contacted Padre Iván to tell him of the destruction of the shed. The Padre felt bad for us and contacted the APG; then, supported by CIPCA, Teko Guaraní, and Caritas, he initiated a court case.

Elías Rocca: There was a trial, which we lost because we had no written proof of the *dueña*'s authorisation, so in August the *patrones* tore the chapel down. They also told us to leave, so we went to Santa Cruz to take a lawyer to make an appeal with the help of CIPCA. We won a trial that gave us the right to stay on the land, but the *patrones* appealed, and a ministry commission was sent from La Paz to see if anyone really lived in Itakua, and to evaluate the situation.

Luz Medina: The *patrones* cut down and burned all the trees around the houses, which the people used for shade, to get them to leave. They also accused the *comunarios* of cattle theft.

Rogelio Torres: The *patrones* killed one of Don Germán's cows and burned down some trees on which the chickens were sleeping, so the poor chickens had to sleep on the ground.

Luz Medina: The *patrones* in Itakua didn't want the *comunarios* to sow crops, so to keep them from doing it they put wire fencing around some of the houses.

Apolonia Medina: To get the people to leave, Sadoth put barbed wire around the ravine where we went to get water; it was the only place where we could get water. To get the water they needed to live, the people crawled underneath the barbed wire, and one time my shirt got ripped at the back; it made me cry because of the pain. So I sent my little daughter instead, she could enter under the wire more easily, and I held up the wire for her.

Elías Rocca: The commission from La Paz decided that we should leave, but that we should be paid for the work we had carried out on the *patrones'* land. But the *patrones* didn't want that.

Christmas and New Year passed peacefully. In March, the lawyers went to Santa Cruz to see if the Vannuccis really had a legal title for Itakua. They did have some documents, and the lawyers also found out that the Urundaiti land had been given to the *comunarios* to live on in the 1953 Agrarian Reform.

The role of any particular actor in the events cannot always easily be pinned down but depends on the requirements of the circumstances. This can be seen in the case of the organisations intervening on behalf of the *comunarios*, where 'development organisations' suddenly become political actors. In the case of CIPCA, which has long been providing legal and practical aid for disadvantaged rural people in Bolivia (Gianotten 2006), this does not constitute something out of the ordinary. The same goes for Teko Guaraní, in that education (for whom, and by whom?) is an issue intimately bound up with politics in Latin America (see Gustafson 2009; Grindle 2004).

Luz Medina: I was eight years old and in the first year of school when the problems started. I went to school in Urundaiti, since the Itakua school had been closed because there weren't enough students. My mother didn't want me to go, she was afraid because the *patrones* said they would kill the children if they met them on the road, they would run them over, because they hated us all.

Apolonia Medina: Rubén Bruno was *mburuvicha* at the time.

Luz Medina: Padre Iván Nasini of Teko Guaraní bought a cart and horse for the children to go to school in, and he left Rubén Bruno in charge of it. For one week, he was driving them to school and back and everything was fine, but then an accident happened.

On the day before San Juan [i.e., the 23rd of June, before the Christian holiday of St John], Rubén Bruno dropped the children off as usual, but they found that there was no one at the school and there were no classes. So the children started to walk back on foot.

At mid-day, Don Rubén left to pick the children up again, but he never arrived at the school.

Aurelio Rocca: We had the cart for one week when one of the horses killed Rubén. They were about to leave Itakua, and Rubén was putting the bridles on the horses when one of them got scared by something and ran off, dragging Rubén over 200m, then breaking his skull with its hoof.

Luz Medina: They found the overturned cart halfway. The horse had run off. Don Rubén was found close to his own house by his daughter's oldest son, his first grandson. The horse had smashed his head in so the brain was spilling out of the skull. His heart was still beating, but he soon died. One of his sons was the same age as I; the two youngest were so small they probably hardly remember their father now.

Aurelio Rocca: When Sadoth heard about the accident, he said that for all that Rubén had wanted land (*tierra*), he was now under the earth (*tierra*), and claimed to have paid a witch doctor in Camiri to kill him by witchcraft.

Luz Medina: Later, the *patrón*'s own workers (*peones*) sold the *patrón* out, they told the *comunarios* that the *patrones* had brought a witch from Brazil to kill my father as well, so my mother went all over the place to get him cured [i.e., they got several witch doctors (*curanderos*) to perform magic to counter the witch's magic] to save his life, and it worked.

The *patrones* even burned the cross and the decorations on Rubén Bruno's grave and replaced the candles the *comunarios* had left there with red candles of evil to bring even more people down (*hacer caer a más gente*).

The alleged role of witchcraft in the killing of Rubén Bruno constitutes a whole dimension of the conflict that is absent from the legal documents entirely. The difficulties that emerge in cases where such 'partially connected' indigenous and nonindigenous ontologies (see De la Cadena 2010) are made to interact in court have been described by Tristan Platt on the basis of an intriguing case of a clash between the Bolivian legal system and the moral and ritual codes pertaining to highland shamanic practice (2014b). Likewise, while Michel's historical document possessed an inherent legal power lacking from the *comunarios*' memories, it could not, by its very nature, contain this rather important aspect of their experience.

Aurelio Rocca: Once the court case had started, Sadoth Palenque told us to leave immediately and move to a different place, where we would be able to do what we wanted. He told us to go to Cañón de Segura, which didn't have an owner, but then he attempted to get legal ownership of it himself.

Luz Medina: A week before we went to Cañón, Sadoth came out of his house and told us, 'Tonight, blood will flow.' So the people locked themselves inside their houses, but nothing happened. It seemed that Sadoth had found out about the plan to move to Cañón and got annoyed because he and his family wanted to claim the land as their own. To show that he'd been working the land in Cañón, Sadoth dug a well, but there was only sand in it, no water, and also a water reservoir that didn't have any water either and was very small.

Elías Rocca: In August 1992, three *comunarios* went to La Paz to look in the office of the Agrarian Reform whether the *patrones* really had a title to Cañón de Segura as they were claiming, and they didn't. After the three returned, they called a meeting and told the rest of the *comunarios* that Cañón was vacant land (*tierra baldía*), and we all decided to go there to live.

In September, the lawyers found out that Eloy Palenque had put in a solici-
tude for the land to be titled to his family.

Aurelio Rocca: The trial was held in the name of Sadoth's father Eloy
Palenque because Sadoth was only sixteen years old at the time.

Elías Rocca: Two days after the three *comunarios'* return from La Paz, the
patrones came with police to take two of them and two others to the prison in
Camiri. They pretended to take them to Camiri to sign some documents, but
this was only a pretext (*engaño*), and really they were locked up and accused
of cattle theft. A woman employee of the Vannuccis wrote a letter of lies to
claim that the four had stolen cattle, but none of it was true, and really they
were taken because they were all leaders: one was *capitán*, another secretary,
the third *vocal*, and the fourth leader of the women's group.

The *comunarios* decided that Germán Medina [Luz's father] should be the
new *capitán*, and he started to organise the move. Two of the *comunarios*
didn't stay in jail long, but the remaining two stayed in jail for two years
because the land battle had priority over the cattle case, so it was taken care
of first. The *patrones* had started the cattle case because they saw that they
were losing the land battle.

Aurelio Rocca: There was an on-site inspection (*audiencia*) in Itakua, to
see from where the cattle had been stolen. Eloy Palenque went, saying that
they would present their own witnesses, but then failed to do so. The *patrones*
claimed that the *comunarios* had taken cows from here or there and tied them
up in the forest, but there was no proof. The Santa Cruz lawyers got angry
with the Palenques' lawyers and told them that they should have demanded
proof of the allegations before defending their clients, and that their duty was
not just to make money.

Little by little, the police understood that the problem was really to do with
land, not with cattle. One of the lawyers defending the *comunarios* was from
the APG, the other one a defence lawyer of the poor, for people who can't
afford a lawyer. One other one left the trial because he was paid by the Vannuccis, even though he was an old Camireño and knew the history well. The
Vannuccis also bribed the judge and the police, but the *comunarios* had six
witnesses to confirm that the cattle theft allegations were wrong whereas the
Vannuccis had none, so after a year or so of court battle the judge had to give
in and declare the *comunarios* winners of the trial.

Elías Rocca: In the cattle case, lawyers came from Santa Cruz to interview
the witnesses about the theft, but those could not agree on the exact numbers,
so they were revealed as liars. The accused went to Santa Cruz for a final
hearing, but neither the Palenques nor their lawyers showed up, so they were
cleared of the accusations.

The cattle theft case provides an instance in which the documentary evidence is as contradictory as the *comunarios*' memories: on at least two occasions, the persona of one *comunario* is mixed up with one of his uncles in the witness accounts (IDAC: Chilo 1992; IDAC: Rueda 1992; IDAC: M. Justiniano and Torrez 1992), and on one occasion the testimony originally given by one witness suddenly appears in the name of another (IDAC: V. Guzman 1992; IDAC: M. Justiniano and Torrez 1992).

Elías Rocca: In Cañón, meanwhile, the work had begun of clearing space for houses, which was carried out with the support of the APG, so people came from all the neighbouring *comunidades* to help. So when the last two *comunarios* got out of jail, the houses were already built, of wattle and daub (*tabique*) at first.

Rogelio Torres: We first came from Itakua over the hill, in the night to avoid the *patrones*, to start constructing the houses. I was the very first one to stay in Cañón, it was very lonely. There was only a narrow path through the canyon, so we cleared spaces in the forest. People came from Urundaiti, Piedritas, and as far as Eiti and Alto Parapeti to help us clear the spaces for our *chacos* and houses.[9] We built the houses quickly, with the support of CIPCA, they gave us materials. The central school building was the first one we built, that's why we haven't torn it down yet even though it's very simple; it's historical.

The *patrón* and his hired hands would sometimes come to try to get us out. Once, a truck full of the *patrón's* men arrived, who wanted to cause trouble, but they didn't realise how many Guaraní there were working in the fields and everywhere, so they left quickly when they found themselves surrounded by some 150 men with machetes. Someone tried pulling a gun, but the *comunarios* threatened to peel him like an onion if he didn't put the gun away, so he did.

After we built our first houses, some others and I lived in Cañón for about two months before all the rest of the people followed. CIPCA also helped us in our final move by providing a truck in which everyone, with their animals and household belongings and everything, was brought to Cañón.

We all got together in the school building to decide who was going to build their house where. The only rule was to keep at least 100 meters distance between houses to avoid conflicts over chickens going into the neighbors' gardens, that kind of thing. There was one man who wanted the spot of my wife Filomena's mother's house so he could be closer to the centre [i.e., the school], but he ended up with a plot way at the other end of the village. He has gone to Santa Cruz to live now. A few other people changed their minds about where they wanted to make their houses, so they took their roofs and other things and went somewhere else with them. At that time, the houses were built like my fence, with poles of wood only [i.e., wattle and daub], so it was easy to move them.

Apolonia Medina: In Cañón, there was only forest, with a lot of ticks and mosquitoes. My family had built a house in the place where my house is now when I arrived, but it was all made of sticks and mud. There was no water, and the children were suffering because of the many insects (*bichos*), they would crawl into their eyes and make them cry. We had to get water from far away; we did that at night. But even so, the water was never enough, it was just enough to cook and wash one's face, but in the hot season we would have needed a lot more.

Rogelio Torres: At first, we had to go to Itakua to fetch water during the night, because during the day we were all working. We only got our own water supply (*cañería*) in 1996.

Caritas gave us the corrugated metal for the roofs and some mesh (*malla*).[10] They were meant to provide concrete floors and doors and windows as well, but they ran out of money before they could supply them. The people in the organisations often go to work there to put the money into their own pockets.

The three accounts of the move from Itakua presented above nicely demonstrate the different registers in which different *comunarios* talked about it: Don Elías's is sparse and matter-of-fact, Don Rogelio's is emotionally charged, with an almost swashbuckling quality to it that underlines the danger and rebelliousness of the act, and that of Doña Apolonia recalls the suffering the *comunarios* endured during this initial period. While almost certainly also reflective of the narrators' personalities, these differences also reflect the different roles they played in the occurrences: Don Elías, having been one of the *comunarios* accused of cattle theft, had been absent for most of the move. Doña Apolonia remembered it from an almost purely domestic viewpoint that conveyed her anxiety about not being able to look after her family properly. Don Rogelio, meanwhile, was involved in the guerrilla-style pioneer work of clearing the forest at a time when the conflict with the *patrones* had not yet been officially resolved, and so witnessed a particularly high amount of friction. Interestingly, Don Rogelio was the only non-Guaraní *comunario* living in Cañón at the time, yet he was also the one with the greatest interest in keeping its history alive. We also find in his account some of the themes I will discuss more closely in chapter 4; that is, that of the *comunidad*'s spatial organisation, internal mobility, and the disruptive effect of jealousy on community life.

Luz Medina: The first to move to Cañón were Filomena, Apolonia, and their whole family, who went in July or August. My family was the last to go in

September. I went to stay with my uncle Virgilio for a little while because my other uncle Aurelio's son and I were the only ones still left to go to school in Urundaiti, which was far, and we were scared. The *patrones* left us alone though, because papers had already been signed to say that they had to. The last families to leave apart from us were Aurelio's and Elías's.

Aurelio Rocca: After the case was closed, I stayed in Santa Cruz for one more month because I was afraid that I would be murdered. I was told not to assume any responsibilities for three more years, not to go to meetings, because the Vannuccis might try to get revenge somehow, but I didn't follow the advice and instead organised the installation of two water pumps.

Elías Rocca: At the time of the move, various people left and went to live in other places because they were afraid. One of them was Jacinto, who only returned in 2003. There is a video of the Itakua story [made by Teko Guaraní] that shows him ever so well, cutting down trees for the *patrones* (*cabalito se ve cortando árboles para los patrones*). He was working for them at the time.

Apolonia Medina: Don Jacinto was working for the *patrón* all that time, helping him do the dirty work because he paid him.

Rogelio Torres: The *patrones* were spending a lot of money on lawyers to get us out, but the *comunarios* stayed because they were in the right, so before the *patrones* had to sell all their cattle to pay for the legal fees, they finally gave up.

Elías Rocca: A transfer was done in La Paz, and the Vannuccis' request for the title to Cañón was annulled. Padre Iván, CIPCA, and some others helped pay for the trials, and an organisation for the support of land matters paid the US$5,000 which we had to pay for the wire fencing and other work done by the Vannuccis in Cañón. All this was settled in a meeting in Camiri. The *patrones* never paid anything for the *comunarios'* work on their land.

In the end, it all worked out well for us though, because the land in Itakua over which we were fighting at first was only some 100 hectares, and now we have close to 3,000 hectares.

Apolonia Medina: In the end, things turned out a lot better for us than they had been before, because now we have peace and quiet and lots of space for sowing crops and other things.

Elías Rocca: This is all part of the *comunidad*'s vision of achievements (*visión a lograr*): to live free of the *patrones*. We have already achieved the improvement of the houses, that was a Caritas project in 2001. We have the cattle project that started in 1998. And the *comunidad* also has a water supply system, which I did with Caritas in 2000. We are also going to have our own veterinarian soon, Don Germán's son Valerio. He is still studying, but he will be finished with his studies soon; he will be a professional soon, and then we are going to start a pig breeding project here in the *comunidad*. Of course, there's still a lot missing, but little by little things are improving.

We can see in the *comunarios'* accounts how this political edge to local development creates a continuum between the *comunarios'* first acts of resistance and the ongoing development of the *comunidad* in which the initial support rendered by some of the organisations (in the form of lawyers' fees, transportation, building materials for the first houses, etc.) and the projects subsequently provided by them and others (the municipality's cattle project, Caritas's water and housing projects, etc.) merge seamlessly into one another in what Elías referred to as one unitary 'vision of achievements.'

While this last point becomes most apparent in the account of Don Elías, who had a particularly strong interest in Cañón's development, there are certain aspects that appear as fixtures in almost all the versions I was told by the *comunarios*. Those are the identification of 'good' and 'evil' forces that find their epitome in the figures of Rubén Bruno and Sadoth Palenque, respectively.

'Skinny Guy'

The account of 'Skinny Guy'[11] came out of a chance conversation I had with a couple of former schoolmates of my Camireña friend Viviana's, who had met at her house to celebrate their school-leaving anniversary. As fate had it, this drunken encounter was to provide me with the only account that might be called representative of the perspective of the 'other side' involved in the Itakua case. Sitting in Vivi's house with several bottles of beer in front of us, Vivi's schoolmates and I talked about all kinds of things happening in the world for a bit, and I was impressed by the knowledge of European history of the skinny guy. Then, the talk turned to the topic of Bolivia and its current state of affairs, from where it soon turned to Evo's government. They both agreed that Bolivia was 'under development' and had to be developed European-style, then Skinny Guy launched a speech that began like this: 'I'm not against the poor and indigenous people having better chances in life and wanting to better themselves, that's a good thing and totally okay . . .' (I should have seen it coming, but the vehemence of what followed took me by surprise) '. . . but this government of this shitty Indian (*indio de mierda*) isn't worth anything. I mean, I'm an accountant, but I only know the smallest bit about what there is to know about accountancy, so how can a Constituent Assembly made up of *campesinos* who don't know anything rewrite the Constitution?' And so on.

I was going to say to him that I agreed up to a point, but that the argument for having *campesinos* in the Constituent Assembly was that they knew a lot more about the needs of the poor people than any lawyer, that there were in fact quite a few lawyers in the Assembly (besides other 'professionals'), and that it was in no way guaranteed that 'professional' politicians always knew what they were doing; but I didn't get another word in. 'Skinny Guy' ranted on about how Evo's government was screwing the people, just look at what happened to our mate Sadoth in his court case.

At this point I interrupted him to ask what his friend's full name was; he replied: Sadoth Palenque.

I told him I was doing an investigation in Cañón and asked him to tell me more about this case, and, as was to be expected, the version he gave me was very different from those of the *comunarios*.

The *comunarios*, he said, had taken the land in Cañón away from his friend, who, out of the goodness of his heart, gave it to them in the end, even though he had won the court case over it.[12] I told them that I didn't think this was true, that the land had been bought, at which they both shouted that this was a lie. I told them about the US$5,000 the *comunarios* had had to pay for 'improvements' Palenque had made, and Skinny Guy asked me, did I think that was a justified price for such a big piece of land? He then started railing against Padre Iván, who, he said, had caused a lot of hassle for the family and even banned one of the Vannucci sisters from going to mass. Poor Sadoth had had to interrupt his studies in Sucre and return home in order to sort things out.

There was some confusion as to the location of the old community—I mentioned Itakua, but Skinny Guy insisted that there had never been any people living in Itakua, but that they were all living in Urundaiti. He kept repeating how, out of the goodness of his heart, Sadoth Palenque had given the *comunarios* the land so they could go and live there, and how they weren't doing anything with it. Both men alleged to have seen various tractors standing around there uselessly ('*parados*'), which they said had been given to the *comunarios*.[13] They also told me how, when they had visited the *comunidad*, the *comunarios* had threatened them.

I told them that, obviously, I couldn't know what had happened fifteen years ago, but that I had seen their *chacos* now and they were enormous. They said, maybe, but back then the *campesinos* weren't doing anything. I asked how the whole trouble had started, and they told me that it had been due to the *comunarios*' wanting to take the land away from Sadoth, which was rightfully his.

As can be gathered from my own documents-based reconstruction in chapter 1 and the opinions voiced by 'Skinny Guy,' the occurrences preceding and following the incident of Palenque's destruction of the communal building were sparked, as well as received, by a large number of often opposing attitudes, all equally convinced of their own righteousness. Rather than constituting the only——or, indeed, arguably even the most central—of these oppositions, the one between Rubén Bruno and Sadoth Palenque thus only constitutes one in a series of oppositions that could be highlighted: Padre Iván Nasini vs. Olga Vannucci; Eloy Palenque vs. the APG; the Rocca family vs. the Vannucci-Palenque family; the Rocca family vs. the Bolivian legal system and its representatives; the *comunarios*' lawyers vs. the lawyers of the *patrones*; etc. Further, a number of mediating agents and helpers appeared at various stages of the conflict (Franz Michel, CIPCA, AGACAM, PDCC, etc.), who, albeit never completely neutral, did not directly form part of the conflict but rather intervened in it with the aim of bringing it to a swift conclusion.

We can thus see that the foregrounding of the figures of Rubén Bruno and Sadoth Palenque is a reduction. Its importance, I would argue, lies in its ability to fix in place the sides in an otherwise muddled and complex interplay of interest groups and ambitions and thereby rendering it com-prehensible. It is, to recall William McNeill's words, an exercise in pattern recognition that allows meaning to be created out of raw facts (or, in the case of the *comunarios*' memories, individual recollections and opinions). 'Mythic' in character like the opposing parties in the Battle of Kuruyuki, the figures of Bruno and Palenque have taken on symbolic properties which allow them to stand in for—and further, to qualify—the two sides in the conflict that lies at the heart of Cañón's coming-into-being as a *comunidad*: the *comunarios* and the Palenque-Vannuccis, Guaraní peons and *karai patrones*, and—ultimately—good and evil.

THE END OF HISTORY . . . BUT NOT THE END

These two positions are further determined by being 'spelled out' in the historical document, as the *comunidad*'s history itself is determined by the medium that contains it. By preserving the events the *comunarios* had lived through in a written format, the document bestowed a permanence and unity on their story that was lacking from their oral accounts. Its author, further, was not any old outsider but one who, as a lawyer, was endowed with the authority to produce texts that were powerful in a representational sense in a way the *comunarios*' memories were not. The way that people specifically referred to this document as 'their history' is telling in more than one way: on the one hand, it marks out 'making history' as something *karai* people do, a practice of powerful outsiders rather than the real-life experiences of the people who constitute its subjects. It also, however, qualifies the end result of this practice as a finished object that can be neither changed nor extended, but to which—like to a tool—a specific use-value can be ascribed.

It was clear that when people were saying that they 'had their history,' this was to be taken quite literally: to have the document meant to *have* the history, to be in charge of it and be able to present it, should it become necessary. The fact that the document is, as its title informs the reader, a 'historical-juridical investigation' is fitting: this is not the kind of history that exists for its own sake, but a history that *does*, a sort of multi-purpose history that is collective memory, political statement, and legal claim all in one.

Having experienced the problematics surrounding landownership in Bolivia firsthand, the *comunarios* were well aware of the importance of having such a document at their disposal. Together with their contract of purchase and an official map of the community's limits, the history document provided them with a fair amount of legitimacy in the eye of national law. However, while to *have* history was clearly one of the important things the *comunarios* of Cañón sought to stress to me in their statement of '*tenemos nuestra historia*,' there is something to be said about the word *our* here as well: unlike the festival of Kuruyuki—which, although historically the commemoration of a defeat, has practically turned into a celebration of Guaraní courage and unity in the face of *karai* oppression—the history of Cañón is not one that seeks to speak for *all* of Bolivia's Guaraní. It is, on the contrary, the very particular history of a place and its people, the most important part of which many of the people whom I met during my fieldwork had lived through themselves. As such, it also functioned to set the people of Cañón apart from the inhabitants of other communities whose experiences were altogether different from their own. It was thus meaningful to the *comunarios* on a personal level a generalised ideological construct like Kuruyuki could not hope to reach.[14]

It is, then, little surprising that the figures of the hero and the villain were not only central to the 'official history' as contained in the document, but also became the pivot around which the *comunarios*' own versions revolved. Fixed in this way, their positions are not negotiable, and hence concurrence with the side of the 'villain' becomes unthinkable. The difficulty accompanying any attempt to hold such a contradictory position is demonstrated by the case of Don Jacinto, a *comunario* who had been 'ostracised' from the community for siding with the *patrones* during the initial stages of the conflict. Jacinto was forced to live with his family at the edge of Cañón's residential area, a position that reflected their uncertain status within the community: although still situated on community land, their house was equally close to the first houses of the other *comunarios* as it was to the abandoned house of the *patrones*, and both Jacinto and his wife continued to carry out occasional work on the *patrones*' property, such as, for example, milking their cows. A friend of mine once pointed out their house to me as 'where the señora lives who looks after the Vannuccis' house,' a description from which I at the time completely failed to gather that this señora was in fact one of the *comunarias*.

Unlike the inflexible positions occupied by the mythified hero and villain of Cañón's 'history,' the positions of such 'real-life' characters as Don Jacinto were a lot more flexible, and he and his family moved back into the centre of the *comunidad* during the time of my stay there. Considering that Jacinto's family was connected to those of other *comunarios* by various kin ties, this development is perhaps not all that surprising. What did, on the other hand, surprise me a great deal was to learn that relations between the *comunarios* and the arch villain of their history, Sadoth Palenque, had also calmed down over time and were now in fact even amiable. However, this piece of information was not volunteered to me but rather came to light only as a result of my specific inquiries on the topic. It was obvious from the responses I got that this current relationship was not one that greatly interested the *comunarios*: they basically limited themselves to assurances that things between them and Palenque were 'just fine' (*'tranquilo nomás'*), and the most detailed account I got on the matter was that Palenque occasionally came to visit the community and even gave *comunarios* lifts in his car when he encountered them in the road.[15] Accounts of Palenque's villainous behavior during the time of the conflict were, on the other hand, always abundant.

The fact that, like with Don Jacinto, things had also moved on between the *comunarios* and Sadoth Palenque since the time of the 'historical' episode, but the *comunarios* nonetheless only seemed interested in portraying the latter as a villain, is revealing, not of any particular maliciousness on their part, but rather of the fact that Sadoth Palenque had since ceased to be of any particular importance to them. The role that had lent him his importance was precisely that of villain in the history-come-founding myth of their *comunidad*, and it was as such that he had been immortalised in the *comunarios'* historical document. History, then, was opposed to lived experience in that it was a thing of the past, unalterable, permanent, and *finished*.

The idea of history as the finished product of the practices of powerful outsiders that finds its embodiment in the document in whose pages it is contained, and which can as such be owned and utilised, is one that cannot be separated from the historical background of the region. Within Latin America, the writing of history was a practice introduced by the agents of colonialism, which has been, and to this day remains, intimately bound up with legal issues (such as, most crucially perhaps, the struggle for land). In the words of the literary critic Roberto González Echevarría, 'Latin American history and fiction, the narrative of Latin America, were first created within the language of the law, a secular totality that guaranteed truth and made its circulation possible' (1998: 10). In this sense, the history contained in the document was a piece of evidence that contained the 'truth' of the rightfulness and lawfulness of the *comunarios*' position vis-à-vis the *patrones*, and which had been written specifically to be presented to the legal authorities in support of the *comunarios*' case. For this purpose, its limited scope was sufficient, and the contract sealing the purchase of their land, together with the map outlining the *comunidad*'s current limits, were all that was necessary to put a full stop to the *comunidad*'s history altogether. Having fulfilled its designated role in the Camiri courts, the 'history'—in its legal function—had become obsolete, except as a kind of insurance policy for the *comunarios* against possible future abuses of their rights.

The use of village archives as a repository of legally powerful documents used to protect a community's rights is a convention that has long been practiced in the Andean highlands (Platt 1992; Platt 2014a). The same longstanding tradition of using documents in this way does not exist in the Bolivian lowlands, however, which differ from the Andean region not only in their ecological makeup, but by extension also in their historical background: whereas indigenous groups in the highlands actually benefitted from the 1953 Agrarian Reform that dismantled the large landholdings (*latifundios*) and gave indigenous people the possibility to apply for individual land titles, the same did not happen for the indigenous populations in the lowlands, whose villages often found themselves located on a piece of land that had at one point or another passed into the possession of a non-indigenous landholder, often as a gift from a contemporary government leader (see chapter 1). Considering the strong insistence of the *patrones* in the Itakua case that Itakua was a 'property' (*propiedad*) rather than a *comunidad*, and also considering what such a difference meant in terms of the rights (or, as it were, the absence thereof) of a place's inhabitants, it is not surprising that a tradition of using archives for the legal defence of communities did not develop in the lowlands. For one, such documents would largely not even have existed in the first place; and further, it is unlikely that many *patrones* would have tolerated the existence of a community archive on what they considered to be their land.

It seems likely that the scarcity of documents that were available to the *comunarios* had played a part in their insistence in equating their 'history' with the one particular document, while at the same time disregarding anything that had happened before as well as after the events therein described. As an 'insurance policy,' there was no need to expand it any further, and thus the writing of the history of Cañón had finished before I started my fieldwork there. However, as we have seen, even though the historical project had ended with the establishment of Cañón as a legally recognised *comunidad indígena*, the *comunarios* regarded their *comunidad* itself as a project that was still ongoing.

In part II of this book, I explore how, instead of 'history,' which was seen as a thing belonging to the past, ideas about 'living well' had become a dominant idiom in *comunarios'* understandings of this process, which were in turn bound up with ideas about 'development.' This shift in focus coincided with the increased presence of institutions other than the Bolivian legal system as influential agents in the shaping of the community and the lives of its inhabitants; that is, governmental and nongovernmental development organisations.

NOTES

1. Cf. Gow (1991), Taylor (2007), and Rappaport (1990) for contrasting models of historicity among South American indigenous peoples.

2. I am using the word in inverted commas here because it is not one the *comunarios* of Cañón ever used to talk about those past inhabitants. At the same time, however, they did acknowledge that they had also been Guaraní and in that sense culturally similar to them. They would, for example, often remark how in the past, the Guaraní did not seem to have used sugar, as the skulls of the skeletons all had 're-ally good teeth', which they would then jokingly compare to their own. Thus, while not providing the *comunarios* with specific genealogies of descent and the like, the bones of the dead were an assertion that their land had in fact been Guaraní land for a considerable length of time, which, in the light of the ongoing tensions between land owners and indigenous groups in Bolivia, can be an important claim to be able to make (cf. Castañón Pinto 2011).

3. For a more detailed account of Kuruyuki and its antecedents and aftermath, see Pifarré (1989: chapter 24) and Gustafson (2009: 34–40).

4. Gastón Gordillo (2012) describes how the APG's usage of this concept has more recently been picked up by Guaraní leaders and activists fighting for land in Jujuy, Argentina. Like in the Bolivian case, Guaraní people in Jujuy are having to defend themselves against accusations of not being 'local' enough, which puts the legitimacy of their land claims in question (cf. chapters 6 and 7). In the Argentine case, there is the further complication of Guaraní people's land claims standing in possible opposition to those of other indigenous groups such as Toba, Ocloya, and Wichí, whose ancestors occupied the territory in question before Guaraní people settled there in the late nineteenth century (ibid.: 154).

5. The use of European-style denominators such as 'nation' for indigenous groups is widespread in South America and goes back to colonial classificatory practices that sought to understand the political scene in the New World by ordering it in terms of familiar categories (Schwartz and Salomon 1999).

6. The University, which has been baptised 'Apiaguaiki Tumpa' in honor of the messianic leader of 1892, was inaugurated on 11 April 2009, together with the Quechua University 'Casimiro Huanca' and the Aymara University 'Tupac Katari.'

Further underlining the centrality of the Kuruyuki 'myth' in present-day Bolivian discourses on the Guaraní, Apiaguaiki himself was officially elevated to the status of 'national hero and martyr in the fight for the liberation, sovereignty, and dignity of the Guaraní people' via Law 4051 of 07 July 2009. The paradox inherent in the nomination of a national hero whose fight for liberation was aimed against the forces of that very nation is worth noting, as it exemplifies the difficulties of Evo Morales's attempts to remodel Bolivia into an egalitarian 'plurinational' society whilst maintaining the framework of a capitalist nation-state (Postero 2017).

7. These conversations were held in Spanish and recorded with the help of a notepad, as various *comunarios* had expressed an aversion to being recorded on tape. The following accounts are therefore paraphrased from my fieldnotes and do not necessarily reproduce the *comunarios'* exact words. The content, however, is in all cases true to what the people in question told me.

8. I was unable to gain access to the Palenque-Vannucci family during the course of my fieldwork. The 'memory' part of this chapter is thus conspicuously one-sided; however, we can at least get an idea of the *patrones'* attitude on the subject from the discussion of the documents in the previous chapter in combination with the account of 'Skinny Guy.'

9. Eiti and Alto Parapetí are different *capitanías*, or Guaraní districts. Urundaiti and Piedritas are *comunidades* located next to Cañón.

10. Rogelio also mentioned 'a project called "Visión Mundial"' in this context; this actually referred to an NGO rather than a project, i.e., the Bolivian incarnation of World Vision, which was conducting Areal Development Programmes (PDA) in Cañón geared especially toward the promotion of children's rights and wellbeing (see chapter 5).

11. For the purpose of anonymising him, I have here nicknamed him—in good Bolivian fashion—according to his physical appearance.

12. The *comunarios* also say they won the court case, but according to the documents the case was dropped as part of a financial settlement between the two parties (see chapter 1).

13. It was obvious from Skinny Guy and his friend's talk that they had only gone to Cañón de Segura once, so even if they had seen a tractor standing idle there, it might just have been a day outside of the sowing season. Being located a fair way off from the nearest river, and having as yet no irrigation system, the *comunarios* were completely reliant on the arrival of the rainy season for their agricultural activities. Their talk of 'several tractors' was almost certainly mistaken—at the time of my fieldwork, there was one tractor being kept in Cañón, which was shared between three communities, and which was being used day and night in order to get all the planting done in all three once the rainy season had started.

14. The way 'history' here functions to promote social coherence on different levels is reminiscent of what Nancy Postero has described for the concept of 'autonomy' in the by now autonomous indigenous district of Charagua (2017).

15. As it happened, I never encountered any member of the Vannucci-Palenque family in Cañón during the time I was there.

Part II

'THIS IS A FREE COMMUNITY'

Comunarios' Ideas about *'Comunidad'*

Chapter Three

Tranquility Beats Reciprocity?

Of Shifting Meanings and Enduring Significance

Given that the *comunarios* had lived in Itakua 'since time immemorial' and thus had attachments of a spiritual as well as a material kind to the land there—after all, many of their relatives lived, and still live, in the neighbouring *comunidad* of Urundaiti, and many of their own dead were buried on Itakua land—I was curious to know how people felt about the move to Cañón on an individual basis. So I asked various people where they had liked living more, in Itakua or in Cañón. The result was unanimous: everyone I spoke to asserted that Cañón was much preferable to Itakua, even those few who expressed a certain nostalgia for their old home. As an explanation, they would tell me, '*Aquí, se puede vivir tranquilo*'—'One can live in peace here.'

In other words, what people were telling me about was their version of what it meant to be able to live well. Ideas of 'living well' (*vivir bien*), or 'the good life' (*vida buena*), permeate the ethnographic literature on South American peoples, and the topics under discussion here are manifold: we hear about the achievement of sociality and conviviality through the balance of positive and negative emotions (Overing and Passes eds. 2000); the maintenance of harmonious community life through the management of (female) reproductive power (Belaunde 2001); and new ideas about the 'good life' emerging as resistance to the power of the state (Sarmiento Barletti 2011), to give but a few examples.

Since the coming into power of Evo Morales and the MAS (Movement toward Socialism) in December of 2005, 'living well' ('*allin kawsay*' or '*sumaq kawsay*' in Quechua and '*suma qataña*' in Aymara) has also become a political catchphrase in Bolivian state politics. The notion forms the ethical principle of the new Bolivian Constitution,[1] Article 8 of which states:

93

The State assumes and promotes as ethical-moral principles of the plural society: ama qhilla, ama llulla, ama suwa (don't be lazy, don't be a liar nor be a thief), suma qamaña (living well), ñandereko (harmonious life), teko kavi (good life), ivi maraei (Land-without-Evil) y qhapaj ñan (noble path or life). (CPE: 2009)

The use of concepts from different indigenous languages here can be seen as mainly an ideological statement reflecting Evo Morales's (at least officially) indigenist politics rather than constituting concrete directions for how to conduct one's life, and is overall rather vague. Besides, the Spanish rendering of such indigenous-language concepts as 'living well' is problematic, as has been pointed out by Xavier Albó (2008a). The translation of *ñande reko* as 'harmonious life,' for example, stretches the concept of *teko* (which in itself is a more neutral term meaning 'way of being,' 'character,' or 'custom') in that it presents an implicit value as explicit meaning, without, however, providing any explanation for this move.

If we ask what exactly this 'harmonious life' may entail for Guaraní people, we find that authors tend to stress the importance of reciprocity in the Guaraní *teko*, a concept that has often been used as synonymous with the idea of 'living well' (see, e.g., Medina ed. 2002). What is termed 'reciprocity' among Guaraní peoples is conventionally represented as a combination of positive reciprocity—the creation of alliances and kinship ties through the redistribution of goods by chiefs (*mburuvicha reta*) in the form of fiestas in exchange for women and their or their families' work—and negative reciprocity based on an ethics of vengeance directed against enemy groups. One the one hand,

[r]eciprocity assumes that someone offers a gift for free and voluntarily. . . . The gift does not create necessary obligations of restitution, although it creates a relation that will in its turn motivate another gift. . . . The best expression of reciprocity is . . . the generous banquet, [for which a chief will receive] multiple forms of generosity: moral support, delivery of women, participation in the work to be achieved, accompaniment in his enterprises. (Melià 1988: 47)

On the other hand,

[t]he tribal universe of the Chiriguano rests on the confrontation between its [various] parties: a completely negative reciprocity, vengeance engages the network of the relatives and allies of one generation and also its descendants. It creates a dynamic within the connections between the 'obliged' (*deudos*),[2] some always being in debt of an offence or affront. This unbalanced antagonism permits the reaffirmation of the establishing tie of society. . . . However, founded on the settling of old scores that are rarely cleared between local and regional groups, it opposes their fusion into a unified political whole. (Saignes 1982: 80)

The common denominator of the two types of reciprocity is the way in which both functioned as an 'identity marker' by establishing a group's (ever-changing) position in relation to other groups, and—on an intra-communal level—through the procurement of personal prestige by distinguished men through the display of generosity and prowess in warfare.

However, interesting as these texts are as historical accounts, they are puzzling when presented in the context of ethnographic works. Quite routinely, texts talking about contemporary Guaraní people's ideas of the 'good life' rely on classic ethnographies such as those by Nordenskiöld, Métraux, or Susnik from the early to later twentieth century, or even colonial sources going back as far as the sixteenth century. This happens particularly in the case of ethnographic investigations that are carried out by NGOs and similar agencies to function as a basis for development projects, where researchers are often tempted to only consult the most well-known texts for reasons of time pressure. One such example is a study of the Guaraní *teko*, entitled *Ñande Reko—La comprensión guaraní de la vida buena*, carried out by the Programme for the Support of Decentralised Governance and the Fight against Poverty (PADEP)[3] of the German Society for Technical Collaboration (GTZ). The GTZ (since 01 January 2011 a part of the German Society for International Collaboration, or GIZ) was an internationally active organisation with the declared aim of 'support[ing] the German Government in . . . provid[ing] viable, forward-looking solutions for political, economic, ecological and social development in a globalised world . . . on a sustainable basis' (http://www.gtz.de/en/689.htm). The GTZ's Camiri office was very active among the local Guaraní populations at the time of my fieldwork, working closely with the Capitanía Kaami to organise workshops, compile reports on development needs in the *comunidades*, and support them in their collaboration with the municipality of Camiri within the framework of 'decentralisation.' The abovementioned study states as its objective the 'divulgence of good information in order to facilitate an intercultural dialogue between the . . . GTZ/PADEP and its clients of the Chaco: the municipalities and the Guaraní Territorial-Based Organisations' (Medina ed. 2002: 7). This being its declared purpose, the selection of texts found in this compilation is surprising: about half of them deal with historical documents from the sixteenth century onward (indiscriminately picking and mixing sources that talk about Guaraní peoples from all over the continent), and the text taken as the main reference for explaining the concept of the 'good life' among the Guaraní is Bartomeu Melià's much-quoted classic *Ñande Reko: Nuestro modo de ser* (1988) whose arguments, again, mainly rely on historical (largely colonial) sources.[4]

I am not denying that such older sources can be of interest to contemporary Guaraní people. However, assuming that their findings reflect people's lived realities today risks 'freezing' Guaraní society and culture in time, when really contemporary Guaraní people's lives occur in contexts that are very different from those encountered by the 'classic' ethnographers, responding to different pressures from the outside and also operating according to different rules internally. In a study on Ashaninka people in Peruvian Amazonia, Juan Pablo Sarmiento draws our attention to the importance of bearing this in mind even when dealing with a supposedly 'traditional' subject such as the 'good life':

> [*K*]*ametsa asaiki* [the good life] is central to any understanding of Ashaninka social life and practices, especially in a context like that of the Bajo Urubamba. This context requires them to find new tools in order to be able to retake their pursuit [of] *kametsa asaiki* that was interrupted by the war [between the Shining Path and the government]. However, the objective in the post-war [era] is not to go back to an idealised past of abundance, sharing and peace but to re-structure and creatively adapt Ashaninka society to the current state of affairs in Peruvian Amazonia . . . *kametsa asaiki* is no longer a communal project of conviviality but it has become a tool for defiance of the Peruvian State and its impositions on their lives. It is a conscious political choice in their fight for the right to have rights. (Sarmiento Barletti 2011: 284–85)

While my aim here cannot be to read the efforts of the *comunarios* of Cañón de Segura purely in terms of resistance, which would be too restricted in the present context (cf. Ortner 1995), the above quote alerts us to the importance of taking into account the various forces currently impacting on their society and thereby shaping their ideas of what life in the *comunidad* is, or should be, about. As Jean Jackson (1989: 132) put it, 'traditional cultural forms that are retained are not necessarily the same if their meaning has changed. This might seem so obvious as to not warrant comment, but such a point is often forgotten because anthropologists and indigenists alike are often interested in discovering the connections between current traditions and earlier ones.'

This chapter takes up the *comunarios'* assertion about the importance of 'living *tranquilo*' and explores what it was they meant by this, and what it meant to them. Taking a more critical approach to generalised notions of Guaraní reciprocity by putting them in relation to the way people talked and acted provides us with a glimpse of what 'living well' in Cañón entailed within the particular circumstances at the time of my fieldwork. What will become clear throughout this discussion is how these ideas were inseparable from the concept of *comunidad*, which not only provided a framework for people's daily lives but was in a way itself constituted by them.

'NO NOS DEJABAN TRABAJAR': THE IMPORTANCE OF BEING ABLE TO WORK IN PEACE

As we have seen, what had most detracted from people's tranquility in Itakua were the *patrones*. Apart from general complaints about them, such as Luz's assertion that 'they would come to molest the people at any moment' (see chapter 2), one of the main grievances people had about them was that they would not let them work in peace: the *patrones* objected to the *comunarios'* keeping animals and only let them cultivate small patches of land, whereas the work they were obliged to do on the *patrones'* land was time-consuming and badly paid. In the words of one *comunario*, who was about thirty-five years old at the time the trouble with the *patrones* started:

> Itakua was a *propiedad*, and the children of the *comunarios* living there could not study enough because all the people had to work for the *patrones*. They were paid about five bolivianos a day at the age of 10. I myself started out earning 1 boliviano a day at the age of 10. I got up to 2.50 bolivianos a day but never reached any wage higher than that [while I was working for them].

In Cañón, there was not only a primary school (for children of up to about thirteen years of age) but there was also enough land to cultivate for everyone, and people could come and go as they pleased to take care of their fields. The keeping of animals, too, was not only possible but in fact encouraged by various projects provided by outside agencies, in which people could take part or not, depending on their personal circumstances and motivation (see chapter 5).

This freedom was also stressed to me whenever I asked about the rules for deciding the size and location of one's field (local Spanish: *chaco*; Guaraní: *ko*): everyone could, people would tell me, make their *chaco* wherever they wanted, and as big as they wanted. When I asked my friend Lupe what happened if two people wanted to make their *chaco* in the same spot and maybe had a fight about it, she said that that didn't happen, as once someone had made their *chaco* in one spot it was already theirs, and no one would be able to contest it. She said, *'Es una comunidad libre'*—'This is a free community.' In this, Cañón was different from Itakua, which—being situated on a privately owned property—could at best qualify as a so-called 'captive community' (*comunidad cautiva*), even though from the point of view of the *patrones* the use of any such terminology was precluded by the question of ownership: Itakua was their property, their *propiedad*, and as such talking about it in terms of *comunidad* was simply incorrect (see chapters 1, 2).

Like the *patrones* in their argumentation in support of their own case, the *comunarios* thus put life in a *comunidad* in opposition to life on a *propiedad*.

However, whereas the *patrones* had used this argument in order to justify their imposition of restrictions and prohibitions on *comunarios*' lives, in the usage of the *comunarios*, the distinction became a declaration of present freedom as opposed to the unfreedom they had suffered in the past.[5] It was also an affirmation of their rights as lawful owners and inhabitants of their own piece of land, and, to an extent, even something of an idealisation of the harmony this free life entailed.

To me, one of the most interesting aspects of this 'freedom' people liked to stress to me when talking about their work was that it was not marked by the total absence of prescriptions, but rather consisted in the fact that work was regulated by rules that were *acceptable* to people. For one, while it was true that there was great freedom for people to choose the location of their *chaco*, all new *chacos* were meant to be made within the same designated planting area since the community had been divided into different usage zones in 2001. The evaluation and measuring of the territory on which this division was based was carried out by the GTZ in line with their Project for the Sustainable Management of Natural Resources (MASRENA; see also Müller 1999) supported by the Prefecture of Santa Cruz. The result was a Plan of Regulations (*Plan de Ordenamiento*) that identified the following eight zones, according to soil type and character of the vegetation:

1. Residential area: for building houses, smaller fields, raising smaller animals, etc.
2. Clean intensive cultivations 1: mainly flat areas designated for making *chacos*.
3. Clean intensive cultivations 2.[6]
4. Pasture: areas with natural and/or sowed pastures with chalky ground or medium inclination for cattle and other larger animals to graze in.
5. Forest pasture.[7]
6. Forest production: can be used for wood production.[8]
7. UPFPR (Protection areas for rivers or ravines): no cutting of trees, no grazing of large animals.
8. Protection: no cutting or burning of trees, no hunting.

The reason the *comunarios* welcomed this division—imposed, as it were, by agents from outside the *comunidad*—was that it came accompanied by the production of a document that a) was in line with Forestry and Agrarian Reform Law,[9] and b) included several maps rendering the outlines and limits of Cañón in great detail. Like the historical document discussed in chapter 2, the MASRENA document thus represented a further legal 'tool' at the disposal of the *comunarios* that helped secure their territory within the realms of law and bureaucracy.

WHOSE RESPONSIBILITY?
COMMUNAL WORK VS. *MOTÏRO*

The fields were located beyond the residential area at the back of the *comunidad* (see map 1). Spaces for new *chacos* were cleared by first making incisions around the stems of trees, which made them dry out and easy to fell. The desired area was then burned, and the burnt tree stems sold as charcoal.[10] (Alternatively, some *comunarios* made use of a chain saw for the purpose.) Crops that were sowed included maize (Guaraní: *avati*), beans (*kumanda*), squashes (*guandaka*), chili peppers (*kɨi*), peanuts (*munduvi*), sugar cane (*tiriku*), and very occasionally melons (*sandía*) and yucca (*mandío*). What people sowed depended on them, but one crop that was planted by everyone was maize. Maize was extremely important in the *comunarios'* production of food, for their own consumption as well as for selling in Camiri, and people would talk about it with great fondness. Maize was often intercropped with beans and squashes, a classic combination in which the different crops aid each other (the bean uses the maize stem to climb up on, and the squash keeps the ground moist with its large leaves, which in turn benefits the maize). Others were sowed separately, like peanut and yucca. Apart from the sowing and harvesting, *chaco* work basically comprised keeping *chacos* clear of weeds.

There was one tractor, shared between the neighbouring communities of Cañón de Segura, Piedritas, and Urundaiti, that had been bought with the money these communities had received from the municipality as compensation for the inconveniences caused the inhabitants by the building of the Santa Cruz-Camiri motorway (which had, for example, cut off their water supply for several months). However, the money had not been enough to also buy the necessary implements to go with it (such as a harrow or a plough), which consequently had to be rented from one of their neighbours. The tractor was looked after by the *mburuvicha*, who tended to have it parked in his patio (*oka*) when it was not in use. Maintenance and repairs were the responsibility of the community's Production team (see PISET below), who, lacking technicians of their own, usually just got someone from Camiri to fix it.

Besides such technical and financial restraints, the most obvious restrictions people faced in their economic activities were those imposed by environmental factors. There was, for example, no irrigation system of any sort, so if it did not rain in the rainy season, there was not much people could do to

save their crops. However, those were not the only difficulties the agriculturalists encountered. When I once asked Don Elías how the work in his *chaco*
was going, he said that he was only planting maize, beans, and squashes. For
more crops, he said, he would need more land—he only had one and a half
hectares because he couldn't manage more beside his work with Caritas in
Camiri. He said he had already sowed the maize, but that the 'worms'[11] had
eaten it all, so he would have to do it all again, double the work. He said
one could spray the plants with insecticide, but that that was bad for the soil.
(Other *comunarios* had, less scrupulously, told me that the reason they did
not use insecticide was that it was too expensive.) This example, then, already
demonstrates four possible complications that could affect *comunarios*' ability to work: environmental forces, work engagements outside the community,
ethical concerns, and lack of money.

As a result of the MASRENA project, the community's *chacos* had been
made close together and were mostly only separated by a row of distinct crops
indicating the limits between one person's *chaco* and another's (such as a row
of beans planted between two *chacos* of maize). People sometimes lamented
the lack of wire for fences to keep the large animals out but always asserted
that there tended to be no problems between the owners of neighbouring *chacos*.[12] Besides the large *chacos* at the back of the *comunidad*, most families
also had an additional field close to their houses. Those were used for the
family's immediate needs and contained such crops as chilies, tomatoes, and
flavouring herbs to add to *mate*, whereas produce from the further away (and
usually larger) field was often sold as well. Some people, when asked, estimated that the relationship between produce consumed and sold was about
half and half, whereby maize was the leading crop in both categories. As far
as I could tell, the only crop that was produced exclusively for sale in Camiri
was peanuts, a crop which had only recently made its way into the community
and was being planted by just a few families. When I asked about the smaller
fields and why they could be made outside the designated area, I was told,
'Oh, those are just gardens (*huertas*),' indicating that as such they did not fall
under the regulations pertaining to *chacos*. These gardens were worked by the
women more often than the larger and more remote *chacos*.

Despite these multiple plantations, there was still a lot of cultivable land
left in the community, which explains why *comunarios* could choose the
location and scale of their *chacos* so freely. Part of the land was even still
being used by the *comunarios* of the neighbouring community of Urundaiti,
with whom—both populations being descendants of the same Itakua peons,
and people still frequently intermarrying between the two *comunidades*—the
Cañón *comunarios* shared close kin ties. However, whereas there were no
papers involved in the organisation of the Cañón *comunarios*' own *chacos*,

Two fields with maize plants separated by a row of beans.
Photo by the author.

there existed a legal contract outlining the conditions on both sides for the Urundaiti people's use of Cañón land, thereby denoting their status as 'outsiders' to the community.

While legally the community as a whole owned the land on which it was situated, individual families or people more or less informally 'owned' the right to use the space on which their houses, *okas*, and *chacos* were located—unless, that is, they left them. I was told that if one left one's house and *oka*, one lost one's right to them, whereas if one stopped using one's *chaco* it still belonged to one, and if someone wanted to use the land, they had to ask permission of the original owner (which was then usually granted). Further, the permission of the communal council (*asamblea*), consisting of all *comunarios* who would attend any meeting that was called to discuss a particular matter, had to be sought before the clearing of space for a new *chaco* could begin. Once the *asamblea* had given its consent (which was generally the case), one could indeed use as much land as one wanted; or rather, as much as one and one's family could manage to work. As a result, family *chacos* rarely exceeded four hectares in size, the average being around two.

Every family was responsible for their own *chaco*. Men did a major part of the work, especially in the clearing of new *chacos*, while women and occasionally children helped out when needed (in particular during the harvest), but otherwise spent a lot of their time in the *oka*. The exception were frequent trips into Camiri, where the women sold the family's produce in the markets. The fact that people would often refer to the designated planting area as the 'communal *chaco*' had confused me at first into thinking of it as one huge *chaco* that belonged to the *comunidad* as a whole, and—having read about the existence of 'communal work' among some Guaraní groups—I asked the *capitán* whether such a practice existed in Cañón. As it turned out, even though communal work had used to exist in Cañón, it had been abolished in the not-so-remote past (only after the community's move), because it had not really worked: in the words of the *capitán*, 'If twelve, fifteen people were meant to be working, only eight actually would.'

What did exist, however, was the *motïro* (in Spanish usually translated as '*faena*,' 'job' or 'work group'), which, he said, was different from communal work per se in that it involved one man inviting those of the others he wanted to help him carry out a certain task that would exceed the capacities of just one family (see, e.g., Melià [1988], *Plan Desarrollo Rural Cordillera* [1986b]). The inviter then had to arrange for *chicha* (maize beer; Guaraní: *kägui*) and food to be prepared, a task performed by the women, which were given to the helpers in recompense for their work after it was finished. Traditionally, it was the chiefs (*mburuvicha reta*) who would invite entire communities to partake in these work parties. Their social importance lay in the reciprocal exchange involved in them, as the work necessarily had to be followed by big fiestas (*arete*):

> The *arete* and the system of reciprocity are not a simple addition to Guaraní life, in the way of a reward for the good success of the work, but an essential element of the economic system in which interplay relations of kinship, of work and production, of social and political relations, and of ritual celebration. (Melià 1988: 51)

Even though the small-scale *motïro* as it was still being practiced in Cañón did not involve the organisation of fiestas as such, the provision of *chicha* seemed to be by far the most important part of the entire enterprise. It was also named as one of the main differences when I asked how the 'communal work' proper had been different from the *motïro*: there was no *chicha* involved with the former, because no one was issuing an invite. Rather, it used to be *comunarios* working together for the good of the whole community—a practice that has been reported as difficult to organise among Guaraní peoples from colonial times onward (see e.g., Melià 1988; Pifarré 1989; Saignes 1990).

The only area where this kind of communal work still existed was in the community's cattle project mentioned in the introduction, where, I was told, it did work for some reason. I strongly suspect that the reason communal work had been successfully maintained in the cattle project was that the cattle project was not only communally owned, but also deemed particularly valuable. Besides the economic value of the project, cattle breeding is an activity that is regarded as prestigious in the area, and the fact that not all families could afford to keep cows of their own made the communal cattle project all the more important. Further, communal work tied to particular projects may well have a different status from the kind of obligatory communal work 'for the communal good' which missionaries tried to introduce, or that imposed on people by *patrones*. This is supported by the fact that a women's workgroup existed in Cañón, whose leader Doña Filomena—contrary to the assertion of the *mburuvicha*—assured me that the women's group frequently engaged in 'communal work.'[13] As it turned out, the communal work the women's group did was almost exclusively tied to such projects as had funding at any given time, such as the production of yoghurt, weavings, or pottery (the latter of which I discuss more closely in chapter 6). The idea that communal projects require the formation of communal work parties was first introduced by CIPCA, the first NGO to implement projects among the Guaraní (Hirsch 2003b: 90–91), and has since become established practice in the Guaraní world (as, for example, in the *comunarios*' insistence that their Urundaiti tenants form work groups to work their rented land in Cañón).

Be that as it may, what all of these forms of 'communal work' had in common was that they were different from the institution of the *motïro*. Nonetheless, what is sometimes titled 'traditional communal work' in the literature is nothing else but today's *motïro* on a larger scale,[14] organised by the *mburuvicha* and involving the entire community, and not the kind of communal work the *capitán* told me the *comunarios* of Cañón had abandoned for the difficulties in making it work. This usage of the label of 'communal work' to designate the *motïro* is misleading in that it facilitates the conflation of two concepts that are quite contrary to one another. In the words of Bartomeu Melià (1996: 205), '[i]f economically the *potirõ* [*motïro*] is collective work, socially it is *pepy*, fiesta;' in short, the difference—and a significant difference it is—is that the *motïro* involves reciprocal exchanges, while other forms of communal work do not.

It is perhaps hardly surprising that, as an imposition by the *patrones* of Itakua rather than a form of organisation that emanated from the *comunarios* themselves (or even their NGO allies), communal work proper disappeared in Cañón shortly after the relocation of the *comunidad* and the resulting freedom from the *patrones'* authority. The reason for the disappearance of large-scale *motïro*, on the other hand, is to be found in the changes the socio-political structure of Bolivian Guaraní communities has undergone over time. More precisely, they are no longer dominated by (male) individuals distinguished by their prestige as orators, warriors, and hosts of fiestas, but nowadays tend to be organised according to more 'democratic' principles, with leaders being elected by the *asamblea* every two years. This leadership structure echoes that of the APG, not only in the practice of the frequent reelections of *capitanes* as a means to preclude community members from monopolising power and/or wealth, but also in the division of leadership duties among a specialised team of 'PISET' officials, who were (at least theoretically) subject to the same election cycle as the *capitán*.[15] PISET is the acronym of the 'Peasant Development Programme' that was cooked up by CIPCA and the then-departmental development agency CORDECRUZ, the two main entities responsible for the founding of the APG in 1987 (Hirsch 2003b: 91). Its initials stand for Production, Infrastructure, health (*Salud*), Education, and land/territory (*Tierra/Territorio*), which were the areas that a joint 1986 survey by CIPCA and CORDECRUZ identified as particularly important for the development of Guaraní communities (*Plan Desarrollo Rural Cordillera* 1986a).[16] To these areas were more recently added those of natural resources, gender, and communication, thus extending the PISET into a 'PISETRNGC' (Caballero et al. 2010: 4); however, for convenience, the acronym 'PISET' remained most commonly used.

Today, most *comunidades* and *capitanías* have a PISET team of their own, the latter of which is often (but not necessarily) made up of leaders from *comunidades* that belong to the *capitanía*. Some few *comunidades* and even *capitanías* had a female *mburuvicha*, but the main trend (encouraged by the increased concern for gender equality of NGOs working with the Guaraní) was toward a female second *mburuvicha*, as was the case in the Capitanía Kaami. The gender official invariably tended to be a woman, in line with Guaraní people's understanding of gender as 'women's work/issues.' In Cañón at the time of my fieldwork, only two of the PISET positions were occupied by women: that of health official, and that of leader of the women's workgroup, a position which amalgamated in itself the roles of 'female *mburuvicha*' and 'gender official.' The explanation for this 'underrepresentation' of women in the PISET team one *comunaria* gave me was that the women were too busy looking after their families and houses to be PISET officials: 'The officials (*responsables*) have to go to meetings in Camiri a lot, they are often even called away at night to attend to an emergency, but the women can't do that very easily because they have to look after the children.' There were no officials for communication and natural resources in Cañón, whereas the production and education officials were each in charge of a team sharing their responsibilities.

With regard to the *motïro*, the effect of this new kind of leadership was a circle of absences that reinforced itself: with the absence of the necessity to distinguish oneself through the traditional means (oratory and warfare), and the consequential absence of individuals with a large labour force at their disposal, also vanishes the possibility of building the kinship alliances necessary for ensuring access to the labour power allowing for the procurement of the means to host fiestas and thus distinguish oneself. As we have seen, work defined life in Cañón not so much because it tied people together in networks of reciprocal relations, but because it was—by allowing people to work in peace—directly opposed to work on the *propiedad*. The importance of work as a definitional feature of life in the *comunidad* thus remained, but for different reasons than in the past, when work was a function of the ability of distinguished males to create and maintain kin and affinal ties through the positive reciprocity of fiestas and the prestige gained through the negative reciprocity practiced in warfare.

What, then, of reciprocity? Given the mostly individualised character of work as it is carried out nowadays, can we safely assume, as is commonly done, that reciprocity does in fact still play an important role in the social relations within the *comunidad*? Or is the value disappearing along with the political organisation and large-scale *motïro* to which it used to be tied? I would like to suggest that the very absence of communal work proper, along with the continuation of the practice of *motïro* on a small scale, highlights the continuing importance of reciprocal relations in Cañón: after all, where there was *chicha*, people were still happy enough to help each other out when needed. However, if we are to look for more evident proof of the importance of reciprocity, we shall have to do so in other areas of the *comunarios'* lives. The following sections take up the question of reciprocity in relation to fiestas and their social significance and resignification.

THE FIESTA AND THE REPRODUCTION OF SOCIALITY

As mentioned above, in the precolonial and colonial periods the fiesta used to function as a ritual to maintain links of reciprocity within and among communities in the context of the *motïro*. However, at the same time it was also an integral part of the acting-out of the 'negative reciprocity' of vengeance and warfare: before going to war, the *kereimba* (Guaraní warriors) would gather their courage by dancing and drinking *chicha* in the fiesta, and after their return a fiesta would be prepared to celebrate their victory and seal new pacts of alliance (Sánchez 1998: 224). Giving expression to the huge importance the fiesta held in Guaraní social and political life, Wálter Sánchez refers to it as the 'source of social cohesion,' and quotes Romano and Cattunar (1916: 165): 'In this way, unity and peace are maintained among the Indians; without these invitations and friendly reunions each one would go their own way [*se independizaría*], and the tribe would dissolve' (Sánchez 1998: 225).

Nowadays largely detached from the context of the *motïro* as from that of warfare, the fiesta nonetheless occupied a central position in the lives of the *comunarios* of Cañón de Segura, and it was also the context in which reciprocal relations among them could be seen at work most clearly. There were four main types of fiesta that would be celebrated with greater or lesser regularity throughout the course of a year, and which varied in their overall setup and the way in which they were organised, while all revolving around a common 'core': children's birthday parties; a set series of fiestas between Christmas and Twelfth Night; the fiestas of carnival in February; and the fiesta of the Virgin of Copacabana,[17] the patron saint of the *comunidad*, in August. What all four types had in common was that they all functioned to draw the community together in a common social setting, usually aided by the consumption of copious amounts of *chicha* and the opportunity to dance to either hired or live music, and that the *comunarios* regarded them as a highly important part of communal life. In short, the historians who so essentialised the Guaraní warrior ethos that they declared Guaraní culture to have departed along with the last of the *kereimba* of 1892 were wrong: the production and consumption of *chicha* may have become dissociated from warfare, but they remain practices of great social significance, and *chicha* a highly meaningful substance. What we are dealing with here is thus not so much a case of a loss of meaning as one of resignification, what Marshall Sahlins has called the 'functional revaluation of categories' (Sahlins 1985). In Sahlins's words,

[i]f culture is as anthropologists claim a meaningful order, still, in actions meanings are always at risk. . . . Culture is therefore a gamble played with nature, in the course of which, wittingly or unwittingly, . . . the old names that are still on everyone's lips acquire connotations that are far removed from their original meaning. (ibid.: ix).

THE FIESTA

The following is an account of the first fiesta to which I was invited in Cañón, which I am using to demonstrate the general dynamics at play in these events. I then go on to outline the differences between the various types of fiesta, and what all these elements can tell us about the ways in which sociality was being produced and constantly reproduced in Cañón at the time.

The fiesta in question was organised by a couple, Doña Filomena and Don Rogelio, on the occasion of their little son's birthday, which also fell around the period of the *comunidad*'s anniversary on 05 May. I went accompanying my friend Lupe and several other people, who had been attending a mass in the school yard. When we arrived at the fiesta's hosts' *oka* (patio), we found a big group of men seated on two benches that had been improvised from wooden boards supported by blocks of wood in the shade underneath some trees, drinking, chatting, and smoking. Only some three women were sitting on chairs in front of the house. The newly arrived group with which we had come managed to fill an additional bench opposite those of the men, and, a bit later, a second one that was quickly put up next to the first one. Children of all ages were running around, the smallest ones sitting on their mothers' laps. I got a seat at the very end of the bench that was closest to the house.

I asked Lupe whether there was always this sex-segregation in the seating arrangements at fiestas, and she said, always. She said that in the town (i.e., Camiri) it was different—there, couples sat together, but here it was women with women and men with men. I kept looking around to see whether any of the women were smoking, but cigarettes, as far as I could see, were only being passed among the men, so I asked Lupe whether the women did not smoke at all, and she confirmed that they did not. When I asked her why, Lupe thought for a bit, then suggested that they probably 'just didn't want to.' I would hear many diverging opinions on the matter of women and '*vicios*' ('vices'; i.e., smoking, drinking, and chewing coca) throughout my stay—while some men at the fiesta assured me that women did in fact smoke and drink, a young man I spoke to on a separate occasion told me that people would get very upset if they saw a *comunaria* smoke,[18] whereas an older lady, after thinking about it for a bit, came to the conclusion that smoking was unheard of among women because 'their mothers probably just don't teach them to.' Judging from later observations and conversations, the women really did not drink as much as the men, and generally only in the fiestas, and I never once saw a woman from the community smoke or chew coca. In short, in the fiesta, the men had the smokes, the coca, and most of the hard drink, while the women had the little children, and the children had an opportunity to get together and play—but what they all had in common was the *chicha*.

There are various alcoholic and non-alcoholic beverages throughout South America that are commonly known as '*chicha*':

> Drinks based on maize (boiled, chewed, and put in earthenware pots to ferment) of the chicha type were used from Mexico to Guatemala, Yucatan, and Darien, and to the high plateau of Bogota in the south; they are also found among the inhabitants of the Andes, in Ecuador, Peru, and Chile to Araucania and eastward from the Orinoco, and in Guiana as far as the territory of the Amazon. (LaBarre 1938: 228)

Guaraní *chicha* (*kägui*) is made from maize that is boiled and then partly chewed by the women to help the fermentation process, and a lighter form of it (*käguiraɨ*; lit.: 'little *chicha*') is often drunk as an everyday refreshment. A fiesta without *chicha* is absolutely unthinkable. At Filomena and Rogelio's fiesta, I was amazed to see even little children grab cups and drink out of the buckets, clay pots, and large metal containers filled with *chicha* that were sitting on the ground in front of people, freely and without anyone reprimanding them. I asked Lupe about this, and she said, 'Ah yes, they love it!' To my question of whether they did not get drunk on it she replied that the *chicha* didn't make one drunk, only 'this stuff' (pointing toward a Tetra Pak filled with wine) and the 'alcohol' did. What people called '*alcohol*,' or '*trago*' ('booze'), was the high-percentage cane liquor that seemed a constant companion of the men even when they went to the fields to work. It tended to be mixed with water when served out at fiestas, but even then it was still pretty nasty. It also happened frequently that the 'owners' (*dueños*; i.e., hosts) of a fiesta spiked their *chicha* with *alcohol* if they felt that it was not strong enough, or that people were not getting drunk fast enough.

The *trago* and the wine were served out in tiny little portions, whereas the *chicha* was given out in mugs and cups. The serving of drink was strictly systematic: one person was given a container of *chicha*, or a carton of wine, or a bottle of *trago*, which they then had to finish by serving the contents out to the other guests. This was done one person after the other, according to seating order. To start with, the person serving the drink had to invite another person by saying, '*Jeu kägui*' ('Take/drink *chicha*!'), or '*Ndegua jau*' ('I'm inviting you,' 'Cheers!'; lit.: 'I drink to you'), then drink themselves, and then make the other person drink. I provided some entertainment by making a number of mistakes: when Lupe asked me to serve out some *chicha*, I went and obediently supplied everyone on the benches on our side of the *oka* with a mugful, only to be told at my return by a laughing Lupe that one was only supposed to serve from one's own (or, in this case, from her) container,

Boiling *chicha* for a fiesta in big metal barrels.
Photo by the author.

whereas I had been refilling my mug from whichever container was closest to the person I was inviting. Of course, no one had told me a word, but all had accepted my *chicha* smiling amiably. I also offered wine to a couple of people I shouldn't have offered it to, including Lupe's fourteen-year-old daughter, whom I invited twice, the second time because I didn't recognise her face in the dark. I then managed to give some women way too much wine, which they drank, but under protest. One of them got me back a little later by serving me half a mugful of the terrible *trago*. She even freely admitted that this was in revenge for the wine when I suggested that this was the case, but it was all in good humour. As I found out later, her name was Doña Apolonia, and she was the mother of our host Doña Filomena. Later that same evening, she told me that she had already been drinking for three days, as she had been to a fiesta in another community before coming to her daughter's one.

It got darker and darker, until the men, who had moved their benches closer now the sun was gone and people were getting animated to dance, were only voices in the dark and the occasional glow of a cigarette.

After a while, Lupe told me that she was feeling sleepy. I said I was too, but when Doña Filomena came to ask me the same question, I didn't want to be rude, so I told her I was all right. This, according to Lupe, had been a mistake, as now Doña Filomena was going to bring me a new pot of *chicha* to serve out, which indeed promptly materialised. Doña Filomena also asked for a photo of me with the *chicha*. I took out the camera I had brought along, and we tried to take some pictures, first I of her with Lupe, then a young boy to whom I explained the camera of Lupe with me. It was tricky, however, as the camera's display did not recognise the minimal lights of the setting and only showed us blackness, so the exact position of the people to be photographed had to be guessed, the process and end results of which caused a lot of merriment.

A couple of people asked me to dance, but I declined, telling them that I didn't know how. Later in the evening, and with a lot more *chicha* and *trago* buzzing round my head, I was persuaded to dance anyway by one of Lupe's cousins, who had been in charge of the music all evening. The repertoire consisted of all the usual fiesta 'classics' of *cumbia* and the odd *chacarera*. Unlike at some fiestas, where hosts got a DJ with an amplifier to come from Camiri, the music here consisted of a stereo connected to a car battery in a wheelbarrow (a setup which I had seen before in my 'host family's' house, where it was used to power a small black-and-white TV around which the family would gather at dusk to watch their favourite soap opera, *Marina*). My first dance finished, I managed to scrounge a cigarette off Lupe's cousin, which was extremely strong, and which made me the object of the curiosity of some giggling children.

When I got back to my spot on the bench, Lupe told me to go serve *chicha* to the men, which she suggested I do with two mugs at the same time in order to empty our bucket faster. On my round I encountered some acquaintances, like Don Pedro, my neighbour, and the father of my host family Don Germán, who introduced me to his nephew from Santa Cruz. The nephew, very drunkenly (as they all were by that time), asked me whether I would not forget about Cañón de Segura when I went back to my own country, and whether there was maybe a project that I could do with them. I told him that I would do whatever I could, but that I could not promise anything just yet. He went on about how we would stay in touch via e-mail after I left, and how the Capitanía Kaami could always use 'professionals' to work together with them. Don Germán said, wasn't it nice that I was here with them, sharing *chicha*?, and that I would have to remember this fiesta when I went back, and tell the people of my own place about the Guaraní culture.

My 'men round' took a lot longer than expected, as several others also talked to me, some asking me about my country, my family, or my work, others just having a laugh with me. Don Germán's brother Don Sergio called me '*chekuña*' and tried to tell me that it meant 'my sister'—I didn't tell him I knew that it really meant 'my woman,' I just said, yes, quite right, we're all brothers and sisters. Lupe's brother Abel strong-armed me back onto the dance floor where he insisted that my dancing was fine, and kept making fun of Doña Filomena and another woman who were dancing together for being so stiff.

Don Rogelio at some point intercepted me and talked at me for quite some time, telling me how this day was his birthday, his son's birthday, and also the anniversary of the community, and how he always organised a fiesta to commemorate it; how three of the *comunarios* had gone to prison, and Don Rubén Bruno had died fighting for the land, and how he himself had actually come from Chuquisaca but had met Doña Filomena while working in Camiri years ago and settled here,[19] and how he now had his fields and house here, all *tranquilo*, and how that was all thanks to those who had fought for this land, which now was his land as well, and how every year they read a bit out of the history of the community to remember this.

And then he suddenly changed the topic and asked me whether I would, if I could at all, maybe do something for their school, as they needed a roof for the children under which they could have their breakfast, and maybe if I showed them pictures of the poor little Cañón children having their breakfast in the rain, someone in Austria would want to give them a roof. Again, I said I would do what I could. I then made him drink a shot of wine and went on to my next 'victim.'

As the night wore on, more couples danced, and the occasional man came over to the women's side to sit for short periods of time and chat. There did not seem to be a problem with people dancing together who did not form part of a formal couple. I asked Lupe whether it was always the men who asked the women to dance, and she said always, unless it was two women dancing together, which could be done as well. The combination of two men, on the other hand, was a strict no-no.

When our *chicha* had finally run out, Lupe and I again conspired to leave. She said we would have to sneak away, as otherwise they would not let us go but tell us to stay longer. A little earlier, there had been a discussion between her and her brother, who was utterly drunk but insisting that he was perfectly sober, and who wanted to take us down the road in his car.[20] Lupe did not want that because she thought he was too drunk to drive, so she tried to get out of it by using the *gringa*—me—as an excuse. In the end we all left on foot, and pretty openly, with Doña Filomena even coming over to say goodbye. We walked down the road, Lupe with her two boys 'Niño' and 'Bebé,' Abel's wife Leticia with her little one, who had been woken up and was crying, and I. The moon was still quite bright, so finding our way was not too difficult. I left the others at the gate to the school, and they walked on, whereas I had to go round the school wall to get up to my little house because the gate had been locked for the weekend. I went to bed without even bothering to light the gas lamp in my room. The music could still be heard in the distance, and it continued when I woke up in the early hours of morning.

Looking at the above account a little more closely, we can see how these fiestas were events that fulfilled social functions on various levels. For one, it was striking how everyone was 'put in their place' by the seating arrangements—the women on one side, the men on the other, with the children running wherever they wanted. I observed similar seating arrangements in workshops and meetings of the *asamblea*, where the men would cluster at the front of the meeting room, while the women generally sat further to the back. Again, children of both genders had license even here to roam about freely and even climb up on the laps of men who were speaking at the moment, and I was more than once surprised at how much noise people were willing to tolerate from them. This, it seemed, was part of people's understanding of what children were like, which was something they did not seem to feel they could (or, for that matter, should) do anything about.

While the fiesta on the one hand separated people in that it assigned each one their proper position according to their age and gender, which came accompanied by certain patterns of behaviour, it also, on the other hand, drew the community closer together by uniting everyone in one place where food, drink, and activities could be shared. As we have seen, this, again, had to be done according to a set of rules, and the consumption of alcohol in particular was highly ritualised, the main focus being the more or less equal distribution of the available beverages among the adult guests.[21] While with the stronger drink it was sometimes possible to negotiate the amount one was to receive, refusing a drink altogether was hard to impossible if no very good reason could be given. Age, as in Lupe's daughter's case, was one of the few acceptable excuses, as was religion (Evangelicals were allowed to abstain). The result of this obligatory sharing was usually a pervasively inebriated body of guests, the drunker of whom would often provide involuntary diversion for the less drunk, without offence being taken if on occasion propriety went out of the window.

Fiestas provided the *comunarios'* favourite form of entertainment, which included not only the event itself but also people's subsequent exchanging of gossip about what had happened at any fiesta they had recently been to. They would comment on the quality of the DJ; the drunk guy from the neighbouring community who had made a fool of himself again; the fight that almost broke out between two brothers-in-law; the two old ladies who had fallen over dancing; or the *gringuita* who had missed the bench when sitting down and ended up on the ground. When passing the final verdict, it would often be the case that a fiesta was judged unsatisfactory because the *chicha* had run out too soon or had not been up to standard, no matter how elaborately organised the fiesta had been in any other respect.

Chicha, as we have seen, is a substance of great social importance among Guaraní people, historically as today.[22] Its production already relies on the activation of social networks, as neither the sowing and harvesting nor the chewing of the maize that is performed by the women in order to help fermentation can be done by one person alone. When Lupe was making *chicha* for her daughter's *quinceaños* (see 'Children's Fiestas' further on), she recruited the help of some neighbours, relatives, and friends. We gathered in her *oka* in the early morning after the maize had been boiling all night, and sat before the buckets of boiled maize Lupe had put in front of us, sleepily chatting as we fished out the coarser grains and spit them back into the bucket once they had been chewed. As Alfred Gell put it,

> consumption as a general phenomenon really has nothing to do with the destruction of goods and wealth, but with their reincorporation into the system that produced them in some other guise. . . . [E]ven quite ephemeral items, such as the comestibles served at a feast, live on in the form of the social relations they produce, and which are in turn responsible for reproducing the comestibles. (Gell 1986: 112)

A fiesta was an elaborate event in which a lot of people were involved from its planning phase to its aftermath, and which was from start to finish pervaded by a spirit of sharing and reciprocity. Even antagonisms between *comunarios* had a chance to come out at such times, and—aided by the license-giving influence of alcohol—be expressed, if not permanently resolved, before again disappearing under the routine of daily life. Under the influence of *chicha* and the other alcoholic substances, *comunarios* (especially men) would moan about the grievances in their lives, voice their resentments to or about each other, and even occasionally get into physical fights. From what I could tell, grudges were rarely held as a result of such drunken transgressions.[23]

What follows is an outline of the specificities surrounding the different types of fiesta that were celebrated in Cañón on different occasions, and what they can tell us about the *comunidad*'s functioning as a social unit.

CHILDREN'S FIESTAS

Children, as we have seen, were not fixed in the same way as grownups were, but rather gradually grew into their respective roles, with adolescents occupying a position somewhere in between the two, as can be seen in the example of Lupe's young daughter who sat with the women but would not engage in all the activities of the adults (such as drinking and dancing). In Cañón, there were no special rituals tied to a young person's growing-up, except that some people would hold a fiesta for the first hair-cutting of little boys, whose hair would be tied into strands that were cut off one by one and sold to the guests for a moderate contribution.[24] Special celebrations were also sometimes held for a girl's fifteenth birthday (generally referred to as '*quinceaños*,' meaning 'fifteen years'), which is a coming-of-age celebration that is popular all over Bolivia (and, indeed, large parts of Latin America). These fiestas differed from other children's birthdays in that they were a lot more elaborately organised: while a regular children's birthday would consist of a children's party involving balloons, cake, soda, and the destruction of a *piñata*,[25] followed by

Birthday girl pulling the string on her Barbie *piñata* to release the contents.
Photo by the author.

an adults' fiesta like the one described above,[26] a *quinceaños* celebration additionally required a dress and a gold ring for the debutante, and keepsakes (*recuerdos*) for her and all the guests. In order to meet the expenses tied to the organisation of her daughter's *quinceaños*, Lupe named a whole bunch of 'godparents' (*madrinas* and *padrinos*) among her friends and acquaintances, who were to sponsor a particular element of the fiesta. I was named '*madrina del recuerdo*,' which required me to take lots of photographs and purchase a big cuddly toy for the birthday girl.

Since the hosts of a fiesta were always under a lot of pressure to make a good job of it, this naming of 'godparents' to help pay for fiestas was common practice, even though it was also frowned upon by some. I heard people say on occasion that those who couldn't afford to pay for their own fiestas shouldn't be hosting them at all. If a person managed to secure a lot of sponsorship for their fiesta, they also frequently became the object of the jealousy of others, especially if those others thought that they themselves should have been the beneficiaries. Such difficulties, however, seemed inbuilt in the system, without threatening its ability to work. It heavily relied on the activation of kinship and similar relations such as *compadrazgo* (relations between godfathers and -mothers), and requests for sponsorship were—like the drink in the fiestas—hard to refuse. A fiesta could, therefore, be a collective event even in its organisational phase, and people who attended or asked for financial help from their godparents could be sure to be expected to host a fiesta themselves at some point in the future or be themselves asked to act as godparents. In short, there was a strong reciprocal element in the arrangement of fiestas, even if it was not always harmonious or as systematically regulated as the big chiefly banquets of the past might have been.

CHRISTMAS, NEW YEAR'S, AND TWELFTH NIGHT

The fiestas that were held on these three dates were identical in their overall makeup: each had an 'owner' (*dueño*) who had to organise the entire fiesta, and each was held in honour of a '*Niño*' (lit.: 'boy child'; a little plaster statue of Baby Jesus), which was ceremonially passed from one year's *dueño* to the next at the point that marked the end of the religious part of the fiesta. The *Niño* of the fiesta would be displayed on a table, together with a couple of privately owned *Niños* belonging to some of the families, and surrounded by little plastic figures of animals and other forms of decoration to form a sort of 'crib.' This display was the object of the 'adoration' of the children, which meant that they danced in front of it to the sound of a special tape of 'adoration music' played by the *comunidad*'s catechist. It was the fiesta's owners'

Two *Niños* in their 'crib' in front of a tape recorder, Christmas 2007.
Photo by the author.

prerogative to decide the point at which the adoration part of the fiesta ended and the normal fiesta with food, *chicha*, and dancing started (although there was some consensus among the *comunarios* that 22:00 was a good time for this). This latter, more mundane part of the fiesta was then presided over by next year's fiesta's owners, who, indicated by hats decorated with colourful paper, had the duty to serve out *chicha* to the guests until the morning.

These three fiestas, I was told, used to be communally organised, but that had been changed for the same reason as the communal work had been abandoned, namely, that some people always ended up contributing more than others. This change was interesting to me in that it constituted another case in which a move away from the collective organisation one might think of as more egalitarian and therefore more 'traditionally Guaraní' was precisely meant to ensure greater equality among the *comunarios*. Thus, like with the communal work, the practice of the communal fiestas was being lost, but the spirit behind it proved to be more enduring.

THE FIESTAS OF CARNIVAL (*ARETE*)

The carnival fiestas, or *arete guasu*,[27] occupied a kind of middle ground between single fiestas of individuals and the joint fiestas of the past in that they were organised by as many individual families as could afford (or be bothered) to make *chicha*. The guests would move on from one fiesta to the next once the *chicha* had run out. This could theoretically go on for a very long time. The year I was in Cañón to witness the carnival celebrations (2008), only three women had made *chicha*. This, I was assured, was very little, especially when compared to the splendid fiestas of the past that used to involve several *comunidades* rather than just families within the same *comunidad*. Despite this decline, however, the carnival fiestas were still regarded as particularly 'cultural' events, as they involved a lot of traditional elements that were not present in the other fiestas (cf. Ortiz García 2002).

For one, instead of the usual hired DJ or tape player blasting locally popular music through huge speakers, the musical accompaniment in the *arete guasu* was provided by musicians from the *comunidad* playing a combination of flutes and drums.[28] There were only a couple of accomplished flautists left in Cañón, who were therefore in high demand during these fiestas; especially Don Martín, originally from a captive community in Alto Parapetí, did not get much sleep over the three days the fiesta lasted, during which he was forced to play and drink pretty much incessantly. People would dance to this music in the 'traditional' style (one slow step followed by two fast ones, with dancers holding hands in a circle), or skip quickly around a cross decorated with the yellow 'carnival flower' (*cassia carnavalis*; Guaraní: *taperigua*), while masqueraded 'devils' (*aña*) and an '*abuelita*' (Guaraní: *yari*; a man in a wooden mask depicting an old woman and wearing women's clothes)[29] would skip among them, howling, and pull people up from the benches to make sure that everyone was getting their share of the dancing in.

The carnival celebrations resumed after a break toward the end of February, to be concluded with a series of games. The first one was the fight between the jaguar and the bull (*yagua yagua* and *toro toro*), again impersonated by two masked men. Both were backed up by a group of devils egging them on. I was told that either one could potentially win, but on this occasion the jaguar triumphed in the end—apparently, he had bribed the other one's devils to switch over to his side. While the fight was going on, a large round of people was skipping around the flowery cross, and inside this circle a group of four was going in the opposite direction, carrying a 'tent' made up of two blankets tied to poles. Inside, a man and a woman were hidden, who were then to emerge dressed in the opposite sex's clothes. In the end, however, the tent simply disappeared into the house, and the two re-emerged unchanged. The devils, meanwhile, were handing out cobs of maize to each other. The dancing continued long after the game had finished, and there was a lot of laughter as people told funny stories and the devils kept performing their antics.

The next day, the fiesta continued at a different house, where more games were to conclude the *arete* celebrations. For the *kuchi kuchi* (Guaraní: *kuchi*

Yarɨ dancing in front of traditional musicians, a bucket of *chicha* and two bottles of *trago* at her feet.
Photo by the author.

= pig), some boys took a bath in a mud pool and rubbed themselves on the dancers forming a big wheel around a tree trunk in the middle of the *oka*. Then they came running after the onlookers to subject them to the same treatment. After this had been repeated a few times, a man and a woman danced inside and outside a circle of dancers in opposite directions, both carrying an improvised 'flag' and a maize cob. When the circle approached the tree, someone took the flags off them and they had to chase each other, the one being chased hiding among the dancers, and 'rape' each other with the maize cob. This, too, was repeated various times, then the dancers formed two long lines and the first couple started dancing at their end, then ran back and forth in between the lines a couple of times, twisting around each other at each end, and finished up on the other end of the line. This was repeated until all the couples were done. The last game consisted of people throwing the end bits of squashes at each other's feet.

By the time the games finished, it was already quite late. A *comunaria* lamented the fact that nowadays, no one knew how to do the carnival well anymore—Doña Sabina, the late *ipaye* of Cañón, had known, and Rubén Bruno, too, who had known how to make people cry with his speeches. At this point, Don Aurelio began talking about how in the next carnival some people might not be there anymore, followed by a similar speech by the host of the fiesta, and suddenly people were in fact weeping everywhere, including the speaker himself.

The *arete* finished with the 'chucking' (*botar*) of the carnival. Someone grabbed the flowery cross, and the rest went after him in pairs. Doña Apolonia, who was going with me, got her foot stuck in a mud hole and lost her shoe, but she didn't seem to mind and forced me to dance up and down the road with her anyway, so I never in fact saw where they chucked the cross, together with all the improvised masks. Some people went home at this point, but others returned to the fiesta, where the dancing continued with the usual popular music from a tape player: after carnival had been chucked, there was to be no more flute and drum music.

While a detailed analysis of these fiestas is beyond the scope of this chapter,[30] it is clear that the *arete* as it was celebrated by the *comunarios* of Cañón in February of 2008 combined a range of elements pertaining to indigenous culture with Christian-Hispanic elements. For example, the pre-Columbian form of the fiesta as a fertility ritual can be discerned from the centrality of maize (in the form of *chicha* as well as cobs of maize used during the games), whereas the presence of European pagan and Christian symbols (the 'chucking' of the carnival; the cross as central symbol in the dances) and elements reminiscent of the conquest (the use of flags; the bull, an animal from the Old World, opposing the jaguar, which plays a central role in many Amerindian mythologies; cf. Riester [1984] and Saunders ed. [1998]) shows the influence of postconquest Spanish-Bolivian society.

All these things were of great interest to me; however, they did not seem to be of much relevance to my hosts. Rather, as a consequence of my curiosity, I was reminded several times during the *arete* celebrations of what the things were that really mattered. On one occasion, I was watching some people renewing the decoration of carnival flowers on the cross, as the old ones had started to wilt under the intense heat. Wondering what symbolism might be attached to them, I turned to Doña Estefanía, the mother of my 'host family,' who was standing next to me, and asked her whether the flowery cross had some kind of meaning. She looked at me like I had asked something rather daft and replied, 'I suppose it does have some meaning; otherwise, it wouldn't be used.'

The indication of this straightforward answer that seemingly told me nothing about what I wanted to know only struck me after a while: that is, the fact that *what* the things meant was of less importance than the fact *that* they meant something. Similarly, when I asked Doña Apolonia about the motivation for playing the *yagua yagua*, she simply said, 'It's our culture.' Thus, the significance of the various elements in the *arete* lay in the way they kept marking the people who celebrated them out as Guaraní, rather than in a precise science of symbolisms and significations. Of course this is not to say that people did not know any stories about the symbols on display, but rather that they did not offer them as answers to my questions about meanings. Rather, the meanings that were given to me resided in the practices themselves, which reminded people of their shared identity as Guaraní people and as *comunarios* who could dance, laugh, and also mourn together. In short—paraphrasing a *comunario* whom I am quoting more extensively in chapter 6—the answer to the question of what the traditions played out in the *arete* meant to people was, 'a lot.'

THE FIESTA OF THE VIRGEN DE COPACABANA

The only fiesta in Cañón that was still being organised by the community as a whole was the one in honour of the Virgen de Copacabana on the fifth of August, a statue of whom had been donated to the community by a Camireña woman with family links to the *comunidad*. People were not sure why exactly she had done it, but they assumed that it had been in response to a promise she had made to the Virgin for a favour received. The fiesta was preceded by a *novena* (a series of prayer meetings held over nine consecutive days), with people gathering to recite rosaries, culminating in a wake. The fiesta itself lasted for about three days, which were passed with sports events and games, a mass, and a feast with *chicha* and food during which the Virgin, clad in a fancy new gown, would be paraded around the schoolyard to the accompaniment of the banging of fire crackers, and people had the chance to approach her to ask for the granting of favours. The food and drink consumed was made by the women who sold it to those gathered, with the proceeds all going toward the building of a proper chapel for the Virgin, who only had a small shrine in the schoolyard for an abode.

Besides the general importance of fiestas as social events in Cañón, the fiesta of the Virgin was of particular importance to the people because it was another marker of their identity as free *comunarios*: even though it was not clear why exactly the statue had ended up with them, people agreed that she was an important asset. As one *comunario* put it, 'Every *comunidad* has to have their saint; we never used to have one in Itakua, but now we do.' This special significance also explains why the *comunarios* had kept up the custom of collective organisation in this case: much ignored during the rest of the year, the Virgin would make a glorious appearance on this one day as a symbol of their status as inhabitants of a free and recognised *comunidad indígena*.

Moreover, it also identified the *comunarios* as Catholics, an identification that had—with the increased influx of Evangelist missionaries into the region—taken on a surprising link with the old-established tradition of the fiesta. I once mentioned to Doña Estefanía that I had no religious denomination, and thus might not be allowed to act as godmother to any of my friends' children during the baptisms that were planned to be held during the Virgin's fiesta, when she suggested this as a possibility. She replied that she didn't think that would be a problem; what would be a problem, however, was if I were Evangelical, because the Evangelicals, it was said, were a different religion from the Catholics, with different traditions. 'They believe in nothing,' she said, 'not in the saints, not in the holy Virgin, only in Jesus Christ.' In Cañón, she said, there were no Evangelicals because the *comunarios* weren't interested; some missionaries had come a few times, but left again because no one would listen to them. In Urundaiti, she added, there were some, which was causing problems because the people 'weren't the same anymore,'[31] and the Evangelicals would criticise people for drinking alcohol in the fiestas and say that the Devil was sticking his finger up their arses to make them dance, and that they would all burn in hell for it. I remarked that even Jesus drank alcohol sometimes, at which Estefanía interjected, 'Exactly! How can it be of the Devil, if Jesus drank it too? All food and drink is made by God to be consumed by the people, especially the maize—so how can the *chicha* be bad?'[32] So Catholicism was important for the *comunidad* because it ensured that everyone remained 'the same,' and especially with regard to the drinking of *chicha*. We can see here how the consumption of maize/*chicha* has undergone a resignification in terms of Christian Catholic ideology, while at the same time retaining its central role in the lives of the *comunarios*.

To sum it up, the fiesta with its obligatory sharing of *chicha* remained one of the main means of consolidating the *comunidad* as a social unit. Given the uniting power of fiestas, their great entertainment value, and the social pressures attached to their successful arrangement, it is hardly surprising that people attached significant importance to them and went to great lengths to find the means for their organisation. What went into the production of the *chicha* was more than just effort and spit: made from maize that was the product of the *comunarios'* ability to work *tranquilo* in their *chacos*, finished through the women's appeal to their social and kinship networks, and shared by everybody in the fiestas, the *chicha* made by the people of Cañón was a substance that was meaningful not only for forming part of a longstanding Guaraní tradition, but also for being the product of the *comunarios'* own lived experience, the fermentation of an identity and sociality that was specific and general at once. Going back to the question of communal work once more, we can see how, in the case of Cañón, the individual work carried out by the men in their fields and the women in their *okas* was, in a sense, work 'for the good of the whole community,' in that it allowed for the production of maize, and, ultimately, *chicha*, without which the most important communal event—the fiesta—would be rendered impossible. The enduring epitome of reciprocal relations, the meaningfulness of the fiesta itself and the substance indispensable for its celebration had endured despite the fact that circumstances had changed since the times of the valiant *kereimba* and the lavish banquets of the chiefs. The meaningful*ness*, but not the meanings themselves, which ultimately were as flexible as the contexts that produced them.

NOTES

1. Ideas about living well even appeared in Evo's National Development Plan. The plan, entitled 'A Dignified, Sovereign, Productive and Democratic Bolivia for Living Well,' which outlined the economic strategies for the years of 2006–2011, states: 'The propositions and orientations of the National Development Plan (PND) are the basis of the beginning of the dismantling of colonialism and neoliberalism in the country. They also constitute the result of the secular and actual demands of the people for the construction of a pluricultural and communitarian state that will permit the empowerment of the emergent social movements and indigenous peoples. Its principal aspiration is that the women and men of Bolivia *live well*' (my emphasis). Approved on 12 September 2007 via Supreme Decree 29272.

2. This is a word game: the Spanish '*deudo*' really means relative, but looks similar to '*deudor*' (debtor).

3. See http://www.padep.org.bo.

4. An earlier case in point is the 'Rural Development Programme for Cordillera' (1986b) by CIPCA and CORDECRUZ, on the basis of which the organisational structure of the APG and many of the Guaraní *capitanías* and communities was established.

5. Interestingly, while people sometimes talked about their former exploitation being partly due to their ignorance (in terms of lack of school education), I never heard anyone phrase this shift in terms of 'becoming civilised.' 'Becoming civilised' is an idiom that has been widely documented in the usages of Amerindian peoples in reference to different scenarios of liberation from oppression (cf. Gow 1991; Sarmiento Barletti 2011; De la Cadena 1995).

6. Designated cultivation areas one and two both came with a set of recommendations attached to them (such as the installation of windbreakers, rotation of crops, and rotation of agricultural implements), with the difference that in area two soil samples should be taken before the clearing of new *chacos* (MASRENA 2001).

7. Again, the forest pasture area was distinguished from the pasture area by a slight difference in the recommendations given for their management (e.g., in the pasture area, sowing of pastures was supposed to be done in shaded places and trees to be planted where these were missing; MASRENA 2001).

8. This area would mainly be used for the collection of firewood, as the *comunarios* of Cañón did not engage in timber trade.

9. Forestry Law No. 1700, Article 16: 'Lands with forest cover suitable for diverse uses' (12 July 1996), and its by-law, the Supreme Decree No. 24453 (21 December 1996); INRA Act No. 1715, Article 3: 'Constitutional guarantees' (18 October 1996).

10. It was only trees that were felled in the process of making *chacos* that were put to such uses.

11. Spanish: *gusanos*; caterpillars that destroyed a lot of the harvest in Cañón in the season of 2007–2008.

12. At the time of my fieldwork, there was only one *chaco* that had been fenced in, which, ironically, was part of a project called '*sin fronteras*' ('without borders') that had been initiated by the Spanish NGO 'Architects Without Borders' (see http://asfes.org). They had sent an agro-technician who was working together with CIPCA to design *chacos* with crops that could be rotated to prevent exhaustion of the soil.

13. Interestingly, both the *mburivicha's* and Doña Filomena's claims about the nonexistence or existence of communal work were based exclusively on their own gender group. The perception of male and female work among contemporary Guaraní, the relationship between them, and the influence (N)GOs have in shaping them is a topic that is beyond the limits of this book but well worth exploring further.

14. See, e.g., this extract from a PADEP-GTZ development report from 2003 on the valuation of local people's contributions to NGO projects: 'The motivation of the communities for contributing labour power and local materials is principally the need of the infrastructure—self-benefit. Equally important is their socio-cultural predisposition for communal work—community activities of all for all. The Guaraní communities qualify their participation in public works as a . . . tool for negotiating benefits that correspond to it. There exists a high estimation of communal work, and the return service [*contraparte*] is recognised as a contribution of all for the benefit of all—the *mötiro*' (Roduner 2003: 4).

15. In practice, it often happened that the same people kept being reelected because no one else was prepared to take over their responsibilities. This was the case

in both the leaderships of Kaami and Cañón, with the notable exception that a new *mburuvicha* tended to be elected in Cañón so frequently that there were hardly any eligible men left who had not held the position before. This situation had, by the time I left the field, resulted in a young man of twenty-one years of age being elected *capitán*, a move of which some *comunarios* were slightly doubtful (though not enough to voice an objection in the *asamblea*).

16. The components making up PISET bear a striking resemblance to the 'functions of the peasant community' outlined by the 1953 Agrarian Reform: '1.) schooling and extracurricular education; 2.) improvement of housing and elevation of living standards; 3.) care and protection of health; 4.) improvement of production techniques and social and economic relations; 5.) promotion of cooperativism for the creation, through communal effort, of required economic means, and contribution of personal labour to the achievement of local progress' (Article 124).

17. The Virgin of Copacabana is a popular Latin American personification of the Virgin Mary whose cult originated in the town of Copacabana on the shores of Lake Titicaca in the sixteenth century.

18. Outsiders, such as myself and even visitors and kin from Camiri or Santa Cruz, had more license with regard to the *vicios*: the same young man who had told me that people would not tolerate it if a *comunaria* smoked also said that with me it was different as I was from outside and people 'accepted my difference,' and I often heard men comment wonderingly on the amount Cristina, the Spanish engineer of Architects without Borders, was smoking, without there being any apparent negative undertones.

19. Chuquisaca is an interesting department within Bolivia in that it is situated between the departments of Santa Cruz and Tarija, both of which were controlled by right-wing governments opposed to the central government of Evo Morales (the so-called *media luna*), but itself largely supported Evo and his politics. Rogelio himself was sometimes referred to as 'Colla' by other *comunarios* and even himself, which is a name the lowlanders in Bolivia give to the highlanders. ('Colla' can sometimes be—but is not necessarily—used in a derogatory way; see chapter 6.) In this sense, Rogelio came from a background that was both culturally distinct from and politically allied to the people of Cañón.

20. Some of the men in the community sometimes earned some money by driving taxis, which constituted one of the main occupations in Camiri, where most men seemed to either be taxi drivers or lawyers. Abel's car, however, broke down not long after this, and he started a temporary job with the Rural Electricity Cooperative (CRE) instead.

21. I am saying 'more or less equal' here because the men were usually ahead of the women in their alcohol consumption, especially with regard to the *trago*.

22. For historical accounts of the importance of *chicha* among the Guaraní, see Melià (1988), Gutiérrez (1965). For ethnographic accounts of the ritual and social importance of fermented drinks among other Amerindian peoples, see, e.g., Fortis (2015) for Panama, and Weismantel (1991) and Butler (2006) for Ecuador.

23. Contrary to this view, Penelope Harvey has argued that the eruption of 'hostility and social tensions' as a result of festive drunkenness during the celebration

of Peruvian Independence Day in a small Andean town undermines 'the fictions of social cohesion and community' created during the event (Harvey 1997: 38).

24. I am not aware of a longstanding tradition of comparable hair-cutting rituals existing among Guaraní groups. I therefore strongly suspect this tradition of having been adopted from the Andean highlands, where first hair-cutting marks a child's formal introduction into the community (Canessa 1998: 238–39).

25. The *piñata* is a popular prop at children's parties throughout the Spanish-speaking world (and, increasingly, beyond) that comes in various shapes and guises. In the area of Bolivia where I did my fieldwork, it consisted of a large, colourful cardboard box filled with sweets and little plastic toys that could be made to spill its contents by the birthday child's pulling on a string attached to the bottom, at which the little guests would hurl themselves in a heap in order to try to snatch a piece.

26. I have been to children's fiestas that—for financial reasons—were not followed by a 'proper' fiesta at night, but this was not the way it was 'meant to be' and invariably attracted criticism from some of the other *comunarios*.

27. Guaraní: *ara* = day, time; *ete* = real; *guasu* = big, great. In the words of the Isoseño anthropologist Elio Ortiz, 'of all the regular fiestas, this one is the true one[,] the fiesta of all, where all are invited' (Ortiz García 2002: 26).

28. Traditionally, there used to be four types of flutes: the *mimbiyepiasa*, a type of transverse flute; the *mimbiyemboi*, a large double flute; the *pinguyu*, a small flute made from bamboo; and the *mimbiguasu*, a flute similar to the *pinguyu*, but larger than the *mimbiyemboi*. Of the percussion instruments, there were only two: the *anguarai* (made of wood) and the *anguaguasu* (a large drum covered with leather). However, while both types of drums were present in the *arete* of Cañón, most of the flutes simply consisted of metal tubes with holes drilled into them.

29. According to the owner of the *abuela* mask, there used to be an *abuelo* mask to go with it, which had, however, been lost.

30. According to Combès and Lowrey, '[t]oday's *arete guasu*, the harvest festival (now sometimes assimilated to Latin American Carnival) that symbolizes "Guaraní tradition" in Bolivia, is inherited from Chané agricultural traditions and is a complex hybrid ritual through which Chané masks incarnate . . . Guaraní ancestors' (2006: 707; ellipsis in original). For a much more detailed analysis of the symbolism of *arete guasu* celebrations among Argentinian Chané people that feature many of the same elements as the fiestas described here, see Bossert and Villar (2001). It is worth noting, however, that certain parts of their analysis will not apply in the case of Cañón, such as Bossert and Villar's assertion that the production of the *aña* masks from locally sourced wood by the men preceding the *arete* is itself a ritual exchange with the owners of the forest (*kaa iya*), as the masks in Cañón were generally not made from wood but all kinds of other materials such as rags, cardboard, or—in the cases of some schoolboys—even modified backpacks. The only carved wooden mask (that of the *yari*), meanwhile, had been purchased by its owner, and was also not discarded together with the others at the end of the celebrations.

31. A similar case is made by Giovanna Bacchiddu (2016) for the inhabitants of the island of Apiao off the coast of southern Chile in the context of religious festivities held for saints or the community's deceased: whereas the community's mainly

Catholic population regards these festivities and the exchanges tied up with them
(including the sharing of local *chicha*) as indispensable aspects of the local system
of reciprocity, the few Evangelical converts on the island, by refusing to take part
in the festivities, distance themselves from their relatives and *compadres/comadres*
and disrupt the community's social fabric. Apart from the threat of internal division,
Bacchiddu mentions in passing the possibility of the converts' refusal to participate
in the joint festivities also exposing community members to menacing forces from
outside the community: '"The evangelicals don't even believe in the dead," an old
woman once told me, almost whispering, as if she had made an almost sacrilegious
statement. Apiao people take the dead seriously, and they are careful not to disrespect
them, either in words or in behaviour. They can come back and terrify . . . the living
for several reasons. One of these reasons, and certainly the most important, is not
having given the dead a decent funeral, then a proper praying session after death, and
again on the first anniversary of their death. . . . [T]he community's participation [in
these sessions] is crucial' (ibid.: 59).

    32. Cf. Ortiz García (2002: 4): 'The generous one, the inviter, is he who enjoys the
grace of Tüpa, God, the supreme being who thanks to his mercifulness bestowed upon
them [the Guaraní] as their only and principal (and therefore sacred) nourishment the
avati [maize]. Tüpa omee ñandeve avati jese yaiko vaerä–*God gave us maize so that
we should live from it*' (italics in original).

Chapter Four

The Emergent Community

As with the fields (*chacos*), the spatial organisation of Cañón in general was on the one hand restricted by the MASRENA project (see chapter 3), while on the other hand *comunarios* constantly stressed the freedom which they had in deciding its layout. This was particularly true of the houses, where basically the same rules applied as for the *chacos*: everyone, people kept assuring me, could build their house wherever they wanted. It even happened that people moved from their old house and built a new one in a different location, if they decided that they did not like their present one. This had happened to my field assistant Lupe, who told me that she had moved twice since relocating to Cañón from Itakua. First, she used to live somewhere behind my 'host family's' place, but there had been water coming down from the mountain. Then, her family's house was a little further up on the other side of the main road, but there wasn't enough sun, and one lived 'like in a hole,' and there were also big black ants there that bit people. The ruin of the abandoned house could still be seen there, adobe bricks slowly melting away under the onslaught of sun and rain. Lupe then moved to her current location, wedged in between her mother and her brother Abel on the one side, and her sister Valeria on the other, with a lovely view of the mountains opposite. This location, she said, was good now.

This chapter centres on two themes implied in the example above that were central in the spatial and social organisation of the *comunidad*: that of movement, and that of kinship. The first part is largely descriptive and aims to provide the reader with a 'feel' for the *comunidad* as a place. The final sections problematise the *comunarios'* assertions of the freedom and tranquility of community life by turning the focus onto some of the tensions inherent in it, and the way those were bound up with the *comunarios'* aspirations for future improvements of their *comunidad*. Mobility, while valued within the intra-communal context, is thereby revealed to be a double-edged sword, with movements of people and things between the *comunidad* and the towns constituting a kind of necessary evil that constantly put the coherence of the community at risk.

THE SPATIAL LAYOUT OF THE COMMUNITY

Besides the houses located within the residential area, there were a number of conspicuous places in Cañón that could be referred to as 'public,' in the sense that they were not the property of individuals or families, but were intended for use by the community as a whole. The most central was the school compound, which functioned as the social, administrative, and also in a sense as the spiritual centre of the community.[1] Its main function was the teaching of children, which was done by six teachers from outside the *comunidad*, one of whom stayed in a little house within the school during term-time. The school was, however, also used for holding *asambleas* or workshops, which tended to be called by sounding the school bell; for special events other than the fiestas organised by individual people (such as the event described in the Introduction); for communal projects such as the pottery project discussed in chapter 6; for 'friendlies' with the football teams of neighbouring communities; and for attending the infamous church services of Padre Cristián, who came to celebrate mass in Cañón once a month.[2] The school also housed a cistern and a water tank where people could fetch water whenever the water supply to their houses got cut off. There was further a communal kitchen, which was also occasionally used to house guests (such as the 'interns' of the INSPOC institute, a school for bilingual teachers in Camiri, who regularly did placements in Cañón and other *comunidades*), and which also functioned as a storage room (for example, for the pottery produced by the women; see chapter 6). The video room next to it was often used for film presentations at night (mostly of martial arts b-movies with Spanish subtitles), and occasionally for doctors' visits. Next to the school, there was a playground for children with a climbing rack, slide, and swings.

Above the school was the 'health centre' (*posta sanitaria*), where doctors' and nurses' visits usually took place, and where I was living during my stay in Cañón. I occupied the smaller of the two rooms in the building, which had originally been constructed for a live-in nurse, and used the larger one as a kitchen. Since the community's medicine supply and a few instruments were still stored in there from the days when it was used as a consultancy room, I had to remove all my personal things whenever a nurse or NGO doctor came for a check-up. The *posta* also had the only working toilet in the entire community (which, however, didn't resist the frequent use by the schoolchildren for very long).

Further inside the forest, there was a huge concrete water tank, which was where the *comunarios* got their tap water from. Before the installation of this tank, they used to use a water pump inside a well, which also still existed but had fallen out of use. Cumbersome though fetching water from the pump had been, it had already been a huge improvement from not having any water supply at all, which was the case when the *comunarios* first moved to the place in 1991, and people tended to remember that time as one of particular hardship. What was still missing, however, was an irrigation system for the *chacos*, which would make people less dependent on the rainy season.

Apart from the *chacos*, the *comunidad*'s 'productive units' included the cattle corral where the cows of the community's joint cattle project were kept and two enclosures with beehives. The beehives consisted of wooden boxes on stilts inside a fence to keep children and animals out. According to Cristina, an agro-engineer from Spain working with CIPCA, the bee project worked best in Cañón of all the communities she had seen, but the beekeepers faced a constant struggle to keep their bees alive or from migrating elsewhere due to the lack of flowering plants in the area. There were only a few *comunarios* involved in the production of honey, which they sold in Camiri.

The immediately surrounding forest also served as a resource, most importantly for the collection of firewood. Hunting seemed to be the only activity people carried out in the deeper forest farther from the houses, but it was not very common: there were only some three people in the entire community who owned rifles, and nobody hunted with bows and arrows. Animals hunted included wild boar (*taitetu*), deer (*guasu*), some species of birds, and apparently very occasionally wild cats, to which people referred as 'lions' (*leones*), and which, they said, had a very 'strong' meat, in the sense that it made one strong when eaten. Certain plants of the forest were also used, but overall very little. Those included edible ones, such as custard apples (*chirimoya*) and other fruits, spices and herbs (such as a wild variety of chilli [*kɨɨ*] and certain leaves used to mix with the *yerba mate* to make it milder), and medicinal plants. I was once given some leaves and twigs from which to make a tea to cure an upset stomach, but generally people claimed ignorance of these things; there was, at the time of my fieldwork, only one very old *abuelita* in the *comunidad* who was said to know about curing with plants.

There was a cemetery not far from the main tank, which was still rather small due to the fact that the community had only existed for some fourteen years when I got there. Graves were mostly humble and only marked by iron crosses, and were decorated with the usual *coronas* (lit.: 'crowns'; wreaths of coloured plastic flowers). There was another cemetery in Itakua, which the *comunarios* visited on All Saints to pray by the graves, exchange *masitas* (maize flour biscuits and sweet bread made only for this occasion), and leave new *coronas* on the graves. Some few *comunarios* who had been able to afford it had transferred their dead from Itakua to the new cemetery, but most of them had remained where they had been buried.

These public places as structures were more or less fixtures, but many had, nonetheless, a high internal mobility, as exemplified by the constant oscillation of purposes—and the resulting flux of objects and people—of the *posta sanitaria* and the school. As Crivos et al. have noted for Mbya Guaraní communities in Argentina,

> Processes of spatial mobility among the *Mbya* are of interest in anthropological . . . studies, as these processes are related to transformations in the landscape and the environment. Despite this, ethnographic literature usually focuses on the mobility of *Guaraní* communities from the perspective of population dynamics on a regional scale. (Crivos et al. 2007)

What first alerted me to the high internal mobility in Cañón was one incidence in the early stages of my fieldwork when I went looking for Doña Estefanía's house and, failing to remember the way, asked another woman about its location. 'It's just down the road and to the left,' she replied. 'Where they sell bread.' Bread was about the only food product in Cañón that was both produced by the women and regularly sold to other *comunarios*. As in Camiri, houses where bread could be bought were marked by a stick with a white rag or plastic bag wrapped around the top, which could be propped up or stuck in the ground next to the road outside the house. These markers were removed again as soon as the bread had run out. 'Where they sell bread' was thus an indicator that could only be used as long as the selling of a particular batch of bread was ongoing, rather than a permanent marker of location. In order to understand this kind of directions, you thus had to either know who of the women had recently been making bread, or physically go out looking for the stick with the plastic bag. This kind of mobility was even more conspicuous when it came to the organisation of particular houses.

LIVING SPACES AND LIVED-IN SPACES

The houses (Guaraní: *o*, *tëta*) in Cañón were located relatively far from one another, surrounded by forest (except for the patio, which was cleared), and connected by footpaths. They were mostly small, with entire families sharing one to two rooms. Their main function seemed to be as 'storage facilities' for clothes and other belongings and shelter from the rain; most houses did not contain much more than a bed or two, a wardrobe, and some adornments on the walls. In short, thinking of a house in Cañón as the kind of living space 'Westerners' (or even townspeople in Bolivia) are used to would be misleading—in fact, they hardly even constituted the centre of the lived-in space, but rather formed one of the components only of the *oka*, the patio. A lot of the integral parts of the household were situated outside, like the 'kitchen,' 'bathroom,' and living/eating area, and I hardly ever saw anyone invite a visitor into their house. Social life (except for cases in which it was being deliberately hidden from others) largely happened outside in the *oka*. This outside space corresponded to what in *karai* houses was on the inside: in the towns, people also spent a lot of time in the open air, but there the houses were built to enclose the patios whereas in the country the patios stretched out in front of, and in some cases around, the houses.

The houses as they were at the time of my fieldwork had been built by the *comunarios*, using largely (but not exclusively) local materials. They were mostly made of adobe bricks and wood, with additional corrugated metal sheets for making roofs, nails, mesh (to put in front of windows to keep insects out), and lime having been donated by Caritas. When the people had first moved from their 'captive community' in Itakua in 1994 (see chapters 1 and 2), they had built preliminary houses made of wattle-and-daub, which in most cases were replaced by adobe buildings later on.[3] Even the building of the adobe houses was a gradual process; as the *capitán grande* put it, 'We are building the houses little by little—you see, they don't even have [glass] windows yet.'

There were plans by the local government to build brick houses for the *comunarios*, along with providing them with electricity and then gas, but not everyone was happy about that. Some people were worried that with such a change 'bad habits' from the town would make their way into Cañón, inspired by things seen on TV, and that the *tranquilidad* they so appreciated in Cañón would be lost. Though people were undoubtedly aware of similar developments already affecting the *comunidades* in more urban settings (cf. Postero 2017), these examples seemed to be the expression of a generalised uneasiness about *comunarios* becoming more *karai*-like rather than specific worries, as the 'bad habits' people talked about remained mysteriously vague, and TVs in fact already existed in various households, without evidently having caused any particular problems. This concern was echoed in the worry that the new houses would bring a new spatial order with them, in the image of an urban centre with a central plaza and houses that were located close to one another, which, people said, had caused a lot of trouble already in other communities: in Cañón, one didn't, for example, have any problems raising chickens, whereas where the houses were too close together these things could cause fights if one family's animals invaded another's gardens.

One person also uttered the concern that the current freedom of movement would be lost with the construction of solid-brick buildings. As it was, abandoned houses like Lupe's could just be left to slowly make their way back to being part of the natural environment as the adobe disintegrated, which would not be possible anymore with houses built of brick. The concept of houses was thus undergoing a process of change at the time I was living in Cañón, from another potentially mobile element of the *oka* to a more central and more firmly fixed position. From the misgivings that the *comunarios* had voiced about this shift, it was clear that they perceived it as a risky development that would involve the adoption of a more town-like, *karai* order. This, people felt, would impinge on their current '*tranquilo*' way of life, and they therefore anticipated it not without a certain sense of anxiety.

As indicated above, the main living space of the Cañón inhabitants was not the house but the *oka*, a space that had been cleared of the forest where most of people's 'domestic' activities took place (such as cooking, eating, doing laundry, and receiving guests), a kind of 'human space' within the forest. It usually included a fireplace, or 'kitchen' (people did use the Spanish word '*cocina*' for these spaces, even when speaking in Guaraní), made up of some bricks or stones with iron bars laid across them to place pots on, as well as the pots, kettles, and pans themselves, which people bought in Camiri. The kitchen was usually, but not always, surrounded by a wooden frame with a roof and spaces where to hang utensils up called a *chapapa*.[4] In one household, I saw the bottom of the *avatío* (lit.: 'house of maize'), a raised wooden construction used for storing dry maize, being employed in such a way.

While pretty much all of the houses had a fireplace, there were other elements that could be present in the *oka* or not, such as a shower, which was often just another wooden frame surrounded by opened-out sacks or pieces of tarpaulin, or (more rarely) brick walls; a toilet (that, however, was a rare luxury indeed; normally, people just used the surrounding forest); a baking oven made of adobe bricks in which people made bread, *humintas*,[5] and other things; a small chicken coop; an eating space with a table; an *ita* (lit.: stone; a saddle quern consisting of a stone slab and a rounded grinding stone with which vegetables, maize, charqui, and so on were ground); a *takú*, which was a mortar of a different kind, made out of a piece of tree trunk that had been hollowed on top, in which one could pound maize (or, indeed, pottery shards; see chapter 6) with the help of wooden poles; and the above-mentioned *avatío* for storing maize. Many people also had water tanks to fall back on when the piped supply broke down, which happened rather a lot due to such interferences as repairs, road works, and cleaning of the tank. Those without tanks had to fetch water from the school or use the ravine next to the Santa Cruz motorway to wash their clothes and bathe in, but the water there was not very clean.

Typical *oka* setting
featuring kitchen, wood
mortar, table, and two
houses (top), and a quern
stone and clay oven (left).
Photos by the author.

Chairs, benches, and all kinds of kitchen utensils always moved about the *oka*; visitors were often given a chair where they stood, sometimes in the middle of the *oka*, sometimes even almost with their backs to the hosts or quite a distance away from them. There did not seem to be a fixed rule for this, except that chairs were usually put in the shade. Household items such as machetes, cups, cutlery, clothes, or schoolbooks were often left lying around on the ground and were picked up and cleaned when needed. This casualness with regard to the treatment of personal possessions was also noted by Stephen Kidd for the Enxet people of the Paraguayan Chaco; Kidd came to the conclusion that

> [t]he rapid deterioration of Enxet possessions may be explained by the fact that they are not interested in 'having' possessions . . . but in 'using' them. . . . They do not anticipate retaining a particular object for a number of years hence but are interested in taking advantage of it in the here and now. Therefore, while Europeans could be described as a '[to] have and to hold' people, the Enxet could be characterized as a 'to have and to use' people. (Kidd 2000: 251, ft. 28)

Though this approach to material objects can easily be interpreted as carelessness when seen from a Euro-American preservationist perspective, viewed in a different light it is also a reflection of a great degree of flexibility and spontaneous innovative ingenuity:[6] among the Guaraní, even the larger features of the *oka*, such as the kitchen or table, were subject to this continual mobility, so that the appearance of the *oka* could change almost completely from one day to another to accommodate the momentary needs or preferences of its inhabitants. 'Modern' things such as schoolbooks and even TVs got subjected to the same mobility as benches, pots, and tables: Luz's younger sister Marilyn, for example, used to wheel the family TV out in a wheelbarrow that also held the car battery that powered it, and fasten its antenna to a second one that led up high into the trees to get a signal. The same wheelbarrow was later in the evening used as a 'pushchair' to wheel Luz's toddler daughter Cindy around to put her to sleep. Stereos would be brought from town for fiestas, and radios would be hung up in trees during the day and often just left on in the background, with people gathering round them if anything important and worth discussing came on. Besides this constant physical movement of objects, they were also 'mobile' with regard to their uses, and things were frequently diverted from their intended purposes: *takú* could, for example, be put onto their side to serve as 'legs' for additional benches at fiestas, blankets could be made into hammocks for babies, and rucksacks could be transformed into carnival masks.

The 'human space' constituted by the *oka* was also inhabited by certain animals, where some types—such as chickens, ducks, dogs, and the occa-

Children wearing carnival masks made from cardboard and rucksacks with holes cut into them.
Photo by the author.

sional cat—belonged more to the *oka* than others. The bigger ones, such as pigs, cows, and goats, were only occasionally permitted in to drink or feed, but were usually driven out with the help of the dogs. Wild forest creatures (except for toads, lizards, and creepy-crawlies of all kinds) did not usually come close to the *oka* or immediately surrounding forest, which was mostly inhabited by the larger domestic animals that roamed freely during the day and either came back to their owners at night or had to be fetched by them. Now and again, one might encounter a snake or scorpion, but these were usually killed by the *comunarios*. Like the arrangement of the *oka's* features, what was 'human' and what 'animal' space within the *oka* was constantly being redefined: certain spaces, such as the *ita*, were only 'human' and prohibited to animals when they were being used by the people, whereas the rest of the time the animals were free to climb about on them. Others, such as tables, were always prohibited to any kind of animal. People and animals were, however, in constant close contact with each other, and people would often eat or drink things that had been pecked at by chickens or even tried by one of the dogs. Chicken feathers, but also insects, leaves, dust, and other forest materials, frequently landed in the food as well so that most meals included a certain dose of 'non-human environment' as an unintentional ingredient.

Due to this close proximity of the non-human realm, human spaces constantly had to be reclaimed from 'nature' (cf. Gow 1991: 78), which quickly invaded not only the *oka* but also the houses if given the opportunity. I once left the *posta* for about a month when I went home over Christmas, and when I came back, I not only found spiders and all kinds of other forest creatures in it, but also a substantial amount of dust. The space in front of the house had completely overgrown and had to be cleared with a machete. Consequently, the *oka* were swept first thing every morning and cleared of all animal waste, leaves, and rubbish that had accumulated during the previous day, all of which would be expelled into the forest. The organic waste products that were produced during cooking were normally instantly cleared up by the animals (chickens and dogs inside the *oka*, and additionally pigs at its outer edges). Unfortunately, the non-human realm, which tends to be the only 'rubbish disposal system' in the *comunidades*, has no way of disposing of other types of rubbish, and thus older communities that have inhabited their territory over a longer time period (such as, for example, Itanambikua on the outskirts of Camiri) are often swamped with non-biodegradable rubbish.

While the *oka* were mostly cleared of vegetation, they tended to include some natural features that were used as part of the 'home furniture': trees and shrubs could make do for cupboards and shelves on which to hang things up and store things stuck between their branches, and holes in the ground served as rubbish dumps. Despite the 'natural' appearance such features bestowed on the *oka*, they were in fact thoroughly constructed spaces, as even trees were sometimes planted specifically where people wanted them in order to provide storage space, shelter from rain, and—most importantly—shade: an *oka* without shade was not really deemed fit for habitation, and *comunarios* often recalled Sadoth Palenque's burning of their trees in Itakua as one of his most despicable acts. Interestingly, Varese reports a strikingly similar case from the Mexican colonial era:

> In 1768 the Totonacs of Papantla, in the Mexican Southeast, rose in rebellion against the Spanish authorities in defense of their trees, which had been threatened by the mayor. A Spanish source mentions the Indians' reasons: 'The trees give shade to people and help them to persevere, are useful to tie animals, protect houses from fires, and the branches and leaves are used as fodder for animals.' (Taylor 1979: 137, quoted in Varese 1996: 61)

Bearing in mind the importance of the trees in the functioning of the *comunarios*' living spaces, Palenque's act of felling them takes on the character, not merely of a vindictive act of violence, but of a systematic assault on their way of living in which the physical setup of their surroundings played a crucial role.

The same can be said about the *patrones'* restriction of the *comunarios'* movements by such means as allegedly fencing them in with barbed wire. As mentioned, Cañón was crisscrossed by many footpaths, hidden among the trees, that connected the houses with one another, but also penetrated by the dirt road that led to the motorway connecting Camiri with Santa Cruz. These different paths allowed for people to be mobile in different ways. Adults came and went on the road that connects Cañón with the motorway and Camiri, often making use of the regular *trufis* (taxis), wearing their Sunday best. In Cañón, they moved along forest paths, wearing their everyday clothes. These paths were quite different from the road: they could only be navigated on foot, and people were not nearly as visible moving along them as they were on the road. When I first came to Cañón, I explored these paths on my own, getting myself lost in the dense vegetation, eventually resurfacing at houses I had never been to before. Later, I went on guided tours with Lupe, which slowly provided me with a better sense of the layout of the place. As I discovered on these occasions, even the *comunarios* themselves were not all equally familiar with these paths. Thus, it happened several times on our tours that Lupe had to ask one of her children for directions when we reached a fork in one of the paths; the children, it turned out, seemed to know the forest paths best because they were always roaming about outside, whereas the adults were a lot more habitual in the routes they took on a daily basis (to the *chacos* at the back of the community; to their neighbours'/mother's/friend's house; to collect firewood in the surrounding forest; etc.), which were closely bound up with the roles they inhabited in community life.

EXTRAORDINARY PLACES WITHIN THE *COMUNIDAD*

While the forest constituted a non-human space, with human presence decreasing as you moved into it to a similar degree as animal presence decreased the closer you moved into the *okas*,[7] it was nonetheless not an uninhabited space by any means. I soon found out that, besides the forest animals, there were other beings living in various locations around the *comunarios'* houses. It all started with Lupe telling me about a tree located in the main *chaco* area (which she christened the 'tree of death'), under which a fugitive woman was said to have killed her husband. The husband had pursued her and reached her at this point, where the woman had killed him and put him in a sitting position and left him there. That was how he was later found by someone passing by (who, however, was not a *comunario*, as this story stemmed from a time before the existence of the *comunidad*). From the 'tree of death,' the conversation quickly turned to other extraordinary places within the *comunidad* that were the locations of sightings of 'spirit' beings, to which the *comunarios* generally referred as '*bichos*' (Sp.: creepy-crawly, creature). I have discussed the *comunarios*' relationships with the various entities found in these places elsewhere in greater detail (Groke 2015); however, they deserve a mention here because, for one, they form part of the spatial layout of the *comunidad*, and further, because they show that Cañón was never an uninhabited wilderness even before the *comunarios* settled there but rather came with various histories already 'implicated' in its topography (Gow 1995: 50–53). Several of these places were marked by the discovery of old clay pots, which were frequently found in ravines, and some of which contained burials. The terrain in Cañón was arid and unstable, and not only did the main road get pretty much destroyed every year with the arrival of the rainy season, but the opening of new ravines and shifting of old ones sometimes brought pottery to the surface that had been buried or left long before Cañón existed. People were generally scared of the 'owners' (Guaraní: *iya reta*; Spanish: *dueños*) of such pots, many of whom were evil and would haunt people in their dreams, and possibly even make them fall ill or die, when disturbed.

In the ravine crossing the main road, a white 'ghost pig' used to appear at night to scare people who were walking by. It could also appear in the shape of other animals, whereby there was some confusion about whether this pig was the same as all the other creatures that had been sighted around that area or not. Sometimes, it would only be heard but not seen. When I asked about the origin of these creatures, I was told that they were often the deceased owners of vessels filled with money or silver ('*plata*'), which they had buried in the place where they appeared, and which they were now guarding. On the same main road, a 'widow' (*viudita*) had appeared to people driving by at night. In one account I heard, she was dressed in white with long hair hiding her face; in the other she was dressed in black with glowing eyes.

The *abuelita* who died shortly after I arrived in Cañón had, I was told, once seen a huge snake in one of the hills, which almost scared her to death. This *abuelita* also socialised with a mysterious man who lived in the hill behind her house, and to whom people referred as the 'owner of the hill.' He had noticed that she was living on her own and wanted her to come live with him to keep him company, as he too was alone, even though he was rich and kept all kinds of animals. Apparently, she used to be reluctant to tell people too much about this owner, but it was known that he appeared to her a lot in her dreams.

There also used to be a sort of goblin (*duende*) that lived in the school, where it scared the children and sometimes stole babies, who were usually found again when they started to cry. Another one used to live in one of the smaller *chacos*, where it used to follow one of the girls around because it had fallen in love with her. She had had to get it 'exorcised' by an *abuelita* to get rid of it. *Duendes* are creatures commonly known to people throughout Latin

America and not limited to the Guaraní universe. In Camiri and surrounding areas, they are usually described as tiny little men with huge sombreros.

Although an overall motley crew with many differences between them (not least their different cultural origins), two things all these creatures had in common were that they inhabited spaces that belonged to another realm, which was the reason their houses were generally invisible to people, and that they seemed to be disappearing one after the other as the presence and activities of the *comunarios* further and further encroached on their domains. Where they appeared to people, it was usually in their dreams, or when they were walking home from a fiesta at night drunk.

There were also other mysterious places people could not tell me much about, such as a marker stone indicating the location of a house that had existed before the *comunarios* came, and a stone in the shape of a mortar (Guaraní: *itangúa*, 'stone mortar') hidden deep in the forest, about whose origin they could only speculate. These, however, were generally thought to be the remnants of former human presence rather than the products of spirit activity.

While their own 'history' was what had first brought the *comunarios* to Cañón (and was thus, in a sense, itself a history of movement), these local (hi)stories were taken up by the *comunarios* to fulfil a role similar to that of memories described by Peter Gow for a community of Piro people in the Bajo Urubamba (Gow 1991, 1995). There is, however, at least one fundamental difference between the two cases: for the Piro people described by Gow, their community was a landscape that had been (and was being) shaped by the constant place-making activities of adult people in their performances of relationships of kinship and affinity (such as garden making or building houses). Consequently, to local people their landscape was 'historical' in that in it those who remembered could discern the traces of the work and relationships of past generations. In the case of Cañón, however, the landscape-shaping efforts of its inhabitants had only started little over a decade ago, and thus the process of relationships being implicated in its landscape was still in its beginnings. While the role of 'history' had been taken on by one particular document (see chapter 2), the stories about '*bichos*' in the *comunidad* functioned, in the absence of people's memories of their own, to form connections between the land and the people, differentiate the space of the landscape, and enable people to relate to it on a personal level. The *comunarios*' interactions with these 'internal outsiders' allow us to see the process of place-making in Cañón as the ongoing negotiation of a shared space between a set of old and one of new 'owners' (owners of animals, places, and *plata*, as opposed to legal owners of land) (Groke 2015). They also remind us of the fact that *comunidades* cannot be assumed to be internally heterogeneous (or, for that matter, conflict free).

KINSHIP

As in Lupe's case, the places where people had chosen to build their houses often reflected their kinship relations within the *comunidad*. Rather than representing a fixed state of reality at any point in time, however, the position of houses only gives an indication of such a reality, in that the composition of the particular households tended to be in a constant state of flux (cf. Gow 1995). While some people tended to stay more or less put, others came and went on a regular basis. This constituted a problem for the compilation of censuses and other such records meant to provide an overview of the population of Cañón at any particular time: did, for example, the fourteen-year-old granddaughter of the house's main owners, who spent most of her time living with other relatives in Camiri (whose house in Cañón, incidentally, had been standing empty for years) because there was no money for her daily bus fare to get her to school and back, constitute a regular 'inhabitant' of the *comunidad*? Or what was the situation of the young man whose wife lived alone with their little children because he was working as a contractor in Santa Cruz? It even happened with the most 'steady' *comunarios* that they moved away for a while to take on work outside the *comunidad* when the need arose for them to earn some money quickly, and while households were mainly based on the cohabiting of nuclear families, people often 'lent' or 'outsourced' their children to relatives in such situations, or indeed in cases where those relatives were in need of company.

As we have seen, despite the fact that, as a legal-geographical entity, Cañón was a precisely defined space with fixed boundaries, mobility was a feature that was inbuilt in the *comunarios'* lifestyles on many levels. It was reflected in the movements of people, animals, and objects (and their purposes) in and out of and within the *comunidad*, and was even reflected in the uses of the space within people's own domestic domains.[8] However, as with the MASRENA project ordering the community's supposedly 'free' internal space, there were also certain factors that constricted people's freedom of movement. To some extent, the flexibility of *comunarios'* movements was limited by the forces of kinship (in its sense of blood, conjugal, and affinal relations), which tended to draw people together in clusters of nuclear families. However, since most of the *comunarios* were related in one way or another, and since there was no discernible pattern indicating a preference for either uxorilocal or virilocal residence, the way they chose to place themselves in relation to other *comunarios* was still largely a reflection of preference. Kinship, however, was not the only influence in the organisation of Cañón as a social space: in some cases, people were compelled to leave the *comunidad* out of necessity, whereas in others, people's choice of location could even be seen as a political statement. Some families, for example, had built their houses deeper in the forest than others and seemed to play a more marginal role in the goings-on of communal life; recall also the case of Don Jacinto and his family, who had been 'ostracised' from the community centre because of the role they had played in the struggle with the *patrones* (see chapter 2) and only moved back into a more central location when the woman's mother died in 2007 and they took over her house.

In short, to the outsider it was plain to see that behind all their 'freedom' there were various forces pulling the *comunarios* in different, sometimes opposing, directions that constantly had to be negotiated. In the light of all this, the *comunarios'* assertions of their freedom seem all the more striking: to them, Cañón, despite all the limitations I could see in it, was a space of peace and quiet, a 'free *comunidad*'—a label that, used in the self-explanatory way in which Lupe had spoken it, was charged with the power to evoke and describe an entire way of life. Part of this power can be explained by the fact that the much-mentioned freedom of movement put Cañón as a *comunidad* in opposition with the *propiedad*: in Itakua, people had needed the *patrones'* permission if they wanted to move, and the available space had been very limited. In a sense, then, the move from Itakua to Cañón had also been a move from a not-so-good life to a better life that was traceable in the local geography as well as in *comunarios'* memories and the documents produced by the bureaucracy of the legal institutions and the state (cf. Gordillo 2006).

At the same time as the traces of kinship became visible, or, in the words of Peter Gow (1995: 50–53), 'implicated,' in the space of the *comunidad* through the *comunarios'* decisions to construct their houses in certain patterns and their daily movements and activities, this space also became a reflection of their ability to live *tranquilo*. If we recall the violence directed against people's lived-in spaces by the *patrones* in Itakua that sparked off the conflict that ultimately resulted in their move to Cañón (burning of the trees surrounding the *comunarios'* houses, destruction of the communal meeting hall), the significance of this becomes clear: living in Cañón meant inhabiting a space that was defined by the *comunarios'* present ability to 'live and work *tranquilo*' and 'do what they wanted' to such a degree, not because this ability was unlimited, but because of their memories of its *absence* in their previous location. In that sense, Cañón's space was lived and lived-in 'good life,' and inhabiting it a daily enactment of *comunidad*. In other words, the concept of *comunidad* was important to people, not because it described a fixed entity of a particular character (as that represented in the documents containing its 'history,' title, and outlines) but, on the contrary, because it contained in itself the potential of movement and flexibility the *comunarios* saw as so crucial to their ideal of what it meant to 'live *tranquilo*.'

THE DISRUPTIVE POWER OF JEALOUSY

The formation of Cañón as a free *comunidad* where people could 'live *tranquilo*' had not come to its complete conclusion with the signing of the documents of ownership or even the *comunarios'* physical move to their new home. While 'living *tranquilo*' and 'being able to do what we want' were the dominant idioms people used to describe life in Cañón, they were, to some degree, ideals rather than reflections of an already attained reality. There was certainly a sense that life in Cañón afforded the *comunarios* more freedom than life on the Vannuccis' property had done, but this went hand in hand with a certain sense of lack. This sentiment was expressed either directly, in people's talk about what was still needed in order to make Cañón the kind of functioning place they envisioned it to be, or indirectly, in people's daily struggles. The following sections deal with these discrepancies between discourse and reality on two levels: firstly, I use the example of jealousy to demonstrate that, despite the efforts that the *comunarios* put into living well together (as epitomised in the fiesta), life within the community was not always harmonious. This was particularly true for the *comunarios'* dealings with forces emanating from outside the *comunidad*, which had the potential of transforming the mobility people valued so greatly in their lives within Cañón into something subversive to communal cohesion. Secondly, I discuss what the *comunarios* themselves said was still missing in Cañón. These issues are important in that both the tensions and the aspirations that were present in daily life in Cañón can shed some additional light on people's ideas of how *comunarios* were meant to live together.

I have shown above how the move from Itakua to the community's current location became a defining event that produced the *comunidad*'s identification in opposition to the *propiedad* of the *patrones*. This, however, was not the only opposition which the *comunarios* of Cañón used in this way. Rather, they would say very similar things about the difference between life in the *comunidad* and life in the town: Cañón, people would tell me, was a lot better than Camiri because here, one could do what one wanted, whereas life in Camiri was all about money ('*Camiri es pura plata*'). Without money, a young girl from a different community who was doing her teacher training in Cañón told me once, you didn't eat in Camiri, whereas in the *comunidades* people shared food and sometimes even money and helped each other out. Or, in the words of my neighbour Don Pedro: 'I don't like towns. I can only stand Santa Cruz for a week, no longer. I've been to La Paz as well, it's better than Santa Cruz, but it's also *pura plata*, and so is Camiri: they'll charge you for going to the loo there.'

This concern about money reflects a sort of double standard in the lives of the *comunarios*, in that they liked to make a point of stressing their independence of and dislike for the money economy, at the same time as the performance of their daily lives required them to engage in it. While it was true that the use of money in the *comunidad* was very limited in comparison with the town, this limitation was offset by the *comunarios'* limited capacity to earn money, which they needed in order to buy household goods and suchlike from the Camiri market and pay for medical treatments, and—perhaps most importantly—for the organisation of fiestas. This discrepancy resulted from the way in which, despite their demonstrative aversion toward the money economy as it was practiced in 'the town,' the *comunarios* of Cañón were in fact very much bound up in it: besides the temporary labourers who went as far as Santa Cruz and Brazil in order to earn money if need be, the taxis that provided rides to and from Camiri at cheap rates several times a day were always filled with women carrying products that were destined for sale in the urban markets. The same women would then return having done the necessary shopping for foodstuffs, clothes, petrol, and whatever else they needed at home but couldn't get hold of in Cañón.

In addition, Cañón itself was not a completely market-free zone either: for emergency needs, *comunarios* could, if they were lucky, fall back on the 'shops' that two of the women had established within the *comunidad*, each of which sold particular items they acquired in Camiri and stocked in their houses. Doña Estefanía, my 'host mother,' specialised in foodstuffs such as rice, pasta, and packets of *refresco* (powdered soft drinks that were popular as alternatives to *käguirai*), while Doña Apolonia was the one to approach if the *vicios* (alcohol and cigarettes) ran out during a fiesta, or if one needed cigarettes to smoke out malignant spirits. Much like the bread sellers mentioned above, however, these 'shops' were unpredictable and could not be relied on to have any particular item in stock, and it happened frequently that children who had been sent to buy things from one of the tradeswomen had to go home empty-handed. In short, much as the *comunarios* might help each other out, there were a number of items that they simply could not get hold of without money. These ranged from small occasional luxuries such as chewing gum for the kids, and daily necessities such as metal pots and pans, to comparatively huge items such as the implements for the tractor the *comunarios* had to rent every year in order to be able to put it to its intended use of ploughing the fields.

The complexities surrounding the use of money in primarily non-monetary economies have been well documented across South America (e.g., Colloredo-Mansfeld 1999; Harris 1995; Kidd 2000; Ferraro 2011).

As briefly mentioned in chapter 3, in Cañón, one way of dealing with the more immediate money crises was the activation of kinship and friendship circuits for the purpose of borrowing money. I myself (who, as a '*gringa*,' was generally perceived as relatively affluent) soon found myself involved in this convention, which—common though it was—was not without its political complexities. On one occasion, for example, it happened that three people borrowed money from me within two days (one to buy remedies for an ongoing health problem, and two in order to be able to take loans out in Camiri, which they needed to finance a fiesta) at the same time as another couple cautioned me not to lend people money, unaware that one of their children already owed me a, by local standards, fairly substantial sum. While I tried to be as discrete as possible about these transactions, there was no way to avoid gossip altogether, and I was acutely aware of the jealousy that was sometimes sparked by my giving (or even lending) things to people who other people thought should not have received them.

Jealousy, in fact, seemed to be one of the most powerful forces that detracted from the tranquility in Cañón. People were jealous of each other, not only where money was concerned, but also in relation to personal achievements and romantic relationships. There is an abundant ethnographic literature on the disruptive and antisocial force of jealousy, not only in Latin America (cf. Sarmiento Barletti 2011; Overing and Passes eds. 2000) but all over the world, in particular with reference to the so-called 'evil eye,' which can be found in any number of cultures (cf. Maloney ed. 1976; Dundes 1981).[9] While 'evil eye' was not a term that the *comunarios* were in the habit of using, I frequently heard mentions of the negative impact of jealous behaviour within the *comunidad*, which could in certain cases involve recourse to magic, as was the case in the following example: a woman went to Camiri, leaving her then ten-year-old daughter home alone, and when she got back, the girl was gone—she could be seen out in the path, but refused to come to the house and only sneaked into her bed once it was already dark. The same happened the next day, so the mother went to fetch her, but the girl ran off into the forest. A witchdoctor (*brujo*) the worried parents consulted in Camiri discovered the source of the girl's strange behaviour: while tending some animals, the girl had stepped on something evil an older girl had left in the path for another girl with whom she was fighting over a boy, and whatever had been left in the path had entered the little girl's body. Her sister, who told me the story, said that these things were like worms, and that one had to go to a *brujo* to get them removed because they could sometimes even kill the victim. The little girl had had to go several times and she was alright now, but, her sister said, this kind of thing never completely left one once one had it. As this case makes clear, jealousy let loose had the potential to harm not only those it was intended to harm, but whomever chance happened to throw in harm's way.

As far as romantic jealousy went, jealousy between couples was particularly common. Sparked by malicious rumours spread by others (whose reason for initiating them was often jealousy as well), or simply a result of certain people's tempers (which tended to be aggravated by excessive drinking), it could cause rifts within families and high degrees of domestic violence. This latter phenomenon was frowned upon but nevertheless not uncommon, and while others sometimes intervened by trying to talk sense into the perpetrators, there seemed to be no standard procedure for settling these disputes. In one case, I was told that the reason an older man whose repeated absence from the fiestas I had noticed did not go to them anymore was that the consumption of alcohol unalterably made him go crazy with jealousy and beat his wife. Chastised by the then-*mburuvicha*, who told him to moderate his behaviour as the wife wasn't an animal to be treated in this way but a human being with parents who loved her, he had stopped attending the fiestas altogether. In other cases, however, well-known wife-beaters just seemed to be left at liberty to carry on as they pleased, and people would restrict themselves to negative comments about their behaviour rather than direct intervention.[10]

In cases where *comunarios'* jealousy was directed toward the possessions of others, people would comment on their jealousy in terms of their 'badness,' predicting that they would 'get annoyed' if they found out about such-and-such a thing, a frequent concern that sometimes caused people to hide things from each other. In other instances, allegations were voiced that certain people were resentful of someone else's status achievements and 'did not want them' to hold a particular post, even though on the other hand people would often comment on how individuals within the leadership of the community and the *capitanía* kept being re-elected because 'no one else wants to do it.' The reason for the coexistence of these two opposing points of view was that people often viewed posts held outside the *comunidad* with a degree of suspicion and assumed them to be particularly lucrative and/or prestigious, even while asserting how disruptive they were to the incumbent's life and work in the *comunidad*. Internally held posts were less problematic, as they (at least theoretically) rotated every two years and were not usually tied to any financial gains.

While holding prestigious or influential positions outside the *comunidad* (such as positions in the leadership of the *capitanía*) was not necessarily connected with financial gain either, the suspicion of people in the *comunidades* that this was the case was also not completely unfounded. *Capitanes grandes* heading the leadership of the *capitanías*, as well as the leaders of the APG, not only spend a lot of time away from their *comunidades*, but they are also the ones who mainly interact with outside funding bodies of all kinds, which puts them in a position in which corruption becomes not only possible but in some cases even easy. One particularly prominent example of this phenomenon is found in the Capitanía of the Upper and Lower Isoso (CABI), where the present-day situation requires the *capitanes* to perform the double function of 'communal mediator, arbitrator and leader in the Isoseño communities[, and of] representative and mediator toward the outside, vis-à-vis civil authorities, financiers and institutions' (Combès 2005a: 310). This has led to an increase in authority of the *capitanes* and a corresponding decrease in authority of the communal *asambleas*, which are traditionally meant to stand above the *capitán* (ibid.). Further, it has had the effect of *capitanes* spending a lot of time away from the communities, which has caused a rift between them and the people whom they are meant to represent: on the one hand, the CABI has to apply for projects that are 'trendy' with the funding bodies at any point in time, which means that they do not necessarily correspond to communities' real needs (Combès 2005a: 320); on the other hand, CABI leaders are being accused of hoarding power and money for their own benefit (Combès 2005a: 325–26).

Tensions between external and internal demands on indigenous leaders of political organisations and accusations of corruption are 'modern' problems that increasingly affect the traditionally more egalitarian societies of South America (cf. Brown 1993; High 2006; Rubenstein 2007). During my own fieldwork experience, I came across various cases in which corruption was suspected on the part of *capitanía* and even community leaders. On one occasion, I happened to be sitting next to the former *capitán* of a *comunidad* during a fiesta who had just been voted out of power by the *asamblea*. Already quite inebriated, he started lamenting the fact to me that he had been 'demoted' (*degradado*) by his fellow *comunarios* because they had accused him of corruption. He told me that they had said that he had been misappropriating money to spend on girls. I asked, as jokingly as I could, 'Well, is it true?,' and he replied, somewhat enigmatically: 'Nobody's saying that it's a lie.' While in this case the communal *asamblea* had been able to act on the corruption charge against their *capitán*, deposing leaders at the level of *capitanía* or APG is more difficult, as is even finding out about and proving cases of corruption among them, since they tend to spend so much of their time in the towns. This lack of transparency marking the outside dealings of influential *comunarios* makes it understandable that there should be a high degree of mistrust against them (especially where they are in a position to pocket money for themselves that was really meant to benefit all *comunarios*).

THE DESIRE FOR AUTONOMY

Mistrust and jealousy, however, were not the only forces disrupting people's lives in Cañón; ironically, people's attempts to earn more money, which could spark such jealousy in others, could prove to be highly disruptive themselves. As mentioned above, *comunarios* sometimes left the *comunidad* in order to take jobs in the towns. Besides borrowing money, this was another way of acting on urgent financial needs. However, as in the case of Don Elías, whose work for Caritas drastically limited his capacity for working in his field in the *comunidad*, outside work could seriously affect the lives of those left behind: children of working mothers had to be left with other relatives, wives of working men struggled to manage on their own, and entire houses could stand empty for years and have to be looked after by younger siblings or other family members. Leaving the *comunidad* (if only for a short time) for reasons other than the search for money likewise was not always a choice born out of preference, but often a result of necessity. My friend's fifteen-year-old daughter Ángela for example, was unhappy about having to go to live with one of the Cañón teachers in Chorety (a suburb of Camiri) where she was going to school because her parents could not afford her daily taxi fare into town and back. 'Being able to do what one wanted' was thus not always an option even in *'tranquilo'* Cañón, but rather an ideal to which people aspired, but which they never quite managed to reach.

The literature is full of accounts of how the 'good life' among Amerindian peoples is not a given, but rather something that has to be actively pursued and constantly recreated. Take, for example, Belaunde on the Airo-Pai of Peruvian Amazonia:

> Practices of reclusion for menstruating women, alimentary and sexual restrictions for the parents of recently born children, and practices of generosity, reciprocity, and solidarity in the daily activities of adult women and men have for an objective the management of one's own rage and that of others, converting it into a positive element. . . . Another key element in the maintenance of conviviality is commensality, or the repeated and reciprocal sharing of foods and drinks, since together with the food and drink a series of positive physical and moral characteristics are shared that further unite the people. Generosity, control of emotions, and commensality are indispensable elements for the achievement of a *paihueña*, 'the place of the people,' that is, a *comunidad* where people 'know how to live well.' (Belaunde 2001: 17)

Belaunde's beautiful ethnography describes all the classic elements of Amazonian sociality (transforming negative emotions into positive ones, conviviality, commensality, reciprocity, generosity . . .). As we have seen, generosity, reciprocity, and commensality also played an important role in the active efforts of the *comunarios* of Cañón to live well together as a free *comunidad*. However, there were other ideas that people had with regard to how life in the community could be improved yet further that were rather less 'typically' Amerindian. One main theme here was that of Guaraní communities having their own professionals, as mentioned by Don Rogelio in the event described in the Introduction to this book. Having their own teachers, nurses, and technicians was seen as desirable because, in the *comunarios'* opinion, it would reduce their dependence on outside sources: if one of the *comunarios* knew how to fix the tractor, one wouldn't have to take the risk of getting ripped off by a mechanic in town; a local doctor or nurse would eliminate the need for *comunarios* to have to walk into town in the middle of the night to seek the help of a *karai* doctor in the case of emergencies, as had happened in the past; and having their own vet would broaden the possibilities for community livestock projects, which at the time mostly relied on the vets who were sent by the various organisations that were conducting projects in the *comunidad*.[11]

While independence was thus a part of the *comunarios'* vision of their improved future *comunidad* as far as 'human resources' were concerned, what was particularly interesting to me was the talk of 'autonomy' that had become fashionable beyond the circles of the Santa Cruz elites at the time of my fieldwork. When I first heard talk about 'indigenous autonomy' (which was later ratified in Articles 289–296 of the new Constitution of 2009), I had assumed that the concept somehow involved a notion of economic independence. However, what it turned out Guaraní people meant when they said they wanted to be 'autonomous' was more along the lines of, 'to be able to dispose of the money we get from the government and other sources without being accountable to anyone.' Financial independence, then, was not part of their vision; or rather, only insofar as the *use* of specific funds was concerned, but not necessarily with regard to their *procurement*.

This attitude again reflects the ambivalent relationship the *comunarios* had with money: on the one hand, they did not want to worry about where the money for the improvement of their *comunidad* came from, whereas on the other hand they were adamant that they wanted control over it. This statement may read like the anti-indigenist discourses the opponents of Evo Morales's government were fond of issuing at the time of my fieldwork, of whom there were many in Camiri, and who liked to portray indigenous people as lazy freeloaders if it suited their own agendas (see chapter 6). However, I believe that what is behind this kind of attitude is something else entirely, namely, a different understanding of the market economy that is perhaps best explained through the following example: talking about the municipality's planned improvement of the houses with my neighbour Don Pedro, he told me that they were to be built of bricks, and when I asked whether the *comunarios* would be making the bricks themselves, he said that they were to be provided by the municipality. He said the *comunarios* would put in the work, but materials would be paid for by the municipal government, and added, 'Of course, if I work, I have to be paid for it [in this case, in materials], even if it's to construct my own house.'

Although not as markedly as perhaps in more isolated communities—as, for example, the Paraguayan Guaraní community described by Reed (1995), in which money transactions were restricted to trade with outsiders altogether—exchanges involving money in Cañón were associated with the outside to the degree that (with the notable exception of bread) only goods purchased from the town were sold on to other *comunarios*; local produce, on the other hand, tended to be given away.

While Pedro's logic with regard to work did not apply to the kind of work people did of their own accord every day (such as work in the *chacos* for subsistence purposes), the kind of work that was prompted by the outside fell into the category of 'payable work.' This perspective was encouraged (and had perhaps been shaped) by the local government and various NGOs that implemented projects in the *comunidades*, whose representatives would talk about the *comunarios'* work in terms of their 'return service' (*contraparte*) for the livestock, seeds, building materials, or whatever else the project needed which they were providing. Accepting projects from these agencies was thus not like the acceptance of a gift, but rather like the agreement of a deal, and those taking part in such deals often put a lot of effort into making them work.

Further, the fact that Guaraní people in Bolivia were campaigning for more control over the resources invested in their communities to decide for themselves what improvements they wanted to carry out suggests that the passivity with which they were in the habit of accepting all kinds of (often completely unrelated) projects from different outside agents was a result of the system rather than of the people's lack of interest in these matters.[12] In Cañón, a good example of this issue was that of the planned improvement of the houses. As I mentioned earlier, some people were concerned about the changes this improvement might bring about (an urban-style layout with a main plaza and houses that were too close together for people's comfort, as well as a decrease in people's internal mobility). These fears, however, did not prevent people from being excited about the prospect of having houses made of higher-quality materials, as well as the promised gas and electricity. While it might not have been a way of completely resolving the tensions between these two perspectives (which, it should be added, were often held simultaneously rather than being mutually exclusive), giving the *comunarios* authority over the way in which the redevelopment of their houses was to be carried out would at least have rid them of their concerns about the layout. As I discuss in chapter 7, however, there were issues of politics attached to the relationship between municipality and Capitanía that put obstacles in the way of advancing decentralisation in this way.

What all of these latter cases demonstrate is that what was needed and desirable from the *comunarios'* point of view was more of a fusion of outside and inside forces than development agencies were at the time willing or able to provide: rather than only having professionals provided to help out with projects, the *comunarios* also wanted their own people to be educated in the necessary skills; and while projects were on the whole welcome, their implementation was something the *comunarios* wanted to be able to decide for themselves (or at least have a say in). What I want to stress here is that I am not suggesting that all outside interventions were unwelcome in the *comunidad*; rather, the point is that what the *comunarios* envisioned for their future was a continuation of the interactions with outside agencies that was, if not diminished, then at least balanced differently.

THE STRUGGLE FOR EQUALITY

While the kind of jealousy that often results in wife-beating is perhaps indicative of a traditional macho culture in which drinking strong liquors has become a sort of social obligation among men, the envy that people felt about the possessions and statuses of others can be interpreted as the reaction of the Guaraní's oft-mentioned egalitarianism to material and social inequalities creeping in from the outside. Reed describes a case of a Paraguayan Guaraní family that was forced to leave their community as a result of becoming too much like *patrones* and 'not sufficiently "Guaraní"' (1995: 142) in the eyes of their fellow *comunarios* after opening a shop in their house. The problem in this case, Reed stresses, was not the fact that the family was engaging in the market economy as such, but that they had by the end largely replaced the reciprocal exchanges that are usual among kin with commercial exchanges revolving around monetary transactions.

The uneasy relationship the *comunarios* of Cañón had with money can perhaps be explained by the fact that, while the personal jealousies between people could be counterbalanced, if not resolved, by the uniting forces of reciprocity, kinship ties, and the fiesta (or even, as in the case of the bewitched girl, with magic), there was no social mechanism in place for ensuring that any possible encroachment of *patrón-peón*-like relations that might develop between *comunarios* with greater and those with less financial power would be checked successfully. While the egalitarianism that is practiced by Guaraní people like the *comunarios* described in this book may not be a complete one,[13] there was nevertheless a notion that it was important. We may, for example, recall Doña Estefanía's discontent with the Evangelical conversions in the neighbouring community that had resulted in people 'not being the same anymore,' and an attempt to fight the *karai*-style inequalities described above with *karai*-style means was in fact made during my stay by formally incorporating a prohibition of *patrón-peón* relations between *comunarios* in the statute of the *comunidad*.

A similar point can be made about education: whereas education had for a long time been firmly in the hands of *karai* (first Spanish colonists and, later, their *criollo* descendants), at the time when I began my fieldwork, the Pluriethnic Superior Teachers' Institute of the *Oriente* and Chaco (INSPOC) in Camiri had been training bilingual teachers for over ten years (Gustafson 2009), several of whom I got to meet when they were doing their teacher training in Cañón. Guaraní was used alongside Spanish as language of instruction in the school in Cañón, with the first couple of years being taught purely in Guaraní. From the beginning of secondary school onward, however, students had no choice but to transfer to one of the schools in Camiri if they wanted to carry on with their studies, where teaching was provided exclusively in Spanish, and the same applied to those who were planning to continue their education at the university level. The future professionals of the *comunidades* could thus still be expected to be the product of the *karai* educational system. There was, however, at least the promise of an imminent change: shortly before I was leaving Bolivia, word began to spread about a planned Guaraní university in Kuruyuki, the location of the legendary battle of 1892. The university, which was baptised 'Apiaguaiki Tumpa' in honour of the battle's messianic leader, was inaugurated on 11 April 2009, together with the Quechua university 'Casimiro Huanca' and the Aymara university 'Tupac Katari,' and the teaching of courses commenced in August 2009. The choice of courses offered by the 'Apiaguaiki Tumpa' was telling: fossil fuels, forest engineering, pisciculture, and veterinary medicine and zootechnics. Putting the education of the longed-for professionals itself into Guaraní hands thus promised a 'de-colonisation of intellectuality,' to borrow a phrase from Joanna Overing (2008), on top of the de-*karai*sation of community economies promised by the eventual arrival of these professionals and financial autonomy.

Ultimately, the oppositions between *comunidad* and *propiedad* on the one hand, and *comunidad* and town on the other hand, were related in that a town was seen as a place where people engaged in *patrón-peón*-like relations (that is, unequal relations between those who can pay and those who are paid).

Work that was initiated from the outside (such as projects) had to be paid for because it was part of the town system and this was how the town system worked, whereas *motïro* work that *comunarios* could request of each other was meant to be recompensed exclusively through the substances of reciprocity, food and *chicha*, which were exchanged between equals. We can now see what made the ideas of Guaraní professionals and financial autonomy so appealing: that is, the reassurance that the economic development of the *comunidad* was firmly in the hands of the *comunarios* themselves, and thereby not threatening to turn *comunarios* into *patrones* and *comunidades* into towns. In short, we can see here how, while internal mobility in its various guises was desirable as a necessary element of functioning community life, outside mobility (*comunarios* leaving the *comunidad* for work in the town, and *karai* goods, money, and possibly habits entering the *comunidad*) was as necessary to the maintenance of this life as it was dangerous to it, and the way people negotiated this danger, and—crucially—anticipated the ways in which they would negotiate it in future, played an integral part in forming their lived experiences (cf. Hewlett 2017).[14] As expressed in the words of the *comunaria* quoted in chapter 2 ('We have to keep going forward'), and Don Elías's talk of the community's 'vision of achievements,' there was a strong optimism among the *comunarios* that their *comunidad* was moving forward in time in such a way that it was improving more and more, advancing, as it were, from the initial unfree state that was now confined to their past to something that, it seemed, had to be even better than the present, despite the struggles that would necessarily wait for the *comunarios* along the way.

Part III discusses some cases of outsiders to the *comunidad* impacting on the lives of its people through their different perspectives on what *comunidades* are, or should be, about. By showing the great variety of angles *karai* people could take on this subject, I suggest that rather than seeing *comunidades* as particular entities that can be positioned in certain ways, we can understand them as possessing a range of potentialities which different actors seek to activate for their own ends.

NOTES

1. Cf. Gow (1995: 230) on the centrality of schools for the status of *comunidades nativas* in the Bajo Urubamba.

2. Padre Cristián was an Italian Jesuit priest based in Camiri who was in charge of delivering church services to the surrounding *comunidades*, and who came to Cañón every first Saturday of the month. He had a rather curious relationship with the *comunarios* that involved a lot of shouting and attempts at 'blackmailing' them into becoming better Christians by threatening to withhold the money sent to some of

the children by foreign 'godparents,' while the *comunarios*' conduct toward him was marked by a lot of polite smiling.

3. Wattle-and-daub (locally called *tabique*), although a common material for building houses throughout the Chaco region, has the great disadvantage of attracting vinchucas (*triatoma infestans*) to nest in the walls, which can transmit Chagas disease. At the time of my fieldwork, there was a government-sponsored eradication and prevention campaign going on that involved the counting of vinchucas and spraying with insecticide of constructions deemed at risk in the *comunidades*.

4. As far as I am aware, *chapapa* is originally a Quechua word, which was, however, the word used by the *comunarios*.

5. Guaraní: *mbiape*; maize cakes made of soft ground maize, some sort of fat, salt, and sometimes additional sugar or cheese.

6. I discuss this issue more closely in chapter 5.

7. Cf. Gow (1991: 78): 'The house site and the remote primary forest are the opposite poles of a spectrum which leads from most intense to least intense human landscape modification.'

8. A word that, given the centrality of the *oka* rather than the house as central living space, seems a bit inadequate.

9. Daniela Castellanos makes a case for envy among potters in Aguabuena, Colombia constituting a 'form of relating' that produces 'entanglements linking envy, closeness, and reciprocity' (2015: 21), which in a way help to draw people closer together. I can see certain aspects of this in Cañón also; however, the way the *comunarios* themselves spoke about envy and jealousy among them was always negative: if a person was said to be very jealous, this was often phrased in terms of their 'being bad' (see above).

10. The phenomenon of drunken wife-beating constitutes an instance in which the cathartic function of the Guaraní fiesta is undermined. However, seeing that—unlike in other Latin American settings (cf. Harvey 1994)—it is not a practice that is generally seen as acceptable, I would stand by my interpretation of the fiesta as maintainer and reproducer of sociality within the community. This interpretation is further supported by the aforementioned man's self-removal from the fiestas because of the anti-social effect participating in them had on him.

11. For a more in-depth discussion of people's desire for Guaraní professionals and the economy of projects in Cañón, see chapter 5.

12. The desire for more self-determination in the field of development is an ongoing one that predates Evo's coming-into-power. Consider the following extract from a 2003 'Declaration' by Justa Cabrera of the Capitanía Santa Cruz: 'We see how in the name of globalisation we are offered what we do not want and at the same time the little land we have is taken away from us. . . . Globalisation should achieve that all human beings are able to live in dignity instead of serving the ambitions of a few people or transnational enterprises. . . . We know that globalisation is something that has occurred and that we cannot control, but we ask for the respect of our cultures and of our right to decide what the development is that we ourselves wish for.'

13. I am particularly thinking of gender relations, which are widely known to be highly unequal among Guaraní people. The Camiri Literacy Lady's remark that

Guaraní men were '*muy machistas*' (quoted in the Introduction) was one I often found echoed by people working for NGOs, but also Guaraní people (chiefly women) themselves. These, however, seemed inequalities which the *comunarios* were willing (or, at least, more willing) to accept because they were not seen to threaten the way that *comunarios* were meant to live together but were to a certain degree even part of it (think of differentiated gender roles in work and fiestas). Financial inequalities, on the other hand, at least had the potential to severely disrupt the relations between *comunarios* and turn them into something other and less desirable.

14. I am aware that this last point seems to call for an analysis that draws a parallel between the *comunarios*' negotiation of these dangers from the outside and the shamanic taming of threatening or negative outside forces for the benefit of the community that has been reported for many Amazonian societies (e.g., Fausto and Rodgers 1999; Gow 2000; Walker 2009). Andrew Gray (1997) in fact draws such a parallel in his study on Arakmbut people in south-eastern Peru. However, since such an analysis would mean imposing the logic of the highly specialised domain of shamanism onto the life world of an entire community in which such an institution was not present at the time, the risk of misrepresentation seems to me to outweigh any possible insights that might be gleaned from such a move in this case (cf. High 2012).

Part III

MULTIPLE PERSPECTIVES

Negotiating Different Meanings of 'Comunidad'

Chapter Five

(N)GOs and the Economy of *Proyectos*

As I have shown in the previous chapter, a preoccupation with the interactions with outside agencies was a theme that was present as a constant undercurrent in *comunarios'* daily lives, and it was the *quality* of these relations that tended to generate criticism, rather than the fact of the agencies' presence and interventions in the *comunidades* itself. This chapter seeks to shed some light on the agendas of development organisations operating in Cañón during the time of my fieldwork and their relationships with the *comunarios*. As will become clear in the course of the discussion, these relationships were built largely on the basis of contradictory assumptions about the nature of *comunidades*, the role of community leaders, and the purpose of projects, all of which sometimes impeded projects' successful implementation in the communities. Ultimately, however, such contradictions were often in a sense resolved within the context of workshops—not by addressing them openly, but by both interest groups' shared participation in a highly ritualised setting with its own quasi-magical vocabulary that allowed them to talk past each other in an amiable and 'sustainable' way.

In a way, the interactions between NGO staff and Guaraní leaders were similar to the encounters of Portuguese and African traders of the colonial period described by David Graeber (2005): in Graeber's examples, the two different interest groups come together to engage in trading relations and make contracts sealed by the creation of magical 'fetishes,' but with each group acting on radically different assumptions about the nature of 'value': while the principal interest of the Europeans is the acquisition of gold and other 'valuable' objects, the Africans want to acquire objects to use them in the creation of 'valuable' social relations (which, in turn, are of no interest to the Europeans) (Graeber 2005: 431–32). Graeber's article elaborates a complex argument about the nature of power and the workings of social creativity,

but the point I am taking from it for my present purpose is this: it is possible
for people to engage in what appears to be the same activity, while really
attaching radically different significance to it *and still bring about mutually
beneficial (and, in this case, unexpected and unintentional) effects*. This last
point takes us one step further from Sahlins's work on the ambiguous and
elusive quality of 'events' with which we started this journey into the world
of Guaraní communities, in that it renders people's willingness to keep engaging in these shared activities despite the many frustrations they inevitably
involve more understandable.

I begin my discussion with an outline of the activities of development
organisations in my fieldwork area and from there move into an analysis of
a typical workshop scenario that highlights some of the problems complicating these activities. In the end, I propose that an unintended positive effect
is generated for both NGO workers and Guaraní *comunarios* by the illusion
of 'speaking the same language,' in this case with particular reference to the
concept of 'capacity building' (Spanish: *capacitación*).

AGENTS OF DEVELOPMENT: (N)GOS IN CAMIRI

The ever-increasing presence of governmental and nongovernmental organisations (GOs and NGOs) in Cañón since its establishment in the 1990s had,
by the time I started my fieldwork in 2006, led to the development of a system
of project-implementation whose dynamics at first puzzled me a great deal.
What struck me as strange about this system was the way in which *comunarios* seemed happy to accept any project at all that was offered to them,
without seemingly discriminating between the merit and even usefulness of
the offered projects, let alone whether they made any particular sense when
considered in their relation to others that were being implemented simultaneously. At the same time, this last point did not seem a concern of the agencies
themselves either, which—with the notable exception of some of the older
organisations—largely tended to limit themselves to 'doing their own thing,'
and among whom there was, as a rule, very limited communication. On the
contrary, NGOs working within the same region often stood in a relationship
of competition with each other, and they sometimes sought to implement
their programmes independently even of the state (cf. Kohl 2003: 157–58).

The development landscape in and around Camiri at the time of my fieldwork was diverse, with various national and international GOs and NGOs being
active in the area. While all of these agencies influenced the lives of the Cañón
comunarios in some way, there were four in particular whose activities had a
large impact on people's lives due to their long-standing involvement with Ca-

ñón and the Capitanía Kaami: CIPCA, Caritas, the GTZ (the German Society for Technical Collaboration; see chapter 3), and the PDA. The PDAs were the Areal Development Programmes of World Vision Bolivia (Visión Mundial).[1] There were at the time thirty-two PDAs in Bolivia, which addressed specific regional needs independently of each other (for example, the PDA Tekove working with the Capitanía Gran Kaipependi specialised in water-related projects, as scarcity of water was an issue in that area). What all PDAs had in common was the focus on Christian values, manifested in such practices as beginning capacity building workshops with a ten-minute prayer session. The PDA Arakavi worked with the *capitanías* of Kaami, Alto Parapetí, and Ivo, where it implemented projects of sheep breeding, honey production, maize cultivation, and promoting leadership capacities in children. In Cañón, fifteen sheep had been lent to the six families that were involved in the PDA's sheep breeding project, on the condition that after the sheep had reproduced enough for the project to keep going they were to return the same number of sheep to the PDA, which would then lend them to other families. The PDA Arakavi was financed by World Vision Germany, which looked for godfathers and -mothers willing to sponsor children in the *comunidades*. This money did not go to the children

Little boy driving his sheep home from the fields in the evening.
Photo by the author.

directly; rather, it was invested in projects. These projects were decided upon
by a 'community assembly,' which was constituted by representatives of each
of the *comunidades* in which the PDA was active.

Like the PDA projects, Caritas projects, too, were implemented at the demand of those whom they were to benefit, often in collaboration with municipal projects ('The *comunidades* make demands to the municipalities who usually tell them that they can only give them part of the money that's needed,
so they come to Caritas to apply for the rest,' as one Caritas employee put
it). Unlike with the PDA, however, religious issues did not usually come into
the implementation of projects. Having been present since the days before the
founding of the APG in 1987, Caritas had become part of a kind of 'develop-
ment-organisational PISET' (with CIPCA taking over the field of production,
the Health Convention that of health,[2] Teko Guaraní that of education, the
APG that of land/territory, and Caritas that of infrastructure). The Caritas office in Camiri was responsible for the entire Chaco region, employing many
Guaraní technicians in their projects. There were three main themes to its
activities: 1) the improvement of housing (including the construction of new
buildings and vinchuca eradication programmes[3]); 2) water (for consumption
and irrigation); and 3) promotion of human rights (such as capacity-building
courses, information transmission via workshops and meetings, promotion of
human-rights-friendly values, and advice pertaining to legal problems). The
woman I spoke to lamented the fact that, although as an old-established and
well-known NGO Caritas did not have to compete with others in the *comunidades*, sometimes an NGO with a lot of money at its disposal would come in
and try to 'outbid' them. These new NGOs, she said, always ran to whatever
topic was fashionable at any particular time (indigenous peoples, women,
'interculturality' . . .), and when the current changed, they all ran on to the
next one, whereas the old NGOs stayed where they were.

Another of the 'old NGOs' of the region, the Centre for the Investigation
and Promotion of the Peasantry, or CIPCA, for Cordillera with head office
in Camiri supported indigenous *capitanías* and *comunidades* in the areas of
farming and livestock projects (such as apiculture, deforestation of new *chacos*, fences for cattle corrals, and forest management), political empowerment
(by, for example, promoting their participation in local, regional, and state
politics), and access to land, which was seen as the precondition for any kind
of development being possible in the *comunidades* in the first place. One of
CIPCA Cordillera's main activities was the organisation of 'formation and
capacity building workshops' in the areas of production and politics, activities that were implemented with funding from the Spanish government and
other international sponsors. Contrary to some other organisations, CIPCA
was working together closely with the APG, in whose founding it had had a

significant involvement, and which it supported in the areas of production, land/territory, and empowerment. The latter point was not exclusively aimed at political representation but included support in legal matters (as had been the case with Cañón de Segura). A more recent case in which CIPCA was taking legal action on behalf of a Guaraní community was a case of land theft the mayor of Camiri had allegedly committed in the *comunidad* of Puente Viejo on the outskirts of Camiri. The person to whom I spoke commented that the involvement in such land conflicts could be dangerous, and that he himself had received various death threats during the twelve years he had been engaged with the issue.

Despite their frequent reluctance to cooperate with other development organisations, it was clear that none of the agencies present operated in a development vacuum but rather in an environment that was shaped by many distinct forces. During my fieldwork, I got the chance to participate in various workshops organised by different organisations; for the sake of brevity, I am limiting myself here to an example provided by a workshop that was organised by CIPCA, which demonstrates the kinds of activities in which the various (N)GOs were engaged in Cañón at the time of my fieldwork and some of the problems bound up with them.

As one of the outside helpers that came to the aid of the *comunarios* in their struggle with the *patrones* (see chapter 2), CIPCA had a particularly well-established relationship with the people of Cañón. It is also undoubtedly one of the organisations with the most serious interest in the indigenous cultures it seeks to support, as its activities are not limited to simple project implementation but include the publication of materials dealing with said projects as well as other aspects of indigenous and peasant life, among them three of the most well-known studies on Bolivian Guaraní people (Bartomeu Melià's *Ñande Reko* [1988], Francisco Pifarré's *Historia de un pueblo* [1989], and Xavier Albó's *La comunidad hoy* [1990]). In a way, this book itself can be said to be a product of CIPCA's activities in the *comunidades* of Kaami, as it was one of their investigator-activists whose good connections with the leaders of the *capitanía* helped me gain access to my fieldwork community in the first place. In the communities, the role in which I predominantly encountered CIPCA staff was as the leaders of workshops.[4] Often, these workshops concerned organisational issues of *capitanías* and *comunidades* (such as the one in Charagua I mention in the Introduction), and often the presenters acted as 'motivators,' seeking to inspire enthusiasm for a particular issue and its proposed solution in the participants and thereby propel them into action.

Given the drawn-out nature of Guaraní *asambleas* (which can go on for whole days and well into the night, after characteristically having started a couple of hours late) and their conventions of debate (which tend to involve participants remaining in silence for a long time after listening to speakers before they start engaging in any discussion), it was not really surprising to me that workshop leaders could get impatient with their audiences on such occasions. This sometimes resulted in their adopting an authoritative or 'schoolmasterly' tone toward the participants, as was frequently the case with a young agro-engineer, nicknamed 'El Chato' ('Shorty'), who was in charge of many of the capacity building workshops CIPCA was organising both within individual *comunidades* and jointly for select representatives from various places. In one such instance, at a 'conflict resolution' workshop in Cañón, Chato told the *comunarios* that they needed to change their 'way of thinking' in order to get rid of internal problems (such as gossip, misunderstandings, or speculations about what people thought other people thought), and also commented that they were 'losing their culture' (in this case, referring particularly to the abandonment of communal work) and their identity, and that that would have to change. While people seemed used to being addressed in this way, and Chato's lectures did not impede the good relationship he had formed with them, the *comunarios* tended to resort to a kind of passive resistance to unwelcome advice, in that they would listen to it all politely and patiently and then simply ignore whatever they disagreed with or regarded as irrelevant. The same strategy was applied to less well-liked outsiders, such as the Italian priest who came to celebrate mass in Cañón once a month, and whose disrespectful behavior had made him unpopular with the *comunarios*. This convention undoubtedly contributed to the frustration experienced by the (N)GO workers, and also prevented them from finding out what the *comunarios* really thought about their proposals.

THE WORKSHOP

The following is a summary of an inter-communitarian CIPCA workshop on 'social control and natural resources' that took place in the Guaraní community of Guirarapo, Capitanía Kaami, in June of 2007, and which demonstrates some of the dynamics at play in these events. The participants were largely communal leaders who had come in representation of their *comunidades* of residence, with some regional leaders also present.

After all the participants had been given some bread and some very sugary tea, the workshop started. In his initialising speech, Chato talked about the municipality being like a parent to the communities (which were its children), who worried about their children's well-being, with the organisations acting like the communities' aunts and uncles.

Chato said that the *comunarios* all knew their rights by now, but that knowing one's rights without putting them into practice was like having an axe which one never used, and that rights as well as axes were meant for working with. CIPCA, he went on, had been going to the *comunidades* for a long time already, but they were still struggling with the same problems: the *comunarios* were valiant when it came to fighting among themselves, but when there was a problem with a third (*karai*) party, they seemed to be afraid and just kept quiet.

The vice-sub-mayor of Kaami responded that things were in fact advancing (not only those with money had land now, Bolivia had an indigenous president, the Guaraní people had their own engineers and technicians),[5] and that it wasn't that they were afraid of others but that the Guaraní always sought the dialogue, which was what had always characterised them.

Chato said that the life of a leader (*dirigente*) didn't have a manual where what was needed was listed point by point, but that a leader needed the capacity to take decisions independently, to evaluate a situation and decide what was needed. He also—somewhat ironically, given his own previous admonition to the *comunarios* of Cañón that they had to stop 'losing their culture'—said that no one had the right to tell the Guaraní how to be, but that they had to decide that for themselves. The word '*comunidad*,' he said, meant a group of people who had something in common and who lived together, but *comunarios* frequently went as far as the APG about issues they should really resolve internally.

While Chato thus stressed *comunarios*' needs for more independence, it was lack of support from outside that was seen as a problem by a number of the workshop participants: in the groupwork session before lunch that followed Chato's opening speech, the first thing that one member of the Kaami leadership in the group I had joined suggested as a problem with regard to natural resources was 'lack of capacity building.' Several of the other groups' posters produced in this session also invoked lack of external support as the core problem.

At the end of the morning session, Chato again put the participants into groups, with delegations from the communities of Imbochi and Alto Camiri forming groups of their own, so that problems could be compared. I joined the Imbochi group, which was formed by the second *capitana* of both Kaami and Imbochi, the Kaami gender official, and the first *capitán* of Imbochi.

The question to be discussed was what the communities were doing to regulate and manage their natural resources. I asked what resources they had in Imbochi, and they said the River Parapetí, trees, and boulders. One of the

Imbochi *comunarios'* main problems was that the site of the community was being used as a rubbish dump for Camiri, putting people at risk and contaminating the river on which the community's water supply relied. The dump had been there for some ten years already, and only now had the municipal government decided that it would clean up its mess and promised to remove the rubbish. It transpired, however, that not all *comunarios* agreed with getting rid of the dump, as some liked to take their pigs there to feed.

With the boulders, the problem was that people took out rocks without permission to use for building houses and also to sell. The same happened with the trees: they were sometimes clandestinely felled to be sold as timber or even firewood. People were meant to apply for permission for the number of trees and the purpose for which they wanted to cut them down to the community authorities, who then signed a permit with which they were meant to go to the 'Forestal' for further approval.[6] But the *comunarios* didn't always follow these procedures; on the contrary, sometimes they got annoyed if they were told that they should.

After a lunch break with soup and *chicha*, we stood around some more chatting, then went back inside for more poster presentations. One Kaami representative talked about how one needed 1) order, 2) strategy, and 3) politics: order, to look at what resources there were; strategy, to hold regional meetings of *comunarios*, implement social control, and look at what activities needed to be organised; and politics, to strengthen the development of natural resources, and to look for allies who would provide capacity building.

Chato held a speech on how the communities needed to decide what it was they wanted and what they wanted to focus on instead of accepting everything that they were being offered by the organisations, because otherwise they would 'fill' (*llenar*) themselves with projects and in the end wouldn't be able to go through with any of them. He said they shouldn't compare themselves with the *karai* to decide what to wish and ask for, but look at what was really needed instead.

The meeting finished with the announcement that a community meeting was to be held subsequently.

Going through this instance step by step, we can see various assumptions about the meaning and functioning of *comunidades* unfold in this event that go a long way in explaining the discrepancies between *comunarios'* simultaneous desire for both more independence and more support from the organisations on the one hand, and the organisations' somewhat contradictory approach in trying to deliver both on the other hand. We can see how the basis of the relationship between organisations and communities is set up as a paternal one in Chato's initialising speech, in which he likens the *comuni-*

dades to children and the municipality and organisations that work with them to parental figures. This move at once assures his audience of CIPCA's good intentions (they, like the municipalities, are there to support the Guaraní people) and justifies the patronising way in which he reproaches them for their failure to learn to stand up for themselves. The vice-sub-mayor's response offers an alternative view of the situation, namely, that what to the CIPCA activists appears as the Guaraní's failure to advance is rather their own failure to recognise the advances there are, and that what they perceive as cowardice is in fact diplomacy ('always seeking the dialogue' was an expression that was commonly presented by people, especially Guaraní leaders when speaking in public, as a particularly characteristic trait of 'Guaraníness').

In the next part of Chato's speech, the need he sees for the Guaraní 'children' to grow up is personified in the figure of the leader. Let us take a step back at this point and for a moment recall the traditional position of Guaraní leaders as we find it described in various historical and anthropological sources from colonial days onward—that is, a man distinguished by his prowess in warfare and eloquence as a speaker, whose main role is that of binding a community together through exchanges of women, work, and *chicha*, and whose authority to exert real power over others is largely limited to periods of war (Saignes 1982: 79; see also chapter 3). Far from being an exclusively Guaraní phenomenon, this figure of the 'powerless chief' was one that was frequently encountered by the first Europeans to arrive to the New World, and which greatly puzzled and exasperated them because it made it impossible for them to clearly identify individuals who were entitled to speak for 'their' people and negotiate on their behalf; in short, someone in a position to represent them.[7]

As mentioned in chapter 3, present-day Guaraní leaders have become precisely that, representatives of their communities. They fulfil this role when it comes to attending *asambleas*, workshops, or other meetings outside the community, or when it comes to receiving anthropologists eager to work in their *comunidades*. However, 'representing' being an activity geared almost exclusively toward the outside,[8] there was still no sense in which leaders had any 'real' power, and the positions which to represent they went to meetings with outsiders were meant to be ones that had been decided in advance by their communities as a whole. The *asamblea*, not the *capitán*, remained the highest authority within a *comunidad* (cf. Caballero et al. 2010: 3), and, as had happened in the example recounted in the previous chapter, *capitanes* who failed to live up to the other *comunarios*' expectations could be stripped of their nominal authority by the real authority of the *asamblea*.

The modern-day Guaraní *capitán* constitutes an attempt to 'have it both ways,' that is, to satisfy the need of *karai* and their institutions for clearly identifiable representatives, while at the same time honouring the authority of the *asamblea*. Chato's characterisation of a leader as someone with the 'capacity to evaluate a situation and take decisions independently' was reminiscent of the rhetoric of a life or business coach trying to train his clients to be dynamic, entrepreneurial individuals. It was not, however, an idea that coincided with the reality of Guaraní leaders' lives, or, in fact, with Guaraní people's ideas of good leadership. Rather, it reflected CIPCA's own concerns and objectives as an institution that had come to see 'capacity building' as one of its main activities. As Christopher Hewlett has noted about capacity building projects in Peruvian Amazonia, 'the entities at which projects aim their efforts (the Christian individual, the independent community) do not always line up with what might already be present, rather than absent in Amerindian settings' (2017: 122).

Capacity building, or capacity development, is a concept that has become fashionable among GOs and NGOs working in development since the 1990s. Its meanings are manifold and defy exact definition. However, '[w]ithin the many definitions, there seems to be an emerging consensus that CD involves the long term, contributes to sustainable social and economic development, and is demand driven [and also increasingly focused on] enhancement and strengthening of existing capacities' (Lusthaus, Adrien, and Perstinger 1999: 5). This sounds slightly dry, whereas CIPCA's ideas, which are founded on liberation theology and the writings of Paulo Freire on the liberating power of education for the poor (Gianotten 2006: 50), have a much more ideological and political ring to them; however, the general idea—'kickstarting' a process of Bolivia's impoverished rural populations taking charge of their own development—is largely the same (cf. Hewlett 2017).

I should point out at this point that the people working for CIPCA and other NGOs involved with the *comunidades* whom I encountered during my fieldwork were by and large well-informed and well-meaning individuals who were more or less familiar with the local people's ways of life. Nonetheless—and perhaps all the more strikingly—there was a discrepancy between their organisations' aims and the internal workings of the *comunidades* in that there was not really any room for individuals' going forth and dynamically and singlehandedly making decisions which concerned the entire community—which was, perhaps, why the CIPCA staff to whom I had spoken about this matter had professed themselves to be frustrated with their efforts' previous results. The impression I got was that, above all, communal *capitanes* were being cultivated to be better *representatives* to the organisations rather than better leaders to 'their' people; in other words, that what was being built and developed was leaders' capacity to be better-functioning interlocutors for the organisations. The need for organisations to engage with individuals who are able to act in ways that are conducive to their own agendas is a common issue in the development business, and one with which CIPCA itself has struggled in the past: beginning with the communally elected so-called 'civic promoters' (*promotores cívicos*) in its initial phase (Gianotten 2006: 60), CIPCA's preferred interlocutors soon became the already existing communal authorities, who seemed to be invested with more legitimacy locally (ibid.: 68).

DEVELOPMENT OF AGENCY? CONFLICTING IDEAS ABOUT 'CAPACITY BUILDING'

The desire to create the people with whom the organisations worked as a kind of 'comprehensible Other' was pervasive in Chato's speech: on the one hand, Guaraní people must learn to be independent ('no one can tell you what to do'), but on the other hand they must do so in ways that fit in with the organisations' ideas ('leaders must act in such-and-such a way,' 'these are conflicts for you to resolve internally,' 'you must preserve your culture').[9] We can see at work here what James Ferguson has famously termed the 'anti-politics machine' of development—that is, the way in which development agencies cast their 'clients' realities in terms of technical problems to be solved and thereby often sweep questions of history and politics under the rug because they are not equipped to deal with them (Ferguson 1994; see also Uvin 1998; Li 2007).[10] In the case of Cañón, 'history' was something that was required as evidence by the courts during the *comunarios*' land struggle but became largely obsolete once the land was obtained and the legal struggle finished (see chapter 2). As we have seen, the *comunarios* had, by the time I arrived in Cañón, taken on board ideas about 'development' as part of their own vision for the further improvement of their *comunidad*, and I have argued that this vision had supplanted 'history,' as a thing of the past, in people's ways of thinking about their *comunidad* in terms of the present and the future. The organisations catering to these desires came with requirements of a new set of evidences: instead of history, the *comunarios* now had to demonstrate their interest in such things as 'capacity,' 'gender relations,' or 'natural resource management.'

If we take a look at the result of the poster session in the workshop described above, and especially the Kaami representative's speech following it, we can see that the Guaraní representatives who were attending the workshop had taken to engaging these categories, as demonstrated (among other things) by their demand for more capacity building. This demand was indirectly echoed in the Imbochi delegation's discussion of the natural resource management in

the *comunidades*, where the main focus was on the various problems that occurred as a result of new resource management efforts rather than the efforts
themselves. Both the case of the rubbish dump and that of the boulders and
trees show the communal dynamic in which there is no space for authoritarian
leaders: in both instances, no consensus had been reached among the *comunarios* because some wanted to take advantage of these 'resources' in their
own way and resented being told to do otherwise. While *capitanes* and PISET
representatives were well versed in NGO speak and familiar with the conventions of workshops, these episodes point toward another problem the system
of individual representation glosses over; that is, the fact that *comunidades*
are units that—despite, or perhaps because of, their emphasis on communal
decision-making—harbour the potential for internal discord.

The demand for more capacity building as a response to these internal
difficulties is indicative of the way that *comunarios* (including the members
of communal leadership) saw the organisations that worked with them on
the improvement of their *comunidades* as responsible for the projects they
sought to implement—recall my neighbour Don Pedro's differentiation between work on such projects and their own agricultural work as payable and
non-payable work respectively (see previous chapter). Kathleen Lowrey has
described a similar phenomenon for the Isoso:

> The centerpieces of the two projects—Isoseño cultural knowledge [in the case
> of a traditional medicine project], and the Isoseño ecosystem [in the case of a
> National Park project], are not produced in fixed units by wage laborers. Isoseño
> culture and Isoseño nature are instead collective products of the cooperative
> labor of many generations of Isoseño people. . . . I would suggest that—with
> respect to these outside projects—Isoseño have come to think of their nature and
> their culture, and their involvement in the production and reproduction of these
> entities, as 'subject to the value regime of wage-labor': in other words, as forms
> of endeavor commensurable with money compensation. They realize very well
> that every member of the community participates in this work and, because they
> have locally created Isoso's nature and Isoso's culture over many generations,
> that there are 'back wages' owed to them from the outset by the outside world
> interested in these goods. (2008: 71)

As Lowrey has noted in another article, in the Chaco region, more traditional
forms of work are increasingly being replaced by 'the "project" market' altogether because of the greater security the latter offers to indigenous people
(2007: 4). There is some irony in the fact that 'capacity building' from the
point of view of the organisations (and especially in the case of CIPCA) is
seen as a way of educating people into independence, while for the *comunarios* it was another service that came attached to their various projects;
however, as we have seen, it is only one among numerous differences in per-

spectives that existed among representatives of organisations and inhabitants and leaderships of *comunidades*.

What both positions agreed on was the way they saw the *comunidades* as recipients of projects. In line with the continuing trend that has been predominant within the development world over the past half century (Rondinelli 1983; Charlton and May 1995; Green 2003), projects were what GOs and NGOs were willing and able to offer the communities, and projects were what the communities had come to expect from the organisations (and, as in my case, sometimes even other outsiders about whose status and influence they were unsure) (cf. Capitanía Kaami 2007; Caballero Espinoza 2008). Again, the difference between their positions lay in the approach to these projects rather than the primary issue of their implementation. Here, Chato's final speech is revealing: to paraphrase his words, the message was that *comunidades* had to carefully pick and choose between the projects available to them in order to be able to come up with a common 'course of action' that would allow them to specialise in an ultimately profitable way. This idea was in line with current ideas about sustainable development; that is, a kind of development that invests in people temporarily in order to enable them to take over the maintenance of their own livelihoods after an initial 'starting-up' period (Mog 2004; Warburton 2009). One of the problems with this approach that is common in the development world is the fact that project design often tends to be formulaic and does not take sufficient account of local specificities (Eade 2007). In this case, Chato expected the *comunarios* to run their *comunidades* like businesses, an expectation that was, however, doomed to failure because of the anti-hierarchical nature of their social structure and the complexities surrounding their internal organisation.

Comunidades are not businesses.

If we are willing to accept this as a fact, what, then, can we say about the *comunarios'* way of dealing with the projects they were being offered? Frustratingly for Chato, and surprisingly to me, the *comunarios* of Cañón (as *comunarios* elsewhere in Kaami) had taken up a strategy of seemingly blindly accepting whatever project was being offered to them. As mentioned before, these projects rarely involved the entire community, but were usually open to whoever was willing to partake in them. There was thus room for individuals and single families to follow their own interests rather than a consensus having to be reached among all each time; however, all these activities would—where reasonably successful—be seen by the *comunarios* to be contributing to the improvement of Cañón as a whole. The reason behind what to Chato and me appeared as a chaotic way of organising the community economy was, I would argue, that the *comunarios* took an approach to the improvement of their community whose strength lay in its flexibility rather than its being planned in a calculating way. The *comunarios* accepted these projects, not out of indifference, but because they saw them as a way to take advantage of the possibilities that were offering themselves to them at a particular point in time, *and perhaps only then*, and which to refuse would therefore seem unwise.

As discussed in the previous chapter, the *comunarios* of Cañón were highly inventive in the ways they organised and reorganised their living spaces and utilised and adapted objects of everyday use. This kind of flexibility and sensitivity to the needs and opportunities of the present moment have received a great deal of attention among anthropologists particularly of Amazonian groups (Harris 2005; Killick 2009; Feather 2010). We also encounter it in the writings of Claude Lévi-Strauss, who found the same adaptability in many indigenous peoples' treatment of myths, and who himself adapted for this phenomenon the term '*bricolage*.'[11] 'The set of the "bricoleur's" means,' says Lévi-Strauss, 'cannot therefore be defined in terms of a project. . . . It is to be defined only by its potential use or, putting this another way and in the language of the "bricoleur" himself, because the elements are collected or retained on the principle that "they may always come in handy"' (1966: 17–18).

This is also the way in which the projects brought to them by (N)GOs were treated by the Guaraní people of Kaami: not, as it were, 'in terms of a project' (that is, as means to a specific end), but as a collection of elements of potential use. If we look at the *comunarios*' approach to 'development' in this way, it becomes a lot less puzzling that these projects should be taken on more or less indiscriminately—nor, indeed, that they were often dropped by those who had taken them on when they were either seen not to be working out or people's labour and/or time was being engaged in something (at least temporarily) more urgent.

Nor could the organisations' efforts to 'capacitate' the people be any more successful than they were as long as they remained in *karai* activists' hands. As expressed in the desire of the people of Cañón for Guaraní professionals, capacity building was not seen as something whose success would be marked by its eventual cessation but which, in the end, would be provided by Guaraní professionals for the people of their *comunidades* rather than by skilled outsiders. The idea that the kinds of skills and knowledge necessary to make any project into a sustainable one will be passed on from one person to the next and thus diffused throughout the *comunidades* is in theory a good one. However, it disregards certain aspects of how 'knowledge' is treated within Guaraní culture. For one, people can sometimes be jealous of the knowledge they possess, which can keep them from passing it on to anyone else. When, for example, I enquired about the existence or not of a shaman (*ipaye*) in Cañón, my friend Lupe told me: 'There is no shaman. There is now only one old *abuelita* who knows about curing and those things. There used to be another one, but she recently died, and she was so jealous of her knowledge that she didn't even tell her own daughter the things she knew.' This kind of intense jealousy is possibly a phenomenon exclusive to shamanic and healing knowledge, whose divulgence can be risky (Groke 2015). More generally, however, the Guaraní language distinguishes between the kind of learning that is passed on from one generation to the other (*arakuaa*) and school learning (*yemboe*), which for the longest time was delivered exclusively by *karai* teachers. Though Gustafson describes how, through the re-writing of textbooks in the context of bilingual education reform in the 1990s, Guaraní scholars sought to 'intentionally rei-magine Guarani as knowledge makers across a fused domain of arakuaa and yemboe' (2009: 89), the distinction still seemed to hold when I did my field-work some ten years later. There was a strong sense among the *comunarios* of Cañón of the importance of obtaining a formal education. When people spoke of their desire for their own 'professionals,' this quite literally referred to young people from among themselves who would go and obtain a formal education at a formally recognised institution. Ideally, not only the profes-sionals would be Guaraní, but also the institutions educating them (such as the indigenous university with Apiaguaiki Tumpa in Kuruyuki); failing this, the important thing was still that they held an officially recognised degree that not only qualified them as 'professionals' in terms of their skills but also in terms of their legitimacy to call themselves thus.

The idea of institutionalising knowledge that was often promoted by the or-ganisations relies on the notion of a kind of 'DIY knowledge' that people will eventually pass on to each other independently of outside initiatives, whereas the Guaraní vision of having professionals from among themselves appeals to the possibility for young people to go and acquire specialist knowledge from the outside. Ironically, it is the former approach that is incompatible with the system of '*bricolage*' in this case because it relies on the internal institutionalisation of a knowledge still largely viewed as external, whereas the Guaraní vision entails the external education of individuals who would then return to constitute another addition to the communal *bricoleur's* toolkit. This, however, is not something which to provide is within the organisations' capacity, whose projects are shaped by their limitations in funds, time, per-sonnel, and knowledge.

THE CASE OF CIPCA

CIPCA, as a home-grown organisation that was started with the express aim of empowering Bolivia's disadvantaged rural populations economically, culturally, and politically, constitutes a somewhat unique case in the Bolivian NGO landscape, and one might feel inclined to argue that using one of their workshops as an example here is a little unfair. Founded in La Paz in 1971 by the three Jesuits Luís Alegre, Francisco Javier Santiago, and Xavier Albó, it had, by the time I started my fieldwork in 2006, grown into a large organisation with six regional offices in El Alto, Cochabamba, Camiri, Santa Cruz, San Ignacio de Moxos, and Riberalta. As the history of CIPCA by Vera Gianotten (published the same year) makes clear, CIPCA has undergone various changes over time, both in its organisational structure and its mission, which often came about in response to the changing political situation in Bolivia and beyond. Founded during a time of great political and social upheaval, with a succession of military dictatorships coinciding with the emergence of an indigenist consciousness and increased political organisation in the highlands (see chapter 1), 'CIPCA started out as a small, informal group of people that slowly converted itself into an institution with precise aims and objectives, and with formal personnel politics in line with these objectives' (Gianotten 2006: 27).[12] Besides such external and structural factors, CIPCA's activities are influenced by the results of its own previous interventions, which initially largely relied on a strategy of trial and error (Gianotten 2006).

As a result of by now five decades of untiring effort, CIPCA's engagement with Bolivian *campesinos* over time has undoubtedly been a fruitful and often mutually beneficial one, and Vera Gianotten has a point when she criticises the (in her view often misinformed and unnecessarily destructive) desire to critique the work of NGOs that is frequently found in the anthropological literature (Gianotten 2006: 30–31). Certainly, the common portrayal of development agencies as 'a bureaucratic force with global reach and an explicitly pro-capitalist agenda, operating as a tool of regimes that seek to perpetuate relations of inequality and dependence between the West and the rest and, through their representation, to perpetuate the construction of others as postcolonial subjects' (Green 2003: 124) can hardly be said to apply here. Without wanting to negate or diminish CIPCA's achievements, however, it strikes me as worth noting that the same problems should occur here that also mar the endeavours of organisations that are a lot less concerned with their 'clients'' history and culture and a lot less worried about their participation in local and national politics. This points toward the ongoing difficulty of reconciling the theoretical and applied sides of CIPCA's mission of 'investigating and promoting'—a difficulty that has, of course, sparked a longstanding debate within the field of anthropology itself over what exactly is (or should be) the relationship between those engaged in the production of knowledge and those engaged in its application (cf. Ferguson 1994; Escobar 1997; Mosse 2005). The paradoxical situation of CIPCA, then, is one in which some of its elements attempt to reinforce indigenous people's lifestyles (by conducting research into them as well as providing such pragmatic support as legal representation), at the same time as other elements seek to transform these lifestyles in order to better adapt them to the requirements of capitalist markets and nation-state politics (cf. Ramos 1994). Or, to put it the other way around: the paradox of the *comunidades* is that they are being impelled to change in order to be able to stay the same (cf. Jackson 1989: 131–32).

Devoted to the economic and political empowerment of Bolivia's disadvantaged rural populations, CIPCA's approach to development has always been marked by a distinctly political edge. However, by 2006, there had not only been a lot of changes in the political landscape of Bolivia and Latin America more generally since the time of CIPCA's founding, but also in the development landscape in which CIPCA found itself operating. In the case of Camiri, the increase of (N)GOs in the area had left its mark on the way CIPCA was perceived and engaged with by the people it worked with. To return to our present example, people had got used to the idea that organisations gave them projects and provided capacity building, and they asked for these things from CIPCA as well. If we add to this the fact that, like Cristina, the Spanish agro-engineer, their staff are often temporary and come from different professional backgrounds, it becomes even more difficult to see CIPCA's activities in an entirely unified way when viewed from any particular vantage point, and even more implausible that CIPCA should be immune to developments occurring within the wider development world. In short, we cannot define CIPCA's work in the Kaami communities at the time of my fieldwork purely in terms of CIPCA's own agendas, but we have to also take the people into account with whom it was working (be that their peasant and indigenous 'clients' or their own staff), and whose own ideas about development and interactions with other (N)GOs equally shaped CIPCA's activities.

BUILDING CAPACITY, BUILDING RELATIONSHIPS: WHY THE WORKSHOP WORKS

So why, then, despite the discrepancies discussed above, did community leaders keep going to these workshops? And why did the organisations keep organising them? For one, there is of course the aspect of convention: capacity building and other workshops have become standard practice in the development business for the simple reason that they are bounded, controllable events about which reports can be written (Green 2003), an obligation created by development organisations' reliance on donor funding and the resulting accountability to funding bodies and individuals. However, besides fulfilling such bureaucratic requirements, workshops have another, unofficial purpose: they build and maintain relationships between people. This is important for NGOs working with Guaraní people. In a sense, these events stood in for the communal fiesta: they were social occasions that brought people together to talk and share food and drink (whereby the latter two were by far not the least important as far as the Guaraní participants were concerned), and people enjoyed them as a form of entertainment. In the case of local government officials, relationship building was often done during joint drinking sessions tied to some semi-official event or other (e.g., two other international volunteers working with Kaami and I prepared typical dishes from our countries on one such occasion, while another was organised in honour of the *capitán grande's* birthday). In the case of NGO workers, it was mainly the workshops that fulfilled this function.

Finally, there is the uncomfortable (and hence often neglected) fact that development organisations as they exist today are entities generated by, and operating according to the rules of, the global capitalist system with its market-oriented rationality. When viewed as such, the kind of sustainable development promoted by their own mission statements is not in fact in their interest (cf. Mosse 2003). Simply put, development organisations need poor, disempowered people in order to exist. As Alcida Ramos put it:

> The indigenist NGOs owe their existence to the fact that the Indians are exploited by the national society at large and, until recently, had no proper channels through which to place their grievances. If, by some unimaginable miracle, all Indian claims and needs were satisfactorily met, the NGOs' mission would come to an end and so would they. (1994: 166)

Whether NGO workers are aware of it or not, 'unsustainable development' in the form of donor-funded projects is in fact the real sustainable development for NGOs, whereas the achievement of local people's economic independence would put them all out of a job.

In light of the above, the mutual interest organisations and *comunarios* held in projects becomes more understandable: for the *comunarios*, they provided a temporary (and, in the case of particularly successful ones such as the honey project, even long term) source of income while they were pursuing their own ideas about the *comunidad*'s development. For the NGO workers, they constituted standard practice. For both parties, they provided a common basis to build on, a process greatly aided by the deployment of a shared vocabulary exchanged and reaffirmed within the ritualised setting of workshops that helped mask the different meanings each party attached to it. Going back to *The Anti-Politics Machine*, James Ferguson has demonstrated how development projects that fail to realise their aims cannot only be interpreted as successes by the agencies that implement them, but also bring about unexpected consequences for the people they involve. Ferguson focused mainly on the negative side of such consequences (such as the extension of state control into remote areas, or the reinterpretation of political issues as technical problems); the capacity building workshop discussed in this chapter in a way constitutes a more positive example of the same mechanism: while, in my experience, going through the motions at such workshops rarely produced any original outcomes,[13] participating in the shared language of NGO speak (of which 'capacity building' is but one example) nonetheless functioned to let all the participants come away from it with a warm feeling of accomplishment.

And why should it not: in a sense—like in the case of Graeber's colonial traders—while the ritual of the workshops produced an agreement that had been reached on, so to speak, 'unequal terms,' the agreement itself was nonetheless real. We could say that the workshops, rather than being the means to an end as which they were envisaged by the organisations, became the means to a means to an end that displaced their successfulness onto a different level, away from the level of human intent.[14] In short, while capacity building was neither going to fulfil the aims of the organisations nor those of their Guaraní clients in the long run, its invocation within the workshops—creating the illusion of 'speaking the same language'—had the very practical and immediate effect of allowing both sides to continue their work, to keep, as it were, 'doing their own thing.'

NOTES

1. These programmes (Spanish: Programas de Desarrollo de Área) were defined on the website of Visión Mundial Bolivia, World Vision's Bolivian branch, as follows: 'intercommunity organisation created through the political volition of the representative leadership of the organised groups within civil society, which assume the binding commitment of initiating proposals and lead processes of sustainable change focusing on childhood, starting from their reality of poverty and their vision of the future, in the approach of Transforming Development, with Christian values where justice and solidarity are necessary conditions for living in dignity and hope' (http://www.visionmundial.org.bo/visionmundial.php?id=326). We can find reflected in this one statement several of the points discussed in this chapter (i.e., their focus on leadership, sustainability of projects, and the assumption of the poverty of those to be developed).

2. The Convenio de Salud, a collaboration between the Apostolic Vicariate of Camiri and the Ministry of Health and Sport, promotes the improvement of health in the Chaco region via capacity building and direction of financial support.

3. Vinchucas, sometimes called 'kissing bugs' in English, are blood-sucking insects that can carry the parasite *trypanosoma cruzi* which can cause infection with Chagas disease in humans. Since vinchucas like to nest in the wattle-and-daub structures that are common throughout the Chaco region, they frequently become the object of eradication campaigns in those areas.

4. It should be pointed out here that the following analysis focuses on CIPCA's dealings with the *comunidades*, and, more particularly, with communal leaders as representatives of *comunidades*. Organisations such as the APG or even Kaami had their own internal dynamics and relationships with NGO workers; however, for reasons of space these are not discussed here.

5. In the words of Nancy Postero, '[The Popular Participation Law (LPP) of 1994] makes provision for the creation of what are called Distritos Municipales Indígenas (DMIs), or Indigenous Municipal Districts, in areas where the entire municipality is within indigenous lands. In this case, the sub-alcalde, or sub mayor, who directs the district is elected by the indigenous organization rather than being appointed by the mayor' (2000: 3, ft.9). The vice-sub-mayor's position was thus that of deputy to the sub-mayor of Kaami.

6. The Cámara Forestal de Bolivia (Bolivian Forestry Chamber), a non-profit organisation that functions as the umbrella organisation and regulating organ of Bolivia's forestry industry.

7. Sabine MacCormack writes about these early encounters: 'Some nomadic groups . . . appeared to have no chief at all. Other chiefs, whatever their ceremonial and military role might have been, were not obeyed in any way that Europeans found intelligible' (MacCormack 1999:109). See also Clastres (1977) for a classic, if meanwhile controversial, treatise on the role of Tupi-Guaraní chiefs in the colonial era.

8. Since anyone is meant to be able to talk in the communal *asamblea* to make their voice heard, the *comunarios* do not need representation of themselves to themselves. There is a sense in which *capitanes* represent outside agencies to the *comunarios*; however, as this is done from an outside position, it might make more sense to talk about the *capitanes'* role as that of 'mediators' in this context.

9. As David Mosse has shown, development organisations' desire for 'comprehensible Others' is often born out of a necessity to prove the 'success' of their projects rather than mere convenience: '[I]t is not uncommon for agency staff to select those people who already possess the characteristics that a project aims to create–the educated, the organised, the innovators, independent, solvent, modernising peasants; that way a measure of success is guaranteed' (2005: 211); cf also Green (2003: 134). Alcida Ramos puts it even more drastically: '[NGOs construct] a model that moulds the Indians' interests to the organization's shape and needs. [There is a tendency toward] the fabrication of the perfect Indian whose virtues, sufferings and untiring stoicism have won for him the right to be defended by the professionals of indigenous rights. That Indian is more real than the real Indian. He is the hyperreal Indian' (1994: 161).

10. This is, of course, a one-sided argument in that it assumes the development organisations to be the only power holders in the equation. In cases like the present one, the anti-politics machine quickly runs out of steam, as Bolivian Guaraní people have a strong presence on the regional and national political scenes, and workshop partici-

pants bring their own politics back in (see the vice-sub-alcalde's remark on Guaraní diplomacy in the above example). However, it serves us here to draw attention to some of the limitations affecting the work of development organisations more generally.

11. French: handicraft, DIY, or makeshift work.

12. Alcida Ramos describes a similar shift in the running of Brazilian indigenous support NGOs in the 1980s that exemplifies the challenges potentially attached to such a restructuring: 'Whereas in the early days of civil indigenism the goal of defending indigenous rights was never lost sight of and the means were improvised, flexible and pragmatic, now the main concern often is with the means, such as fundraising, accounting, salaries, high-tech equipment, report-writing and, in some cases, publishing. The NGOs may be very efficient in doing all that, but the flesh-and-blood Indians have been edged off stage' (1994: 159).

13. This is perhaps hardly surprising if we consider that the largely formulaic, or 'ritualised,' structure of these workshops may even be designed to only produce certain results in the interest of maintaining manageability. As Maia Green has noted for similar workshops in Tanzania: 'The tight organizational structure of facilitation and the construction of workshops as a site for the management of outputs ensure that workshops produce highly limited visions' (2003: 135).

14. A similar point was already made by Charlton and May in an article of 1995: '[T]he criticisms of the deficiencies inherent in contemporary development project work . . . concentrate excessively on the direct, often quantifiable impacts of projects and consequently fail to appreciate fully the potential positive significance for "development" of the indirect effects of development projects, including some whose direct effects may, quite correctly, be deemed failures' (238–39). See also Mosse (2003).

Chapter Six

Beautiful Culture, 'Shitty Indians'

The *Comunidades* in *Karai*
and Guaraní Identity Politics

As we have seen, ideas about what to do with Guaraní *comunidades* in Cordillera diverged even as far as the issue of 'development' was concerned: while *comunarios* had a vision of living '*tranquilo*' in their *comunidades*, free to work on their own land and decide what to do with their money independent of the need for outside specialists, many of the development organisations working in the area came with plans to capacitate the *comunarios* into 'entrepreneurs' and turn the *comunidades* into a version of successful 'businesses.' This latter vision was one that was also of interest to the governmental ambitions of developing their indigenous populations: to insert indigenous people more firmly into the market economy, or in some cases even to make them into a market of their own by promoting the production of 'cultural' items that could be sold to locals and tourists alike. The idea of 'culture' was pervasive in the relationships between *comunidades* and state agencies, not only in the context of economics, but also in that of Cruceño and Camireño *autonomista* identity politics. This chapter looks at *comunarios*' and outsiders' ideas about Guaraní culture and the way the production of material culture in the Department of Santa Cruz was—rather than constituting a purely economic activity—a relational practice bound up with historically charged issues of identity, hierarchy, and ownership.

THE POTTERY PROJECT

One of the things that first captured my attention when I arrived in Cañón de Segura was the making of pottery by the local women. This was first organised by the women's workgroup in early January of 2007 to produce ceramics that were to be sold at the festival in remembrance of the Battle

179

of Kuruyuki of 1892 on 28 January. As mentioned in chapter 2, this battle between Guaraní warriors and Bolivian republican forces, which resulted in a crushing defeat for the Guaraní, used to be seen by many historians as marking the 'death' of the Guaraní as a people in any meaningful sense (see, e.g., Sanabria 1972; Saignes 1990). In recent decades, however, it has been reinvented as a symbol of Guaraní unity by the Guaraní themselves in collaboration with NGOs working with them. The event of its commemoration was first held in 1992 in the *comunidad* of Ivo near Kuruyuki on the occasion of the battle's 100-year anniversary. It also marked the emergence into public consciousness of the Guaraní's recently-founded political organisation, the Assembly of the Guaraní People (APG), which has since become one of the most influential indigenous organisations of Bolivia (see chapters 1 and 2). Since 1992, the APG has been organising the event annually. Its programme includes speeches by Guaraní political leaders and guests, as well as dance performances and the exhibition and sale of food and arts and crafts.

One day close to the date of the festival, I passed a group of three women who were sitting together in the central building of the school. Noticing that one of them was busy mixing what looked like mud with a fine grey powder in a plastic tub, I stopped to ask what they were doing.

'We're making clay for pottery,' one of them told me.

'How interesting,' I said. 'And what is it you're mixing?'

'*Barro y polvo*'–'mud and powder,' was the straightforward (and to me equally unsatisfying) answer.

Being unfamiliar with people's conversational conventions at the time, in which giving seemingly obvious answers to questions was a common feature,[1] I took this as a hint to leave them alone, and so it took me a while longer to find out the origins of the ingredients of the pottery clay: the 'mud' had been extracted from a site in one of the hills in a neighbouring community; the powder, however, had been made by grinding up the sherds of a large vessel the *comunarios* had come across in a close-by part of the forest, where the heavy rains of the rainy season had caused a minor landslide. While this discovery at first dealt a certain blow to my 'Enlightened' sensibilities, which had been conditioned into regarding ancient objects as something that needed to be preserved and investigated, the way pottery-making in Cañón involved this kind of 'recycling' of old pots became an interesting fact in itself the more I thought about it.

The women of Cañón had not been in the habit of producing pottery prior to the time my encounter with the potters took place in January 2007. If ever their ancestors had been potters (and the presence of several large *chicha* pots outside the *patrones*' old house on the other side of the motorway from the *comunidad* suggested that they had), the technique had been lost sometime during the years of their captivity. Guaraní pottery, however, has become a sellable commodity that can be found in the market stalls of Camiri as well as the tourist shops of Santa Cruz, so when a woman was sent to Cañón from what was then the Bolivian Viceministry of Cultures in order to initiate a pottery project,[2] the women's workgroup leapt at the opportunity to invite Doña Graciela, an old lady (*abuelita*) from the neighbouring community of Urundaiti, to come and teach them what she knew. She was the one I had encountered in the school that day, accompanied by two of the local women, mixing 'mud and powder' to prepare the mixture for the pottery clay.

Making pottery was clearly a lot of fun for the women, and, as was usual with communal events, provided the setting for a lot of socialising, gossiping, and laughter, while the ever-present *poro* (*mate*) made its rounds among the project participants. Since I had only recently arrived in the community, I was pleased to be allowed to help with the polishing of a jug, which was done with a smooth black pebble the women had picked up by the river in Camiri, and to be included in their *poro* round. I even learned a new word on the occasion: listening attentively in order to catch something of the conversation, I noticed that one particular word, which sounded like '*jeikua*,' was being repeated over and over, followed by a lot of laughter, as one of the women held up a small pot that had just been fired. When I asked what *jeikua* meant, this caused another burst of laughter, until finally someone explained to me, 'It's a vulgar word, it means "arse"; she's saying that the little arse of this pot has got burned.'

Notwithstanding such minor accidents, by the end of the pottery session the women had produced a good number of pots, flowerpots, jugs, plates, *hüitimimeros* (pots for making *hüiti*, a form of maize cake), and *yerberos* (vessels for keeping *mate* and sugar), which they proudly presented to the vice ministry's 'Culture Lady' at her next visit. Culture Lady was impressed, but had suggestions for improvement: out of her governmental 4x4, she produced an illustrated volume of pottery styles of the world, some of the pages of which she had marked for the women's reference. There were pictures in it of European, Chinese, and Indian pottery of the Neolithic eras, with captions like: 'From the period when the most beautiful pottery was produced in Europe.' Culture Lady pointed out one pot in particular, which she told the women was similar to theirs. I asked whether it was Guaraní, and she said that it was not, but very similar, and that she was showing the women these things so they could get ideas of how to make their pottery more marketable.

The women listened, looked, and nodded politely—and unperturbedly continued to make their pottery the way *abuelita* Graciela was teaching them. This rejection of Culture Lady's suggestions happened matter-of-factly and did not involve any particular aversion against foreign techniques

Making pottery for Kuruyuki, January 2008.
Photo by the author.

per se: apart from the traditionally used red and white paints, derived from the ground particles of a particular stone (*ita pïta*) and white clay respectively, there were several tubes of acrylic paint in different colours, which the women used quite happily to paint their finished pots. When I lamented the lack of any more white paint to put the finishing touches to the jar I had made, the response was, 'Just use the green—this paint goes white during firing anyway.' The idea of making innovations to the production process thus seemed to be acceptable—as long as they fit into the women's ideas about the way things should be done, and the authority to be followed in this respect was clearly Doña Graciela rather than Culture Lady.

CULTURE: AN ONGOING PREDICAMENT

The concept of 'culture' is a slippery one that has been a headache for generations of anthropologists since it was famously coopted for the discipline by
E. B. Tylor in his 1871 work *Primitive Culture*.[3] Tylor was an evolutionist
who wanted to talk about Culture with a capital 'C,' something common to
all humans but farther or less far developed among different groups of people.
Since then, starting with Franz Boas, the 'father of cultural relativism,' who is
generally credited with introducing the idea of multiple and equally valid cultures that was to shape American anthropology (e.g., Boas 1982), the redefi-
nitions of the concept, reflecting the developments (and, indeed, anxieties)
in anthropological theory of the moment, have been too numerous to cover
here in their entirety (see, e.g., Kroeber and Kluckhohn 1952; Stocking 1968;
Geertz 1973; Abu-Lughod 1991). At the time of my fieldwork, a new powerful trend was taking hold in anthropology that would do away with culture altogether and instead made 'ontology' the focus of scholarly attention (Henare
et al. 2007; Carrithers et al. 2010). However, as Shane Greene reminded us in
a 2004 article on Peruvian Aguaruna people's cultural property claims, indigenous people (and, one might add, other non-anthropologists) can hold ideas
about culture that are often quite unrelated to anthropological concerns (2004:
212). Unlike the Aguaruna, the people I worked with were not involved in
any legal disputes about cultural property rights; however, they, as well as
urban *karai* people, did talk about Guaraní culture a great deal, and it is their
ideas with which I am here concerned. While unpacking the whole intricacies
of the 'culture' issue in this context would merit a study of its own, what I
want to concentrate on here are the ways in which ideas about Guaraní culture
were mobilised in both Guaraní and *karai* identity politics, and the way these
ultimately reveal the production of Guaraní culture to be a relational activity.
    From the way the people in Cañón used the Spanish word for 'culture'
(*cultura*), I got the impression that there were at least two different ways in
which it was being applied. One was more or less the Spanish equivalent of
the Guaraní concept of *ñande reko*, meaning 'our way of being.' This was
the way I often heard people talk about 'our culture' or 'Guaraní culture' in
fiestas, or even just visiting them in their *oka*. 'Isn't our culture beautiful!,'
or, 'When you leave, you will tell everyone in your home about the beautiful
Guaraní culture,' were typical phrases that I got to hear on such occasions.
This started with my very first communal event, the feast described in the
Introduction that had been prepared in honor of the Camiri mayor on the
occasion of the anniversary of the community's cattle project. At one point
during this meal, a middle-aged man sat next to me and started asking me
questions—where I was from, what my country was like, and what my pur-

pose was in coming to Cañón. I told him I was doing an investigation into life in the community for my PhD thesis. He replied that there had been a few investigators before me, none of whom, however, had stayed in the community for any length of time. Rather, he said, they would come during the day to visit the houses and ask people questions, then leave again to go back to Camiri for the night.

'The first question they used to always ask us,' he said, 'was whether our culture was important to us.'

'And what do you tell them?' I asked.

'We tell them, very important!' he replied.

When I tried to find out, however, what exactly he meant by 'culture,' I did not succeed in getting a clear answer. Rather, I realised after a while that there simply was no clear answer to this question—the kind of 'culture' to which people would refer when they said 'our culture' or 'Guaraní culture' was not anything that could be easily put into words, but a way of living, *their* way of living, which was Guaraní because they were Guaraní, and which set them apart from other people because they wanted it that way. As Tim Ingold beautifully put it:

> culture is not something that we can ever expect to encounter 'on the ground.' What we find are people whose lives take them on a journey through space and time in environments that seem to them to be full of significance, who use both words and material artefacts to get things done and to communicate with others, and who, in their talk, endlessly spin metaphors so as to weave labyrinthine and ever-expanding networks of symbolic equivalence. What we do *not* find are neatly bounded and mutually exclusive bodies of thought and custom, perfectly shared by all who subscribe to them, and in which their lives and works are fully encapsulated. . . . The isolated culture has been revealed as a figment of the Western anthropological imagination. It might be more realistic, then, to say that people *live culturally* rather than that they *live in cultures*. (1994: 330)

The other way in which people used *cultura* was as more or less a synonym of *artesanía* (craftsmanship); that is, to talk about what could be translated as 'material culture' (Tilley et al. 2006). This was the kind of culture the Culture Lady had come to promote. Consisting of objects rather than an elusive 'way of being' that was hard to put into words but had to be experienced instead, this kind of culture could be promoted in the same sense as it could be consumed: you could tell people to produce it.

Reified culture is a valuable commodity for indigenous people because it is marketable and people buy it (cf. Clifford 1988). This is basically the rationale behind governmental (and also NGO) projects such as Culture Lady's that approach indigenous culture from a developmental angle. What is more, these kinds of projects reveal an equation of indigenous people with 'culture' that was also present in the attitudes of large parts of the Camireño population in general. *Karai* people in Camiri liked to dress their children up in indigenous attire on certain national holidays and decorate restaurants and hotel lobbies with items reminiscent of and made by indigenous people, such as the pots the women of Cañón de Segura were making, while simultaneously rejecting their way of being (about which the *comunarios* had talked with such pride) as inferior and undesirable. Tangible, manageable culture like pottery, weavings, jewelry, woodcarvings, or even cultural performances is what makes indigenous culture into regional or even national culture in the eyes, not only of tourists and governments (Ardren 2004) but also members of the self-identifying nonindigenous population of many post-colonial countries in the Americas (De la Cadena 2000; Canessa ed. 2005; Theodossopoulos 2010) and elsewhere (Byrne 1996; Smits 2014). Many indigenous groups are well aware of this attitude and have learned to use it to their own advantage in different ways, often deliberately resorting to a 'strategic essentialism' that enhances such traits in their self-representation as are deemed particularly 'cultural' (and, hence, particularly valuable) (Conklin 1997; Field 1999; Frankland 2001).

This plays into a further dimension of the importance of material culture; that is, the way in which producing cultural items affirms, and indeed confirms, indigenous people's identities as indigenous people. This confirmation of identity becomes important in a setting where the possibility of maintaining one's culture as a way of being depends on the recognition of one's indigenous status by such institutions as state authorities and NGOs (Lucero 2006; Canessa 2007; Albro 2006). I often heard *karai* people in Camiri talk about Guaraní culture as a register of Guaraní 'authenticity' or even 'realness,' whereby those groups with the most culture were supposed to be the 'realest.' In a kind of mirroring of Tylor's evolutionary scheme, culture-loss in present-day Guaraní people was sometimes (and especially where politically convenient) taken to indicate their degeneration, so to speak, from proper indigenous people into generic rural populations. The use of the sherds of the old burial urns by the women of Cañón in their own pottery could, in this sense, be seen as a reproduction, a kind of 'cloning,' of the culture of the ancient people which would come back to life in a new yet no less 'authentic' or legitimate form.[4]

ALAMBRITO

To complicate matters, however, borrowing from the Guaraní also proved a useful strategy for Camireños as well as Santa Cruz *autonomistas* to create an identity for themselves that was a) identifiably 'Camba,' and b) able to convey their objective of gaining more independence from La Paz. People's use of the word 'Camba' had confused me at first because of its double significance of 'person from Santa Cruz (Department)' (in which case it was often used in opposition to 'Colla,' meaning 'person from the highlands'), and 'Guaraní person' (in which case the usage became derogatory). In order to avoid similar confusion here, I am using the spelling 'Camba' when referring to the idealised Cruceño stereotype and '*camba*' when referring to the term in its derogatory usage to denote 'Guaraní person.' In its idealised form, the term had only fairly recently been adopted by the Cruceño intelligentsia to give expression to a shift in the Cruceños' popular narrative that occurred after the 1952 revolution and gained momentum with the subsequent intensification of the opposition between highlands and eastern lowlands (Plata 2008: 135–36). This shift, intended to increase the Cruceños' legitimacy as a region with an identity of its own, involved the reframing of Cruceño identity—which had been defined in terms of a 'pure' Spanish ancestry (Plata 2008: 134–35)—in terms of a mestizaje that was meant to be superior to that which had occurred in the highlands (Plata 2008: 136).[5] The suggestion was, for one, that the Cruceño Cambas combined in themselves all the best attributes of the races that constituted them, while the Collas had inherited all the negative qualities of theirs (Plata 2008: 136). Further, the Cruceños' indigenous people who were now part of their identity were said to be better than the highland ones in the first place. The latter point was demonstrated by reference to (and exaggeration of) the fearsomeness and bravery of the Guaraní's 'Chiriguano' warrior ancestors (Plata 2008: 137–39).

I was given a prime example of just how considerable people's ability to double-think was when it came to 'their' indigenous people when I stayed with the family of a *karai* friend in Santa Cruz for a few days. Relatively wealthy upper middle class and of a fair complexion, this family embodied many of the Cruceños' favourite virtues. On this particular visit, Doña Mina, a friend of my friend's mother's from Camiri, also happened to be visiting, and when the two women were talking at night a lot of comments were made about the lazy people in the countryside. Her father, Mina told me, had been very poor when he was little but had decided of his own free will to leave his village in the country and—only a child of eleven or twelve—had gone to the city all on his own, where he worked his way up to a position of some prosperity. In her opinion, there was therefore no excuse for poor people to be poor, and moreover, all the talk of people still living in slavery on certain haciendas was rubbish: if one wanted something, one could go and get it, no matter the circumstances. I disagreed, suggesting that not everyone was born with the same chances and dispositions, but was silenced with the argument that people here knew much better what they were talking about than I.

The same evening, my friend's mother Doña Mercedes told us how she had gone to Argentina once and been confronted with some racist attitudes toward the 'Indian' Bolivians there. In response to this, she had proclaimed how she herself was just as 'Indian' as the rest of Bolivia, which, however, was really the wrong word anyway, 'Indian' being a misnomer that had resulted from Columbus's mistake about where he had landed; so really, if they wanted to call her anything, it would have to be 'Guaraní'—and yes, she was Guaraní and proud of it. From this, she and Mina somehow got into a discussion of the shortcomings of Evo, this shitty Indian (*indio de mierda*), and how the Collas in general were ruining Santa Cruz, which used to be such a clean and livable city before migrants had arrived from the highlands and, sadly, had taught the locals their dirty habits instead of picking up the proper Camba ways. This negative depiction of the Collas conveys the Cruceño elite's sense of a threat that is aesthetic as well as political: 'Regionalists see urban Andeans as a spatialized aesthetic threat to Cruceño order and beauty' (Gustafson 2006: 362), and 'the discourse against Andean *avasallamiento* invokes racial fear and disgust by linking it to the wider MAS expansion in the country, which is viewed as a threat against "Cruceño" resources' (2006: 363).

On a different occasion, I overheard a conversation Doña Mercedes was having with another friend, in which she criticised the laziness of their domestic worker, a Guaraní girl nicknamed 'Alambrito.' As it turned out, Alambrito, who had lived with the family since she was a young girl, had a son by Mercedes's brother, whom she was raising with the support of the family since the father showed no interest in looking after them. Mercedes's complaint was that Alambrito had sometimes used to act like the 'mistress of the house,' but she had told her off for that, pointing out that 'You are no relation of mine, and just because you've had my brother's child doesn't make you one either.'

The above examples give us a hint of the complexities involved in inter-ethnic relations in the *oriente*. For one, from a *karai* perspective, Guaraní identities were up for the taking whenever it was strategically convenient for them (for example, to set them apart from 'racist' Argentineans or 'dirty' Collas). The same rules, however, did not apply in the opposite case, and although my friend would refer to Alambrito's child as her 'little brother,' Alambrito herself would always remain an outsider to the family because of her perceived inferiority. While poverty was thus something that was seen as superable, ethnicity was not, and while in reality people in Bolivia, as elsewhere in Latin America, switch between ethnic identities all the time (cf. Schwartz and Salomon 1999; De la Cadena 1995), being perceived as belonging to any particular ethnic group came with a series of expectations attached that blurred the boundaries between 'innate' qualities (Guaraní are lazy) and learned behaviours (Collas are dirty). As my friend once told me, 'Alambrito has already forgotten her heritage; she doesn't speak Guaraní anymore,' completely bypassing the fact that, as a *criada* of the house,[6] Alambrito had been surrounded by monolingual Spanish speakers from an early age and had not really had the opportunity to practice her 'native' language in the first place. In the eyes of her employers, Alambrito's Guaraníness was an established fact, and any divergence from the behaviour which they consequently expected of her was easily put down to acculturation, rather than sparking any suspicion that their own assumptions might be mistaken.

OUR PEOPLE, OUR CULTURE: GUARANÍ CULTURE IN *KARAI* IDENTITY POLITICS

During my fieldwork, an event in which the use of Guaraní cultural elements in local and regional identity politics was particularly visible was the 'Day of Camireño Tradition' of 2007.[7] The spectacle started in the morning with dancing around the central plaza. A large group of young people in colourful *tipoi* and white shirts, some of them wearing masks, danced the '*arete guasu*.'[8] They were the dance troupe from the Guaraní *comunidad* of Itanambikua, located at the outskirts of Camiri, that had earned some renown within the region for its elaborate performances. The dancers came accompanied by two large figures in the shape of the mythical jaguar and bull that were carried by several people and moved about like Chinese dragons. At the lower end of the plaza, some of Camiri's carnival fraternities were getting ready to march, among them a delegation from the Capitanía Kaami. The Prefecture was represented as well, by a contingent of people sporting banners and sombrero sleeves in green and white, the colours of the Department of Santa Cruz. They revealed a 'monument' in the plaza that consisted of a stele with AUTONOMÍA written down its side and danced round it with a group of beauty queens. A group of traditionally dressed Guaraní from Tëtayapɨ posed in front of the monument for pictures, in a style reminiscent of old photographs from a couple of centuries ago.

This sudden burst into public visibility of Guaraní people as the celebrated bearers of 'culture' disrupted their otherwise low-key presence in Camiri everyday life. A similar observation about the Camireño 'Day of Tradition' has been made by Ana María Lema, who quotes an informant as saying, 'One day each year, those who hate the Guaraní dress in *tipoi*, they put sandals on and walk with their *cambas* by their side playing their drums; but for the rest of the year, they keep treating them badly' (2001: 222). However, even in this exceptional celebration of Guaraníness the signs of an underlying inequality shone through. The scene that unfolded around the monument was telling: noisy *autonomía* activists waving flags and dancing round their idol, while next to them the bearers of culture remained static and silent. The hierarchy implicit in the relationship between the two groups finds its expression in the Cruceño colours displayed by the *autonomistas*:

> As Cruceños learn in school, green evokes natural abundance, the rural and frontier riches of the region. White symbolizes purity (*la pureza del linaje*) and nobility (*hidalguía*), a rather transparent invocation of racial distinction inherited from Spanish colonialism . . . these symbols are encapsulated in representations of the ideal Cruceño-Camba bodies, whether that of virile men or 'beautiful' women, all implicitly 'white' in relation to Andean Bolivia and local indigenous peoples. (Gustafson 2006: 356)

If Cruceño Camba bodies encapsulate the 'white' of the flag, Guaraní *camba* bodies encapsulate the 'green,' in that they belong within the realm of rural and frontier resources to be 'harvested' by their 'white' counterparts (as producers of culture and workers on haciendas).[9] What appears as a *karai* celebration of Guaraní culture is thus really an appropriation, as the celebration only takes place within the context of Camireño and Cruceño self-promotion.

What was happening at this event was a conflation on various levels. For one, elements of the *arete*, the source of the reproduction of the Guaraní *teko* par excellence, appeared out of context in a setting that allowed them to be reframed in terms of *cultura* in the sense of cultural objects or objectifications. Secondly, this 'Guaraní culture' was being appropriated as part of 'Camireño culture,' and as such recruited in the Camireños' endeavour to create a distinctive identity for themselves. A popular slogan relating to the subject that often found itself reproduced on T-shirts was, '*Ni camba, ni colla, ni chapaco—camireño, carajo!*' ('Not Camba [in the sense of Cruceño], nor Colla [highland Bolivian], nor Chapaco [person from Tarija]— Camireño, dammit!'). The trouble Camireños have with the question of identity is rooted in the fact that Camiri has experienced extensive in-migration from all over Bolivia since it gained importance as a gas-producing town in the first half of the twentieth century. While the population's loyalties are thus to some degree divided, general consensus has it that Camiri is part of the Chaqueño cultural realm,[10] whose symbolism—most notably the use of a lot of leather in traditional clothing and arts and crafts—is closely associated with the activities of cattle breeding (which has retained its status as a highly desirable occupation) and a romanticised image of country life. As both country dwellers and ex-peons of the local landowning classes, the Guaraní and their culture fit right into this picture, but only in their capacity of silent extras, or even—like the delegation from Tëtayapɨ posing before the *autonomía* monument—picturesque props.[11] There was no space in the Camireño popular imagination for Guaraní people as speaking subjects, despite the fact that, with the growing importance of the APG, their assumption of this position had long since become a political reality.[12]

However, with the revelation of the *autonomía* monument, Guaraní culture was (in direct contradiction to the sentiment expressed in the '*Camireño carajo!*' slogan) given a momentary political significance that marked it out more generally as 'Camba' culture, and which placed it at the heart of the Cruceño autonomy project. This had been gaining in fervour since my arrival in Bolivia in June 2006, when displays of pro-autonomy propaganda in Santa Cruz de la Sierra had dominated the city centre in the weeks prior to the election of the Constituent Assembly and the concurrent autonomy referendum on 02 July. Following the trend in the departmental capital, by the time I left my field site in September 2008, Camiri was in a regular *autonomía* frenzy that had been building up amidst tensions caused by Evo Morales's land redistribution policies (see chapter 7) and his handling of the country's petroleum production. People were generally happy with the idea of nationalising the hydrocarbons industry, but Evo's policies had not gone far enough for them. Especially the continued dominance of transnational concerns in the exploitation of the local gas deposits and the redistribution of the IDH (Direct Hydrocarbons Tax, a tax on oil and gas production created by the Hydrocarbon Law 3058 in 2005) caused a great deal of upheaval among the Cruceño population, who would rather have seen the revenue created by the IDH come back to the departmental government than be spent on funding universities, land reform, old people's pensions, and—most crucially—subsidising the non-gas producing departments of Bolivia.

In August 2008, I attended a meeting of one of Camiri's Civic Committees. Two such committees existed as a result of a split between government-loyal and *autonomista* factions that had occurred over petroleum-related matters in April of that year. Among other matters, the possibility of joining the upcoming hunger strike that had been announced by the president of the Civic Committee of Santa Cruz, Branco Marinkovic, in protest against the redistribution of the IDH was discussed, and tempers were flaring. Standing at the back of the room, I noticed the T-shirt a woman in front of me was wearing, which sported anti-Evo and pro-*autonomista* slogans ('*No MAS Evo, Rubén es autonomía*').[13] When she turned around, I saw that the front was adorned with a Guaraní design above which stood the word: '*Iyambae.*'

As mentioned in chapter 1, Iyambae is the name of an old and powerful family in the Isoso, a Guaraní Capitanía further to the south-east of Camiri. Because of its symbolic capacity—literally translated, it means 'without master'—*iyambae* has also become one of the favourite catchphrases of the APG, which it presents, depending on the context, as one of the defining characteristics of Guaraníness or as an ideal to be achieved in future.[14] During the time of my fieldwork, *iyambae* was also often used to designate indigenous autonomy, for which the APG was campaigning at the time: 'The Assembly of the Guaraní People (APG) poses indigenous autonomy as a strategy founded on the principle of *Iyambae* (to be free . . . without master), which implies the dismantling of the colonising powers and the reconstruction of the state' (Caballero Espinoza 2008: 19).

'Indigenous originary peasant autonomy' was finally ratified in Chapter VII, Articles 289–96 of the Constitution of 2009, where it is described as 'the self-government as the exercise of free determination of the indigenous originary peasant nations and peoples, whose populations share their own territory, culture, history, languages, and juridical, political, social, and economic organisations or institutions' (Article 289). The next article specifies 'ancestral territories, currently inhabited by those peoples and nations, and the willingness of the population' (Article 290) as the basis for the conformation of indigenous autonomy in any one municipality.

However, opinions in Bolivia vary on what should count as an ancestral territory and who should count as an indigenous person (cf. Albó 2008b; Toranzo Roca 2008; Zavaleta Reyles 2008). Shortly before leaving the field, I came across a new artifice devised to deny the Guaraní any land rights altogether on the grounds of their migratory past. As one employee of the municipality of Camiri put it on one occasion, 'There is something you should know about your friends, the Guaraní. According to a very renowned historian, they only got here very shortly before the Spanish, so they are not *originarios* of this region, which, according to the new Constitution, means that they also have no legal basis for the land claims they are making.'[15] Notwithstanding the fact that he was wrong (Article 30 of the Constitution defines *pueblos originarios* as 'any human collectivity that shares a cultural identity, language, historical tradition, institutions, territoriality, and world view whose existence is *prior to the Spanish colonial invasion*'; my emphasis), by this sleight of hand the Guaraní's own strategy of using history as a tool in their struggle for land rights was turned against them in the eyes of the local government and population.

The municipal employee, whom I had previously encountered various times at fiestas held by the Kaami leadership with whom he had been very friendly, had phrased this opinion in a way that made it sound simply informative. However, in other cases expressions of the same idea were a lot more hostile, as is exemplified by the text of an anonymous flyer the Kaami office held among its documents:

> The Guaraní are invaders of the northern Chaco region . . . they arrived some 100 or 200 years before the Spanish invaders; this proves and certifies that they

are neither autochthonous nor *originarios* of the BOLIVIAN NORTHERN CHACO . . . how is it possible that the departmental authorities of Camiri permit that this part of "CORDILLERA" PROVINCE is DECLARED GUARANI TERRITORY. . . . Where agricultural and cattle producers will be damaged; this will bring about fatal consequences of a fight to the last, there will be confrontations and even deaths . . . (Undated document 'For the Attention of the People of Camiri and the Local and National Authorities,' signed 'The Defenders of the Chaco Region.')

While we cannot be certain about the individual identities of this text's authors, it bears a striking resemblance to the document produced by the local cattle breeders' 'Committee for the Defence of Private Property of Cordillera Province' in response to the *comunarios*' occupation of Cañón de Segura quoted in chapter 1, and the reference to 'agricultural and cattle producers' also points in the same direction. Apart from the explicit aggression, what is striking in this document is the way of reasoning it proposes: rather than an affirmation of the authors' *own* rights, this claim works on the basis of a negation of the *others*' rights. The assumption implicit in these examples, that the presumed non-existence of the Guaraní's rights to the land automatically confirms those of any *karai* with a similar claim, is indicative of what Bret Gustafson has called 'a colonial understanding of identity as racial hierarchy' (2006: 373) that was widespread among the Camireño and Cruceño populations at the time. It was the same attitude that made *karai* people celebrate Guaraní culture at the same time as they looked down on the people who produced it, and it was the same attitude that made *autonomía* campaigners print '*iyambae*' on their T-shirts, when what they were campaigning for had nothing to do with the kind of autonomy the Guaraní had in mind (cf. Canessa ed. 2005).

This seems paradoxical at first, considering that in the one instance the Guaraní's indigenous status was celebrated as a source of identity-bestowing 'culture,' whereas in the other it was denied as a fraudulent ruse to lay claim to lands to which they were not entitled. However, the contradiction only exists on a semantic level: the point is simply that indigenous people have a place in *karai* society only as long as they fulfil their supposed functions vis-à-vis the *karai*. Failing this, they forfeit their *raison d'être* as indigenous people, in which case it is up to the *karai* to take that status away from them and reclassify them as 'invaders.' In other words, indigenous people are free to produce culture and other useful products as long as this does not interfere with *karai* interests. This attitude was summed up rather well in the remark of a Camireña friend's brother-in-law with whom I found myself in a drunken argument about Guaraní work ethics one night: 'I'm not a racist,' he started, 'but—what I wanna know is, what have the Guaraní ever done for me?'

The idea that Guaraní people's purpose in life was to do something for the *karai* was one I encountered over and over when speaking with friends and acquaintances in Camiri and Santa Cruz about my work. Instances of Guaraní people's refusal to fit this designated role were seen as something reprehensible, whereby illustrations of this attitude were often formulaic. One popular example was, 'Today, when you say to a Guaraní woman, "You can work for me, you can wash my clothes," she'll tell you, "No, *you* can wash *my* clothes."' This statement is crushing in its simplicity: there is no need to spell out why the Guaraní woman's response is outrageous because her role in life (that is, as domestic worker of a *karai* woman) is implicit in her ethnicity. Her suggestion that the *karai* woman should work for her instead constitutes an upsetting of what is perceived as the natural order of things, and it implies that she is obstinate, lazy, or in fact too well-off to know her place in life, all options that were seen as equally deplorable. According to a popular Bolivian convention, poverty is often depicted as a virtue: people's appraisal of the 'humble people' (*gente bien humilde*) in the country fuses the humbleness of their possessions and social condition with a sense of humility that gives rural/indigenous people some moral superiority. This expression is not limited to indigenous people, with even high-status *karai* in the *oriente* sometimes getting sentimental about a humble grandparent living contentedly in a small hut in the countryside; it does, however, stand in stark contrast to the values of achieving material and career-related success that *karai* people advocate for each other, and which, as a general rule, they do not extend to indigenous people.

On the contrary, *karai* in Camiri sometimes resented the wealth they saw NGOs as pouring into the *comunidades,* and it was a widely held opinion that any investment in them was a waste of money. As another standard example had it: 'The *comunidades* have all this money from abroad nowadays, they are better off than us, but the people in the country are very lazy, they don't work. I myself have seen the tractors standing idle in [insert name of a *comunidad*].' The resentment expressed in such statements exposes the Guaraní's situation as a Catch-22: on the one hand, they are to be resented because of the easy money they are making through NGO funding. On the other hand, however, they are also to be resented because of their unworthiness of this money.[16] Again, the implication is that really, Guaraní people should be not only diligent, but also poor. And in particular, they should be poorer than *karai* people, for whom they should—ideally—be working in order to make a living. Whenever I argued with someone against such assertions of Guaraní people's laziness, the answer I ultimately tended to get was that I, as a foreigner, simply didn't know what I was talking about. Despite the fact that those among my Camireño friends who were the most convinced that 'my *cambas'* were a bunch of loafers (*'unos flojos'*) rarely went to the *comuni-dades* themselves, they were insistent that they knew better what was hap-pening in them because it was 'their people' they were talking about. While there was a certain acknowledgement of a shared nationality and/or regional identity in this notion of 'our people,' it also expressed an idea of ownership when applied to indigenous people, which included the privilege of insulting them freely: words like *indio* ('Indian') in the *oriente* almost came with the qualification *de mierda* ('shitty') inbuilt, all the while most people would vigorously deny any accusations of racism.

In short, *karai* people claimed a knowledge of 'their' indigenous people that was more complete and authoritative than those people's knowledge of themselves. These claims, which were rarely based on first-hand experiences, but often drew on the supposed experiences of third parties (such as 'Skinny Guy's story recounted in chapter 2) or on superficial eyewitness accounts (tractors standing idle in such-and-such a *comunidad* as proof that all Guaraní people are lazy), formed a narrative tradition that constantly reaffirmed itself through repetition, and whose sole requirement for verification was that those partaking in it belonged to the right ethnic and social category. The setup was one in which Guaraní people's opinions even about themselves did not need to be listened to because they could only either confirm those of the *karai* or simply be wrong. In the eyes of a large part of *karai* society, Guaraní people were there to produce and provide (culture and labour), but not to own (land, the labour of others, the products of their own efforts). Ownership was a privilege of the *karai*, and attempts by Guaraní people to claim this privilege for themselves was often met with objection or even hostility, especially where the claims of the latter were seen to impinge on those of the former.

DEYSI

On the one hand, the way in which *karai* people in Camiri and beyond largely treated Guaraní culture constitutes a classic example of 'cultural appropria-tion' (Ziff and Rao eds. 1997), in this case of an indigenous culture by a neo-colonial power base.[17] Following this line of argumentation has the advantage that it allows us to regard the Cruceño and Camireño celebrations of Guaraní culture (in particular in connection with their *autonomía* project of 2008) with a critical eye and uncover the racism that remained embedded in the region's social structure. However, at the same time, it has the distinct disadvantage that it would make of Guaraní people voiceless victims and thus, in a sense, reproduce the *karai* elites' attempted monopolising of the narrative. This would be most unfair, given that the production of *'cultura'* by contemporary

Guaraní people is neither passive nor exclusively geared toward the outside or in line with outside expectations. If we take a closer look at the commemorative event at Kuruyuki for which the women of Cañón had been producing their pottery, a very different picture emerges.

As described above, the *comunarias'* experience of pottery-making involved the acquisition of a 'traditional' skill, which they, however, experienced as new, utilising material that had been produced by Guaraní people who had lived and died in the area a long time before them, and with whom they claimed no kinship other than the acknowledgment of their sociocultural similarity. The incorporation of the ancient materials was thus at the same time an incorporation of Guaraní 'culture,' something that the old people were thought to have had aplenty but which contemporary Guaraní people were often said to be lacking since the proclaimed 'death' of their society following the Battle of Kuruyuki. The pottery itself was, in turn, produced to be sold at an event that was equally made up of elements belonging to remote Guaraní history, assembled in such a way as to serve a particular purpose at a particular point in time, where it would function as the reified proof that Guaraní culture was in fact alive and kicking. Both historical and cultural practice thus became tools for reasserting and making visible a specific sense of identity, of a Guaraníness that had not previously existed in this form, but which was also not constructed out of nothingness—in short, a (re) appropriation by Guaraní people of their own culture (cf. Jackson 1989: 128).

In a sense, the Kuruyuki festival constituted a kind of anti-Day of Camireño Tradition, in that it was a Guaraní-dominated setting in which non-Guaraní people could (and did) participate, but in which the Guaraní actors were certainly not silent. The cultural items and practices on display there had been produced for consumption of Guaraní and non-Guaraní alike, including the pots made by the women from Cañón. While the pottery project in 2007 had produced many pots, only a few women had taken it upon themselves to make pottery the following year, and all the pots from Kaami combined fitted on a single stand. I was put in charge of selling them. There was a great mixture of people present, with delegations of Guaraní people from as far as Argentina and Paraguay mingling with local *karai*, NGO workers from the highlands, journalists, and even a few foreign tourists and other anthropologists. The atmosphere was friendly and relaxed, despite some quite considerable alcohol consumption by the men, with people sharing food and drink, chairs, and even toilet roll when the need arose. Strolling around in the morning before the stand was set up, I got talking to a young Guaraní woman named Deysi, who had come to sell notebooks, folders, and Guaraní textbooks with beautifully designed covers showing scenes from 'traditional' Guaraní life (women pounding maize in a wood mortar, people dressed up in carnival masks, etc.). Casually but smartly dressed in a short skirt and sleeveless blouse, with her hair put up in a bun, she told me that she was—besides being mother to a little girl, who had arrived unplanned but now was her greatest joy in life—a young Guaraní professional trying to establish a business with her notebooks, which were produced by her boyfriend who worked for the APG. Considering the great interest people showed in her things, this seemed like a judicious ambition.

After failing to attend in 2007 (and thereby leaving the stage to more anti-government-minded voices, such as a representative of the Bolivian Oil Company (YPFB) who took the opportunity to try to recruit the Guaraní for the cause of 'taking back the gas'), the Bolivian President Evo Morales also finally made an appearance at the Kuruyuki festival in 2008. In the early afternoon, a group of soldiers suddenly marched across the field where the people were gathered, forming a line leading up to the stage. Shortly after, Evo was flown in by helicopter to great effect. Once on the stage, in between welcoming speeches, he was given a straw hat by one of the *capitanes* (which he kept wearing throughout the event, much to the delight of the audience), and a retired *capitana* served him some *chicha* from one of the Kaami pots. Then, to my great surprise, Deysi suddenly entered the stage, welcoming Evo in the name of the 'young Guaraní professionals,' and, after giving him a peck on the cheek and urging him to remember her name, presented him with a couple of her notebooks. When I asked her later whether she had in fact been part of the programme, she said that she had not, but had decided on the spot that it was too good an opportunity to miss. There were more speeches, during which Evo was both praised for his pro-indigenous politics and reproached for the heavy military presence at the festival (the president of the APG, Wilson Changaray, told him, 'We are not used to seeing so many armed men in our meetings—the Guaraní people in itself is security'), and then he himself spoke at length, among other things announcing the passing of a large land grant in favour of the Guaraní people. Evo got to go home that day with several presents in tow, among them Deysi's notebooks and a particularly fine pot handed to him by a smiling woman in traditional dress.

THE RELATIONAL PRODUCTION OF CULTURE

If, then, we take Kuruyuki as our prime example, we might be inclined to see the Guaraní peoples' use of material culture as proof of Guaraní agency, resilience, or even resistance in the face of ongoing *karai* oppression (cf. Albro 2006; Turner 1991). Both this approach and the 'cultural appropriation'

The young Guaraní professionals: Deisy with Evo, Kuruyuki 2008.
Photo by the author.

one discussed above are not wrong, as we can easily see if we juxtapose the figures of Deysi and Alambrito. Comparable in age, and both urban-based young mothers of small children, their respective situations were nonetheless completely different: one self-confident in her ethnicity and ability to produce cultural items that were both modern and traditional, the other relatively powerless and having accusations of 'acculturation' lobbed at her by the very people who would appropriate her culture for their own purposes. However, taken side by side, these examples demonstrate that both approaches are ultimately too narrow to take account of the situation properly. Rather, I think it is at this point worth reiterating a point made by Jean Jackson with regards to Colombian Tukanoa people: 'We are,' wrote Jackson, 'at tines [sic] tempted to overly focus on and reify culture, downplaying the actors and their motives for adapting themselves to changing social conditions [and] actively searching for solutions to particular circumstances' (1989: 135). So rather than trying to figure out who Guaraní culture belongs to and what it is good for, I want to draw attention to the way the production of Guaraní culture is a product of current Guaraní people's embeddedness in various different-scale political, economic, and social systems.

While the opinions held by the people operating within these different systems sometimes converge—for example, the idea that supposedly pre-colonial indigenous culture is more authentic and hence more valuable than present-day Guaraní cultural ways—there are other areas where their agendas are opposed: the jealousy of the local and regional *karai* elites of Guaraní people's 'wealth,' for example, stands in opposition to the national government's attempts to 'develop' them by inserting them more firmly into the markets. The cultural projects of Guaraní and *karai* in the Department of Santa Cruz were in turn two different, and indeed largely opposing, ones in that the Guaraní produced material culture in order to be able to continue their *ñande reko*, their way of being, while the *karai* merely tolerated its persistence as long as it remained in the service of their own politically motivated identity project. While the *comunarios* regarded their ability to work '*tranquilo*' as crucial to their *ñande reko*, *karai* only tended to regard work that was carried out within the margins of the established power structures as valid. In a word, we could say that *karai* Camba identity and culture sought to contain Guaraní '*camba*' identity and culture, both in the sense of 'encompassing' or 'incorporating' its products (*cultura*) and in the sense of 'keeping in check' the lives of the people who produced it (*ñande reko*).

Despite such oppositions, however, ultimately all levels are involved: the state initiates a culture-promotion project that encourages local Guaraní people to produce 'traditional' cultural items, which get appropriated as symbols by regional elites and other *karai* for their struggle for more autonomy from the selfsame state's government, and which the Guaraní people sell at an international event celebrating their survival and revival as a people in the face of colonial and post-colonial oppression. In short, cultural production cannot be ascribed exclusively to the producers, nor can we pin down a single purpose it serves. 'Guaraní material culture' is not just a product of Guaraní labour and creativity, but also of the communities' embeddedness in and entanglements with various wider contexts, in which there is an interplay between indigenous people showing initiative and reacting to the demands made on them by others. This does not mean that contemporary Bolivian Guaraní culture is in some way less authentically Guaraní than that of the time of the *kereimba*. Rather, it is to say that contemporary Bolivian Guaraní culture is just that: *contemporary Bolivian* Guaraní culture. Its production is, in a word, a relational process (as I suspect all cultural production everywhere has always been, albeit in different ways and to different degrees).

NOTES

1. One frequent example was having people answer questions of where someone had gone with the rather vague words: 'Over there!,' pointing in the indicated direction. This even happened once when I asked some children where a certain path was leading. As Peter Gow remarked on the imprecision in Piro narratives: one either knows where 'over there' refers to, or it doesn't matter to one in the first place (1995: 51).

2. Since February 2008, this ministry has been known as the Ministry of Cultures.

3. In Tylor's classic definition, 'Culture or Civilization, taken in its wide ethnographic sense, is that complex whole which includes knowledge, belief, art, morals, law, custom, and any other capabilities and habits acquired by man as a member of society' (1871: I, 1).

4. For an exploration of changing ideas pertaining to the 'authenticity' of indigenous material culture and the ways in which they affect indigenous people, see, e.g., Clifford (1988); Conklin (1997); Theodossopoulos (2010).

5. See, e.g., this excerpt from a book by the Cruceño hobby historian Orlando Mercado Chávez (2011: 158): 'The *criollo* and *mestizo* society [of the Andes], because of the degrading sociological situation and the aggressiveness of the environment [*naturaleza*], is constituted by two-faced individuals of traitorous, false, and hypocritical qualities. . . . The aggression of these two-faced individuals of the Andean home country is carried forward against the *mestizo* nation and cosmopolitan ethnic group [made up] of Spanish and other peoples such as the Tupi-Guaraní. . . . Because our cosmopolitan society is [a] welcoming [one] because of its inclusion, without any discrimination of race and culture, of people from all over the world, and moreover developed under the hospitable influence of the descendants of the great autochthonous nation of the Tupi-Guaraní peoples. Also, for having lived since [the time of] our ancestors in balance with the benignity of nature itself, because the nation of the plains and the Chiriguano Cordillera to which we are referring was populated by savage tribes who lived free, taking advantage of the goodness of nature and its ecology.' Interestingly, the environmental determinism underlying the author's argument in this passage constitutes a direct inversion of the environmental determinism of the early colonial era that found 'high' and 'low' societies residing in the continent's highlands and lowlands, respectively (see chapter 1).

6. Spanish: 'maid.' The term has a double meaning in Latin America, where the practice of taking in children from poor (often indigenous) families and raising them (Spanish: *criar*) in return for their labour is widespread (cf. Ortiz 2009: 20).

7. *Día de la tradición camireña*; a holiday commemorating the founding of Camiri in 1935 that is celebrated every first Sunday in November.

8. *Tipoi* are traditional women's dresses of the Guaraní. They are nowadays mostly worn on special occasions. '*Arete guasu*' is Guaraní for 'big fiesta,' the biggest Guaraní festival of the year that was traditionally celebrated at the time of the maize harvest and has since become conflated with the celebration of carnival (see chapter 3). Camireños use the phrase metonymically to refer to a Guaraní-derived dance that is done with one slow step followed by two fast ones and is often danced in a circle at fiestas.

9. Cf. Taussig (1987: 23): '[The situation at the Putumayo rubber frontier in the early 20th century] seems to have been a situation in which rights to Indians were similar to rights to farm the forest. The Indians were there for the taking. . . . The first white to get into one of the large communal houses with perhaps upward of one hundred Indians and press trade goods upon them brought to fruition his "rights of conquest."'

10. Geographically speaking, Camiri is in fact located on the outskirts of the Chaco region, between the eastern foothills of the Andes and the River Parapetí.

11. This reflects what Bret Gustafson, writing about Santa Cruz, has called the urban elite's 'gendered and raced codes for the legitimate occupation of public space' (2006: 372).

12. See also Gustafson (2009: 63): 'For karai the region is imagined as one of centers of *cristianos* or *blancos* and peripheries of rural *cambas* (derogatory, Indians, Guarani). Karai centers extract labor, agricultural commodities, and cultural symbols from the Guarani periphery. In this spatial template, the camba subject must remain in its place and under control. Cambas may only enter karai spaces as silent laborers or spectators.'

13. The first part of the slogan is a wordplay on the name of Evo Morales's party, the Movimiento al Socialismo (MAS), and translates as 'No more Evo.' The second part ('Rubén is autonomy') refers to the Prefect of Santa Cruz, Rubén Costas, who was one of the most fervent proponents of departmental autonomy.

14. See, e.g., Caballero Espinoza (2008: 8): 'In our historical context, we have always thought of the Iyambae, that is . . . autonomy . . . an autonomy to be able to manage our own affairs by ourselves, and it has been thanks to the effort of our grandfathers, of our *capitanes*, that a project has been set up, a statute is set up, a PDDI [development plan of the indigenous district] is set up, and then on this base it has been possible to keep working.'

15. The term *originario* has its roots in the Andes of the colonial era, when forced labour obligations (*mita*) caused many indigenous people to escape from their communities and settle on the lands of others. These so-called '*forasteros*' were opposed to the '*originarios*' who remained in their home communities (*comunidades de origen*) (Chocano Mena 2000: 181). Today, the word is often used interchangeably with *indígena*.

16. Kathleen Lowrey has noted very similar attitudes toward Guaraní people among non-Guaraní Paraguayans: '[T]he Guaraní who live in the Paraguayan Chaco generally enjoy higher incomes than their Bolivian counterparts: their houses are made of bricks instead of mud, many families own one or more motorcycles, [and] it is equally common to have a TV. . . . Such possessions would be unthinkable for the great majority of the Bolivian Guaraní, as also for a majority of the other indigenous groups of the Paraguayan Chaco. Because of this, one commentary that is often heard from the nonindigenous residents of the area is that "the Western Guaraní don't seem to be indigenous," or even more critically, that they "aren't" indigenous. This last comment is related to the fact that nowadays being "indigenous" can bring with its certain advantages, advantages from which some critics think the Western Guaraní should not benefit' (2007: 3).

17. Thanks to the internet, articles and opinion pieces on this subject have in recent years reached a vast international audience via online newspapers (Dastagir 2017; Latton 2016), the blogosphere (Feris 2017; Garduño 2017), and social media sites such as Facebook. These concerns even find an echo in academia itself in the debate, initiated by indigenous scholars like Zoe Todd, about whether the temporarily trendy 'ontological turn' that sees itself as an academic decolonising project of sorts (Holbraad et al. 2014) is in fact just another instantiation of the colonial legacy of white 'Western' supremacy, in that it still largely excludes scholars and other knowledge holders from the cultures it purports to celebrate (Todd 2016).

Chapter Seven

Changing Alliances

The Elusive Position of Guaraní
Comunidades in Local and Regional Politics

As I discussed in the previous chapter, the Guaraní featured in the daily lives of many Camireños as a silent presence at best. One brief interruption to this trend came in Rubén Costas's election campaign preceding the recall referendum (*referéndum revocatorio*) called by President Evo Morales in August 2008. A main feature of the *autonomistas'* propaganda, Guaraní people were suddenly brought into the Camireños' public consciousness as speaking subjects. However, events earlier the same year expose these appearances of Guaraní people in the service of the Prefecture, if not as political ventriloquism, then at least as ideological filtration. During these events, the stubborn colonial attitude toward indigenous people that remained common among the *karai* populations of the region (especially the landowning classes) manifested itself in perpetrations of physical violence in response to attempts by the MAS government and the APG to carry out a long-overdue inspection of haciendas in the contested zone of Alto Parapetí. This chapter looks more closely at the infiltration of local social configurations into municipal and departmental politics. The consequences of the activation of these links during a time of national crisis challenge the idea of a decentralisation of power to the municipal level as envisaged by the Popular Participation Law (LPP) of 1994, and further demonstrate the inherent instability of the alliances between Guaraní organisations and local governments that had been brought about by this decentralisation. This instability makes it difficult to give any account of how a community like Cañón de Segura 'fits' into a broader politics, which leads us to question the extent to which indigenous communities can be *positioned* in this political landscape.

THE RECALL REFERENDUM OF 2008

The recall referendum, the first of its kind ever to be held in Bolivia, in which Bolivians were asked to either confirm or reject the mandates of the President of the Republic and eight of the nine departmental prefects,[1] was a response to the increasing cries for autonomy coming from the *media luna* departments. Beginning with Santa Cruz the previous December, these departments had drawn up their own 'autonomic statutes,' declarations of their political self-determination within the Bolivian state. These were, however, met with rejection by the National Electoral Court, which declared them unconstitutional (Assies 2011: 109), as well as wide-ranging international disapproval. The ballot paper used in the referendum contained two questions, arranged one below the other:

> *'Do you agree with the continuation of the process of change led by President Evo Morales Ayma and Vice President Álvaro García Linera?'*

and

> *'Do you agree with the continuation of the politics, actions, and management of the Prefect of the Department?'*

Each of these questions then offered the options of answering 'yes' or 'no' by ticking the relevant box.

Campaigning was fierce on both sides, as well as slightly misleading: since at least in Santa Cruz the MAS stood in opposition to the Prefecture, and the Prefecture of Rubén Costas was certainly opposed to the government of Evo Morales, neither party restricted their campaigns to advertising their own cause but took the opportunity to campaign against the opposition at the same time. As a result, the slogans *'No arriba, sí abajo'* ('no above, yes below') and *'Sí arriba, no abajo'* ('yes above, no below') could be heard and seen everywhere in the weeks before the referendum, creating the erroneous impression that it was only possible to vote 'yes' on one of the questions and 'no' on the other. In order to make sure that the population of Santa Cruz Department knew exactly where to place their crosses, the Prefecture broadcast a range of television ads, several of which featured Guaraní people. In one, a Guaraní man visits a Guaraní woman standing next to an open fireplace in a typical *oka* setting, to whom he shows a ballot paper and explains that she has to tick *'no arriba'* (to say no to Evo) and *'sí abajo'* (to say yes to the Prefect). This is repeated several times to make the slogan of *'no arriba, sí abajo'* stick; the man then tells the woman, 'So you know what to do on the tenth.' Another ad shows the mayor of Camiri at the time, Gonzalo Moreno, giving a public speech in which he praises Rubén Costas, thanks to whom the rural population now has electric light—this, he says, really is progress!

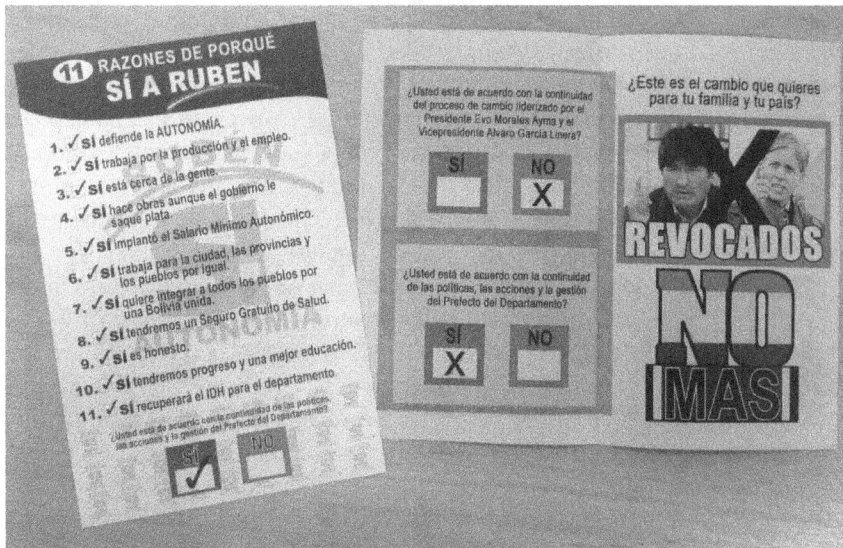

'*No arriba, sí abajo*': propaganda leaflets in support of the Prefecture and in opposition to Evo, Camiri 2008.
Photo by the author.

On the ground, things looked a little different. Costas's 'progressive' electricity project, which promised electricity to all the *comunidades* within the municipality of Camiri, had first reached Cañón in August 2007 and was projected to finish in October. As with the municipality's housing project about which I had been hearing (see chapter 4), people awaited the arrival of the electricity with a mixture of worry and anticipation. Everyone agreed that 'it wouldn't be the same anymore' after the *comunarios* could stay up at all hours and watch TV in their own houses, but while some looked forward to the benefits being able to use appliances such as refrigerators would bring, others worried about the potential increase of unspecified 'bad habits,' as if the wires connecting Cañón to the town might carry the negative aspects of the *karai's* lifestyles along with their electricity. Besides, people were not very clear about how this new luxury was to be afforded—the message was that each family would have to pay for their own consumption, but how much that would be, or how the poorer ones would afford it, were issues that remained unresolved. Such worries aside, however, people remained excited about the prospect, and the more NGO-accustomed *comunarios* assimilated it into their discourses about the *comunidad*'s 'development' and 'achievements' (see chapter 2).

As was the case with other projects, the *comunarios* were expected to contribute a 'return service' (*contraparte*) toward the execution of the electricity project. Thus, men from the *comunidad* were working in collaboration with employees of the Rural Electricity Cooperative (CRE) to put up poles along the main road and closer to the more secluded houses and draw the cables between them. October came with some work still left to do, so a new target date for completion was set for Christmas 2007. However, although the poles and cables had been finished by the time I left Cañón for a couple of months in March of 2008, there was still no sign of any electricity, and by the time I finished my fieldwork altogether in mid-September of the same year, the 'electrification' of Cañón was only just beginning.

This delay did not fail to make an impression on the *comunarios*. On the first day of the fiesta of the community's patron saint, the Virgin of Copacabana, on 04 August, I found myself standing next to Don Aurelio and the *karai* husband of one of the APG leaders whose family lived in Cañón, as I watched the procession of the Virgin in the schoolyard. Chatting about this and that, we got talking about the upcoming referendum, so I asked for whom they were intending to vote. Both asserted that it would have to be Evo. The generally highly popular 'Juancito Pinto' (a yearly bonus of Bs. 200 for all schoolchildren in their first eight years of schooling) was given as one of Evo's merits: both men agreed that such a thing had never been seen before, under any president. Rubén Costas, on the other hand, the APG woman's husband said, was using the *comunarios* for his political purposes; for example, he had promised them electricity, but only two families had it thus far, so it all looked like a big swindle.[2] Besides, Costas was telling lies to discredit Evo, such as that it was Evo's fault that prices in the Camiri market had been rising of late. Really, he said, it was the vendors putting the prices up, not Evo.

The 'contract' between the *comunarios* and the Prefecture that was implied in the electrification project—that is, electricity in return for votes—thus seemed to have broken down because of the Prefecture's perceived failure to deliver the promised electricity.[3] However, neither the fact that, as the date of the referendum approached, there were mostly only poles with cables to show for the Prefecture's efforts but no electricity, nor the fact that the *comunarios* were on the whole unimpressed with the outcome of the project and were therefore not inclined to give their votes in return, stopped the Prefecture from using the electrification project in their television ads in a rather over-enthusiastic way ('Thanks to Rubén Costas, the rural population now has electricity . . .'). Leaving aside the suspicion I could not shake, that the entire project had been part of the campaign in the first place, within the context of the campaign what had really been done in the *comunidades* was clearly not all that important. Notwithstanding that the Prefecture may have lost some *comunidades* due to the non-fulfilment of its promises, the televised images of men putting up poles, supported by the local mayor's assertion that 'this truly was progress,' could still serve in the attempt to convince others.

STICKS AND CARROTS: *AUTONOMISTA*
RESISTANCE TO PLANNED LAND REFORM

The heavy targeting of Guaraní people in the Prefecture's televised propaganda was not arbitrary but tactical. It was aimed to win over a part of the population that had already been alienated by the Prefecture's *autonomía* antics and later outright antagonised by the actions of *media luna*-affiliated landowners earlier the same year. The Assembly of the Guaraní People (APG) disapproved of the Prefecture's plans because it saw them as incommensurate with the Guaraní's own plans for autonomy, which was to be built on ideas of solidarity, egalitarianism, and freedom (APG ed. 2007). The force of these sentiments is demonstrated by this extract of a speech given during an APG meeting that was held in July 2007 to discuss the formulation of a Guaraní autonomic statute:

> The *karai* is individualistic, there is always someone who wants to be in authority, and this is what's happening with the departmental autonomy. The *karai* call this monarchy, that is, the concentration of the power of decision making. How is it possible that we should all be peons of the Prefect of Santa Cruz? That would mean a step back, when what we want is to live in freedom. . . . The departmental government that wants this departmental autonomy has an aristocratic attitude. What does an aristocratic government mean? It's the government of a few; it brings together a few; it doesn't include all. That's why we say, 'Death to the oligarchs!' (Montenegro 2007: 10–11)

The imagery of the Cruceño leadership as aristocrats under whose autonomy the Guaraní would live as peons sums up the unequal standing on which the Cruceño elites were used to dealing with the indigenous people of the department. The Guaraní were not the only ones who worried about the impact of the Cruceños' proposed autonomy: on 31 March 2008, representatives of the five indigenous groups of Santa Cruz (Chiquitano, Ayoreo, Yuracaré-Mojeño, Guarayo, and Guaraní) got together in the departmental capital to sign a resolution rejecting the Cruceños' autonomic statutes, which they called 'exclusionist, separatist, racist, illegal, and unconstitutional' (Resolución de Rechazo . . . 2008). Along with this, they presented their own declaration of autonomy, which included a call to the national government to ratify this autonomy by law, and a declaration that the five groups would not be participating in the 'arbitrary and unconstitutional referendum' (ibid.) that had been called by the Prefecture for 04 May to vote on the ratification of the departmental autonomist statutes.

Among the criticisms made of the Cruceño Autonomic Statutes at the time, one particular bone of contention was its treatment of the issue of land ownership. While the central government was taking a line of increased scrutiny of the legality and use of private estates, with the prospect of expropriation of unproductive properties and those found to be employing workers under conditions of servitude, the Cruceño Statute was formulated in a way that brought the regulation of land ownership and redistribution under the authority of the departmental government.[4] Existing indigenous territories were to be respected (Article 103, II), but the Prefecture's specification of 'local citizens' with a 'farming and livestock vocation' (Article 108, II) as the preferred recipients of state-owned lands made it clear that the kind of large-scale expropriation of big landholdings (*latifundios*) that were often owned by cattle breeders to the benefit of indigenous and peasant communities as envisioned by Evo and the indigenous organisations was not within its scheme.

The land issue had put a strain on relations between the Cruceño elites and the government of the MAS from the start; however, the situation began to escalate after INRA decreed the titling and *saneamiento* of a TCO in the disputed area of Alto Parapetí in February 2008. On 27 February, a delegation of 'municipal authorities, cattle ranchers, and the Civic Committee of Cordillera [Province]' expelled the INRA and APG functionaries from the INRA office in Camiri, 'using psychological violence through intimidations and death threats' (Valle Mandepora 2008). When the officials nonetheless tried to go ahead with their planned inspection, they were ambushed by a group of armed men on the property of a US-American landowner and eventually forced to turn back (ibid.; Gustafson 2010: 58).

The conflict reached its culmination on 13 April, when INRA and APG made a renewed attempt to enter Alto Parapetí. Near Cuevo, the convoy was attacked by a crowd of locals that included cattle breeders as well as district officials and schoolteachers, among the latter the mayor of Cuevo (Gustafson 2010: 61). The attackers separated a young Guaraní lawyer from the group and dragged him into the main plaza, where they tied him to a tree and insulted, threatened, and severely beat him for being an ally of the MAS and a traitor to the region (Gustafson 2010: 51).

Apart from being a prime example of the colonial attitudes that were deeply rooted in Cruceño and Camireño life, these incidents further demonstrate the collusion of economic and political elites in the *oriente*. In the words of the Vice-minister of Lands, Alejandro Almaráz, who was with the convoy when it was ambushed:

> The mayor [of Cuevo] is married to the regional army commander. The local military leader is also a landowner. The district attorneys are controlled by the landowners. The landowners are ready to defend their lands with bullets, since that's how they acquired them. The police are pissed that they now have to serve the Indians. Sure, they do not earn much, but their pockets are filled thanks to

'APG—nest of traitors': graffiti on a house wall in Camiri, 2008.
Photo by the author.

these local powers. [Despite the fact that we are attempting to support indigenous claims] we are working from within a state structure that was designed to do the absolute opposite. (Quoted in Gustafson 2010: 59)

The situation in Camiri was much the same. The spokesman for the cattle breeders who had expelled the INRA officials from their office, Ronald Moreno, was one of three deputies of opposition parties to the MAS who were called by the Parliamentary Brigade of Santa Cruz to form a commission to 'investigate' the accusations of Guaraní slavery on Alto Parapetí haciendas (Viceministerio de Tierras 2008b). They did so with the stated intention of 'show[ing]' the lies that Almaráz tells about the topic of slavery' (Moreno, quoted in Viceministerio . . . 2008b). Unsurprisingly, the commission found no evidence of slavery, only 'extreme poverty.' Its findings ended up being disqualified by the national government for 'lack of impartiality' (Ortiz 2009: 14). At the same time, Moreno, himself a landowner as well as a deputy for the opposition party PODEMOS,[5] was one of an official multi-party delegation in charge of the investigation of the same problem (Viceministerio . . . 2008b). He also happened to be the brother of the mayor of Camiri, Gonzalo Moreno (ibid.), and both were close allies of the Prefect of Santa Cruz.[6] Compelled by motivations of supposed ethnicity (Camba vs. Colla) and civic solidarity, and informed by an opinionated local media, the mood among the *karai* population in those days was mostly tense.[7] The violence committed against a delegation that included government officials had cost the hacendados a fair degree of support among the Camireños; however, there was also a lot of confusion about Evo's planned land reform, which resulted in even small local landowners fearing for their property. Objections to Evo's land policies were often standardised, popularised phrases such as 'Giving to those who don't have anything is good, but it mustn't be done by taking away from those who do,' or 'If you've worked hard to build yourself a big house with many rooms, would you say that it's right to force you to take in a bunch of homeless people?'

The above gives us an idea of the complex situation in Camiri at the time. The connections between different sectors of the population blurred the boundaries between matters of local, regional, and national politics, economics, public opinion, and social life to such a degree as to make any such categories almost meaningless. As a result of these connections, the aggravated relations between the Prefecture and the national government also had an impact on the relations between the municipality and the Capitanía Kaami, which had been working together quite amicably on the implementation of various projects in the *comunidades* when I first arrived (cf. Delgadillo Terceros 2008).

One project that seemed to be working particularly well, and which was very popular within the *comunidades*, was that of the school breakfast (see Caballero Espinoza 2008: 45–46). The school breakfast was part of Kaami's 'Intercultural Governance' programme, which it had initiated in 2002 with the assistance of PADEP-GTZ. It was financed by the municipality and coordinated by the Sub-Alcaldía and the Capitanía, which decided how to divide the designated sum up among the *comunidades* that were part of the Capitanía. Once the supplies bought by the Capitanía had reached the *comunidades*, the breakfast—usually consisting of a gruel made from oats or maize—was prepared by the mothers of the schoolchildren, who took turns to cook it and dish it out to the children. The school breakfast was a prime example of the workings of the decentralisation process initiated by the Popular Participation Law of 1994. The Kaami leadership hoped to see this process developed into the kind of indigenous autonomy that was also envisioned by the *comunarios* of Cañón, which would grant them more direct control over the financial resources at their disposal (see chapter 4).

However, with the deterioration of the relations between INRA and landowners in the region, relations between Kaami and the municipality, too, took a turn for the worse. This development manifested itself in various ways, such as the adoption of new discourses about the Guaraní by members of the municipal government (mentioned in the previous chapter) that portrayed them as 'invaders' of the region with no real legal claims to the land. While, however, this historically-based attack bore direct relevance to the land issue, the municipality leadership also resorted to accusations of corruption in order to undermine the Capitanía's autonomic ambitions. As I learned in a zonal meeting in August 2008, the Alcaldía had accused the sub-mayor of Kaami of pocketing money that was intended for the implementation of projects in the Kaami *comunidades*. The sub-mayor was very upset about the issue and firmly denied the allegations; according to the Kaami leadership, the problem had arisen after some *comunidades* had complained about a cut-back in the provisions they were receiving, which had become necessary due to a general increase in food prices. In any case, there was talk of reversing the process of the decentralisation of projects and putting the municipal government back in charge of the management of resources, which greatly alarmed the Kaami leadership. Concurrently, accusations against the mayor were being voiced by *comunarios* of Puente Viejo, a *comunidad* on the outskirts of Camiri, according to which the mayor had illegally sold part of their community land to a private landowner.

The situation between Capitanía and municipality eventually calmed down again after I left the field, and in a 2010 report by PADEP-GTZ Kaami still appears as one of their most important showcases in successful decentralisation and 'intercultural governance.'[8] There are, however, two important points that can be gathered from the above examples. Firstly, there is the issue of how the state-led process of decentralisation was reversed in Camiri through the particular constellation of power relations in Santa Cruz Department at the time. Rather than bypassing the Prefecture, as was the criticism of the Cruceño Civic Committee when the LPP introduced decentralisation to the municipal level in 1994, it was effectively the national government and its legislation that were being bypassed in this case. It was, in the words of Bret Gustafson, 'a battle over de facto and de jure rule' (2010: 49), in which both sides claimed to be on the side of the law and the Constitution. At the same rate as Evo's government and the Constituent Assembly were churning out laws for the new 'decolonised' state they envisioned, the opposition in the *oriente* kept coming up with arguments that declared their legal reforms illegal in order to justify their increasingly aggressive resistance.[9]

STATES ACTING LIKE MOVEMENTS, ELITES ACTING LIKE STATES: THE AFTERMATH OF THE REFERENDUM

Things really came to a blow when Evo Morales was confirmed as president in the recall referendum on 10 August. In response, the leaderships of the *media luna* called an indefinite civic strike demanding the return of the revenue from the hydrocarbons tax (IDH) to the oil and gas-producing departments. When I left Camiri some three weeks later in September 2008, the strike was still on, and I had to make my way through a series of road blocks obstructing the entire length of the motorway to Santa Cruz. When I finally arrived in the city centre, I walked straight into a riot of masked, bat-swinging autonomy supporters enraged by Evo's victory in the referendum. As I walked the streets that were saturated with the acrid smell of tear gas, I passed the empty and smashed-up office of the national telephone company in the main plaza that had been trashed by a group of rioters earlier that day. I later learned that other government buildings had been sacked as well, and there had also been beatings of indigenous people and suspected MAS sympathisers.

The violence of this '"civic coup" attempt' (Soruco Sologuren 2011: 69) was, however, still outdone by events that took place on 11 September in the town of El Porvenir in the *media luna* department of Pando. Ambushing indigenous and nonindigenous *campesinos* on their way to a (suspected pro-government) union meeting, groups of elite-hired armed thugs massacred eleven people and—recalling the beating of Ramiro Valle Mandepora in the plaza of Cuevo earlier the same year—publicly whipped and tortured several others in the main plaza of Cobija (ibid.).

In an analysis of these events, Ximena Soruco Sologuren explains the *media luna* elites' excessive use of violence as a form of perceived self-defence in the face of world-shattering bafflement at the erosion of the old power structures (2011: 80–83): merging 'colonial reasoning' with 'the modern logic of individualism, the absolute sovereignty of the "I"' (ibid.: 85), these elites sought to annihilate an Other who had failed to fulfil its only acceptable role in an order perceived as natural (ibid.: 84–86). In their attempts to regain control over 'their' territory and 'their' social order, the *autonomistas* claimed for themselves the legitimacy of physical violence that Max Weber famously identified as *the* defining feature of a modern state (Weber 2004: 33). Rather than simply an act of punishment, the attacks on indigenous people and MAS supporters were an expression of a sense of entitlement that claimed a quasi-legal legitimacy for itself, in which the boundaries between being (morally) right and having (legal) rights became blurred, as had also happened in the legal battle over Cañón de Segura (see chapter 1): if the law was against the elites, then the law must be wrong (or even, as people often put it, unlawful).

More innovative than the eastern autonomy supporters' resort to colonial-style violence was their echoing of classical *indigenista* forms of organised resistance. As the national government, itself at least in part the product of decades of indigenous struggle, resorted to 'social movement tactics' that 'relied heavily on public spectacle, seeking to make visible and redefine violence against indigenous peoples and rural workers as an expression of illegitimate feudal and colonial orders that should be dismantled' (Gustafson 2010: 50) in order to consolidate its support base among the population, the departmental and local governments in the *oriente* responded by adopting such means of pressure as the road block (*bloqueo*), which were historically associated with Aymara and later peasant-union-led resistance to (first colonial and then republican) oppressive state leaderships.[10] For almost the entirety of my fieldwork, life in Camiri—and, by extension, Cañón—was frequently interrupted by one protest or another (such as road blocks, civic strikes, or hunger strikes) against Evo's policies and leadership. While the main issues at the heart of these protests were related to the local petroleum industry (demands for a 'proper' nationalisation of the industry; opening of new drilling sites in Camiri; the restoration of the IDH redistribution to its previous form), these tended to get mixed up with issues about departmental autonomy, land distribution, and protests against the Constituent Assembly and the MAS in general, as all the intimately connected interest groups tried to make their concerns heard.[11] Despite the fact that the ones who were most

Road block outside Camiri, February 2007.
Photo by the author.

strongly affected by their actions were the local populations,[12] those Camireños who were involved in these protests saw this adoption of traditionally
indigenist measures of resistance as 'giving Evo a taste of his own medicine.'
In short, while the Eastern elites acted 'state-like' toward 'their' indigenous
people, they also acted 'indigenous-like' in their dealings with the state.

The second point I want to raise with reference to the events described
above is related to this perceived reversal of roles between the highland indigenous sector and the nonindigenous elites in the *oriente* in which the former
relegated the latter from a position of practically unassailable power to that
of 'underdog': that is, the inherent instability of political alliances within the
Bolivian context. As mentioned, the antagonism against Evo and the MAS
that was driven by civic and political leaders in the Prefecture with close links
to local politicians, civics, and landowners had resulted in the demonisation
of Guaraní people, and in particular the APG, as traitors to the region (allies
of the MAS), invaders of land (trying to take away landowners' property),
and false *originarios* (descendants of 'recent arrivals' to the area). This had
culminated in a series of attacks on Guaraní people and their organisations
and supporters: violent, in the case of Alto Parapetí, and moral/ideological
in the case of Kaami. The severity of the violence perpetrated in the former
case, however, caused many Camireños to distance themselves from the
landowners' actions, and, consequently, from the increasingly radicalised
departmental and provincial Civic Committees, thereby deepening the rift
within Camiri's *karai* population that was expressed by the split of the local
Civic Committee earlier the same year.[13] While most Camireños seemed to
agree on the two (unrelated) points that departmental autonomy was a good
idea and that Guaraní people were naturally inferior to *karai* people, many
now took the stance that the expelling of government officials from their offices and public beating of Guaraní people went beyond the entitlements of
the autonomy-propagating elites in the area. Thus, who was on whose side
was by no means always clear, and—echoing the situation in the colonial and
early republican eras (see chapter 1)—alliances between Guaraní and *karai*
interest groups could appear, dissolve, and reappear in quick succession, depending on the political requirements of the moment.

In this confused and increasingly anxious climate, Guaraní people were
suddenly hauled out by the Prefecture of Santa Cruz to appear in Costas's
televised pre-referendum campaign. Although some Guaraní *comunidades*
and *capitanías* did in fact support Costas's politics, the tenor in Kaami was
largely oppositional. Nonetheless, the work the men from the *comunidades*
around Camiri carried out alongside the technicians of the CRE in the Prefecture's electrification project also featured in the televised propaganda in
support of Costas. Their voices, however, remained hidden behind that of

Gonzalo Moreno praising the 'progress' brought by Costas's project. The only Guaraní voices for which there was room in the *karai*-dominated public sphere were those that proclaimed their approval of the existing *karai* leadership, within a context that was controlled by the latter. While I am not suggesting that the Guaraní people who appeared in Costas's ads were 'fake,' the ads were certainly a means to filter Guaraní discourses for those suitable for public consumption. In short, only those in agreement with the Cruceño power base were allowed a voice; the others were silenced with stones, whips, and accusations of corruption.

OF ERODED POSITIONS AND FREED CAPACITIES

Like local and regional *karai* uses of Guaraní 'culture' (see previous chapter), the political situation in Camiri and Santa Cruz in 2008 revealed the colonial attitude that remained prevalent among the Cruceño power elites (and, by extension, large parts of the *karai* population), in that Guaraní people's work and voices were only given visibility and audibility within the margin of *karai* approval. The issue was not so much one of giving the subaltern a voice as of having a chosen subaltern give a voice to the Prefecture, an indigenous voice that could speak for the Prefecture on behalf of a population parts of which were being deliberately alienated by factions from among the Prefecture's own power base. What is striking here is the constant reconfiguration of 'realities' in which the described events took place, which made it possible that conflicting messages were given out by the same interest groups not only in quick succession, but at times even simultaneously. Thus, rather than thinking about the changing positions of the various parties in play with each other in this setting as a constant ebb and flow, it may be more helpful to look at them in terms of the alternating activation of different potentialities that co-existed within the same general framework.

This is similar to a point Marilyn Strathern has made in relation to people's capacities to act in different ways: Strathern argues that a focus on the *positions* of subjects is theoretically problematic because it relies on people's identities at any one time being fixed and independent of the perspectives other people take on them. The notion of *capacity* suggests the different roles or relationships in which a person may act. Acting 'in the capacity of an indigenous person' implies the *potential* to enter into certain kinds of relationships without making any claims on the 'actual' identity of persons (Strathern 1988). In the case of the Guaraní, the overall trend was for politically motivated *karai* actors to treat the *comunidades* and their inhabitants as tools to further whatever their current ambitions, which could mean such diverse things as beating them up in order to keep them in check, or allying themselves with them in order to promote their own public image.

However, the Guaraní people involved in politics in the APG and Kaami whom I encountered were on the whole by no means prepared to simply serve as pawns in *karai* politicians' strategy games. On the contrary, the Guaraní leaderships, too, strategically allied themselves with such national and international groups and organisations (be that INRA, NGOs, human rights organisations, or, indeed, the municipal and departmental governments) as they felt could be of use to their aims at any one time. The result of this was a high degree of instability because of the way in which the relationship between different interest groups could change rapidly from one between friends to one between foes, whereby such a change in attitude toward any respective other was not necessarily mutual.

In short, the political situation that Guaraní people in and around Camiri were facing during the time of my fieldwork was highly unpredictable. This was especially noticeable in the crises surrounding *media luna* demands for autonomy. On the one hand, this political fluidity recalled the shifting alliances of the colonial period, in which Guaraní groups could be the allies of other Guaraní or Spanish groups at one moment and attack them as enemies at the next. On the other hand, however, the Guaraní people who formed part of the constellation of changing alliances in the Department of Santa Cruz in the 2000s were not the same 'savages' of old that could be understood by simply relegating them to a box marked '*indios*,' in the sense that they were active participants of the emerging 'decolonised' state whose presence and influence on the political scene could not be ignored. This contemporary political reality, however, clashed with the colonial attitude of the elites. As a result, the elites saw themselves forced to acknowledge the Guaraní as political agents to be taken seriously, at the same time as they sought to position them in line with their understanding of them as ethnically 'inferior.'

To put it another way, the attitudes of the Cruceño elites were somewhat lagging behind the political reality within the country. However, anachronistic though these attitudes were (certainly when viewed from an outside perspective), they had not been that for all that long: as recently as the 1980s, Guaraní people in Bolivia were largely marginalised and subdued (Healy 1982), and even today there are still those who live in virtual slavery on privately owned haciendas. Bearing this in mind, the Cruceño elites' 'bipolar' approach to the Guaraní in alternately subjecting them to colonial-style violence and wooing them with electricity projects is not all that surprising. In this context, questioning where the *comunidades* 'fit' into the local and regional political landscape is a relatively fruitless exercise. Rather, the difficulty in determining their position on the part of the local and regional elites is an interesting fact in itself, as it reveals the Guaraní as people whose significance within local politics was sufficient for *karai* parties' claims on them granting them multiple and often conflicting capacities for political agency. It may be that the effect of the empowerment of *indigenista* politics in Bolivia in recent decades has been precisely to erode the 'position' of indigenous people in order to free exactly these capacities.

NOTES

1. The Prefect of Chuquisaca Department, Savina Cuellar, had only been elected in June of the same year and was therefore exempt from the referendum.

2. This was not the only time I heard this, and the view that the Prefect had 'lied' about the electricity was even expressed by a member of the Kaami leadership in a zonal meeting the same month.

3. It should be added that Guaraní people are notorious for their unpredictability as voters and the way representatives of political parties often leave with the impression that their cause is being received with favour along with their campaign presents, while in reality the Guaraní merely see them as bringers of 'free stuff' (cf. *Plan Desarrollo* . . . 1986b: 55–56). Thus, it is impossible to say whether the actual completion of the electricity project within the promised timeframe would in fact have changed the *comunarios*' (electoral) minds.

4. Article 171, III of the Statute of the Autonomous Department of Santa Cruz stated: 'The Departmental Institute of Land is a decentralised institution of the Departmental Executive, under the tuition of the corresponding Departmental Secretary, and is responsible for the execution of the ordering (*saneamiento*) of farming and livestock property, regulation of land ownership laws, and application of the policies pertaining to the possession, dotation, awarding, distribution, and expropriation of lands in the Autonomous Department of Santa Cruz.'

5. The 'Democratic and Social Power,' a right-wing party opposed to the MAS that was created out of the 'Nationalist Democratic Action' (ADN) in 2002. The name is a pun: *podemos* in Spanish means 'we can.'

6. Bret Gustafson has called the local elites with ties with Santa Cruz dominating Camiri's municipal government at the time 'a political mafia of sorts' (2011: 179).

7. Having said this, the hold of the Santa Cruz Civic Committee on the civics of Camiri was already waning by the time the recall referendum was coming up, as was made manifest by the split of the Camiri Civic Committee earlier that year (see previous chapter). However, rather than easing the tense atmosphere among the population, this development only added an additional layer of confusion to an already chaotic situation. When, for example, the *autonomista*-loyal Civic Committee called a general strike at the beginning of August, a lot of people were unsure about what to do, as according to the other Committee the strike was not happening.

8. A 2010 report quotes Modesto Condori, the Director of *Comunidades* of the Ministry of Autonomy, as calling Kaami 'the best experience there is in Bolivia in the field of intercultural and indigenous governance' (Condori, quoted in PADEP-GTZ 2010: 15).

9. These included the following: The new Constitution is illegal because the MA-Sistas were keeping Constituent Assembly members of opposition parties away from the voting sessions by having armed guards keep them from entering the building or secretly organising meetings in remote places. (In the MAS version, those opposition members deliberately kept away to boycott the sessions.) Besides, the Assembly should have discussed the issue of the departmental autonomies, on which there had been a public vote, instead of talking about regional and indigenous autonomies, on which there had been none. The recall referendum is illegal because it will take more votes to vote Evo out than it took to vote him in. The redistribution of the IDH to such uses as the old people's pension (*renta dignidad*) is illegal because it robs the people of money that was designated for the improvement of the infrastructure of departments and municipalities in previous legislation (i.e., the Hydrocarbon Law 3058 of 17 May 2005 and modifying Supreme Decrees).

10. In the 1980s, the *cocalero* movement came to the forefront of organised union action in the highlands and, by enlisting the support of other highland peasant unions, managed to organise numerous road blocks and other protests, which in various cases succeeded in causing the state to modify its policies in areas such as 'market control, local rural development, and programs for cocaleaf eradication' (Healy 1991: 91).

11. Occasionally, these more overtly political protests were interspersed by protests of more defined sectors of the population, such as, e.g., a market vendors' protest against the restriction of imports of used clothes in 2007.

12. The modern-day road block is a curious animal that really deserves a study of its own: since towns often opt to block the access to roads in their immediate vicinity, their own population tends to end up at least as inconvenienced as those coming from outside. In the case of Camiri, this frequently resulted in the spontaneous emergence of trading relationships between locals and those they were blocking, as the locals ran out of food supplies and lorry drivers immobilised on the motorway saw their cargoes threatened by the heat. Apart from complicating the lives of the Camireños themselves, the road blocks also aggravated the situation of people in the surrounding *comunidades*, who had to either go through considerable trouble to get their produce to the Camiri markets or accept a reduction in their incomes that in many cases put a serious strain on the household.

13. One of the most dramatic demonstrations of the conflict of interest that could be created for individuals who were invested in both the *karai* and Guaraní sides at this time was the case of a friend of mine who not only had a longstanding involvement with Guaraní organisations and a deep interest in Guaraní culture, but who was also a local landowner and convinced *autonomista*, and as such played an important role in the provincial civic movement. While he maintained both these positions for a while, it appears that he got swept away by the pro-Santa Cruz current in the end: one of the last times I met him, he told me that he was doubtful whether there were in fact any Guaraní people in Bolivia anymore, as most had lost their traditions and language by now. Later, I found out that the APG had denounced him (along with other political and civic personages in the department, province, and municipality) as 'servants of CONFEAGRO [the Bolivian Agriculturalists' Confederation], the COMITÉ PRO SANTA CRUZ, and the separatists of the MEDIA LUNA' (APG 2008; capitals in original).

Conclusions

In 2016, ten years after I first started my fieldwork, I finally got the chance to return to my old field site. As expected, there had been some changes. Most dramatically, the number of houses in Cañón had almost doubled to about fifty, and several of them were now made of bricks. The electricity that had featured so prominently in Rubén Costas's referendum campaign of 2008 had, I knew, arrived shortly after I left the field, a fact that was advertised by the blaring of televisions from some of the houses. At first, I hardly knew where I was, until Lupe rescued me and suggested that she give me the tour of the new 'improved' *comunidad*.

The economy of *proyectos* had left its mark: the school had acquired a set of working toilets and a roof for the football pitch, and facing it a new building was housing the *comunidad*'s very own tractor. A little down the hill from my old house, a new meeting hall had been built, which was, however, being used as storage for the bags of sugar, boxes, and tools required for the much extended honey project that already comprised several dozen beehives. The once-popular sheep project, meanwhile, had died a death, with too many sheep straying up into the mountains and getting killed by 'tigers.'

We went on to visit some of the houses of my old friends and acquaintances, and I was glad to see that—excepting a couple who had taken their families to live in Camiri—they were all still there. Many of the people I had known as children had grown up and now had children of their own, their new houses crowding round those of their parents, grandparents, and siblings. The adults, on the whole, seemed little changed; Doña Apolonia, who rushed to meet me and squeezed me tight when she saw me coming, seemed in fact to have rejuvenated herself, her formerly grey hair having turned jet black. When I asked her about it, she told me that one of the other market women had suggested that all the older women dye their hair because

219

it would make it more likely that people would buy from them. She said she went to Camiri almost every day now to sell *chicha* and other products. When I asked whether she or her granddaughter still wove bags or made pottery, she said they had both given up on it. Even the *arete guasu*, it seemed, wasn't being celebrated anymore. When I asked why, all I got was a wistful, '*Por qué será*'—'I wonder!' 'People here aren't looking after their culture,' one man said. Itanambikua, meanwhile, home of Kaami's most renowned dance troupe, seemed to have further strengthened its cultural focus, despite its much closer proximity to Camiri.

Cañón's connection to Camiri had certainly intensified, with taxis going back and forth much more frequently and longer into the night, and many *comunarios* now owning mobile phones they could even use in the *comunidad* without having to climb one of the surrounding hills to get a reception. The feared town layout hadn't arrived with the new houses, but people remained ambivalent about them. Big compared to most of the adobe ones, with a square layout a quarter of which was taken up by a tiled patio, and boasting bathrooms and large glass windows, they were, all the owners I spoke to agreed, definitely an improvement on the old houses. This assertion was, however, invariably followed by some criticism. Most people said that they disliked the windows, which were very large and easily permitted sunlight and the curious gazes of others to enter into the rooms, and some lamented the inflexibility of the design that didn't allow for any adjustments to particular families' needs. Lupe's sister, who continued to live in Camiri and hold a position with the APG, blamed the ever-present televisions for the intrusion of bad habits in some *comunidades*, where she said many young people had started smoking marijuana or engaging in prostitution.

Camiri, too, was much 'improved': it now had a bus station, several of the hotels were advertising wi-fi, and a lot of new shops had sprung up all over the centre, including an arts and crafts centre up the road from the Capitanía Kaami that was selling local Guaraní products such as pots, masks, and *tipoi*. The plaza had acquired a new monument, an imposing array of seven statues commemorating the Cruceños' 'first cry for freedom' from Spanish rule in September 1810, as a plaque bearing the names of Rubén Costas and Gonzalo Moreno informed the observer.

More surprisingly, Camiri (as well as Santa Cruz) sported a fair amount of pro-Evo propaganda, with cute Evo cartoon faces alongside slogans such as 'With Evo, we do have a future' painted on open sewers, walls, and even mountains along the motorway. Camiri's new mayor, it turned out, was a MASista—a thing that would have been unthinkable at the time I had last been there some eight years before. In Cañón, the political tide had turned the other way: Evo, I was told, had been in office too long and was getting 'tired,'

'With Evo, we do have a future': graffiti on a wall in Camiri, 2016.
Photo by the author.

and the same people who had been telling me about the former mayor's vices were now filled with nostalgia for the time of his leadership. When I asked about the problems people had told me they had had with him, one *comunario* said that while it was true that there had been some at first, they had got over them after a while. At least, several others said, the old mayor had 'done things,' whereas this new one hadn't 'done anything yet.'

The disillusionment with Evo and his politics went further than Cañón or even Kaami. After the lowland indigenous populations' and organisations' opposition to the government's planned 'development' of the Isiboro-Securé National Park and Indigenous Territory (TIPNIS) escalated in 2011, the lowland indigenous umbrella organisation CIDOB had been taken over by a government-friendly leadership (Postero 2017). The APG had separated from CIDOB in protest in 2015, citing CIDOB's partiality and failure to back the Guaraní people in their conflict with the state over the compensation payment owed them for the YPFB's hydrocarbons extraction in the *capitania* of Takovo Mora as reasons (Vargas 2015). The Guaraní claimed that the payment had been too small, and that the Ministry for Hydrocarbons and Energy had failed to carry out the previous consultation of affected communities it was legally required to conduct; the ministry, meanwhile, claimed that such a consultation had not been necessary due to the extraction sites' location on private properties bordering the *capitanía*'s lands (Defensoría del Pueblo 2016). In 'retaliation,' as my APG contact put it, the government had excluded the APG from access to the Fondo de Desarrollo Indígena, a government fund financing projects in indigenous communities with money derived from the IDH that was established in 2015 when its predecessor, the Fondo Indígena, was dissolved amidst accusations of corruption and mismanagement of funds on a large scale (CNN Español 2015).

In this situation of relative financial insecurity, the YPFB swooped in with the promise of alternative funding in the form of compensation payments for the exploration of potential drilling sites in six Guaraní *capitanías* in Cordillera Province, including Kaami. For the previous consultation, a two-day meeting was organised in Cañón, for which a representative of the YPFB Andina had come from the Ministry for Hydrocarbons in La Paz to give a talk. Equipped with a power point, the representative handed out bilingual booklets and started to set out the YPFB's plan of action for the *comunarios* and leaders from the APG, Kaami, and other *comunidades* who had come to participate. There were to be more workshops and local inspections to determine what places had to be avoided, and what the social, environmental, technical, and legal impacts were going to be. The shape the finished project would take, which was hugely important for the Bolivian economy as a whole, she said, depended on the outcome of this investigation.

While most of day one was taken up by the ministry representative's presentation, with only little input by the Guaraní participants, day two was a different matter. More delegations had arrived from other *comunidades*, among them a group of seven from Puente Viejo almost entirely made up by young women, one of whom came pushing a pink pram. The YPFB woman had moved on to crunching numbers for the next planned meetings when the *capitán* of Itanambikua stood up and started to speak. The Guaraní were one people, he said, and they were not going to allow the government to divide them as they had done in the past. Others were quick to follow suit: for the Guaraní, a Kaami representative said, the *kaa*, the forest, was sacred, and the YPFB needed to look at Kaami like at a human body. Besides, they were going to disturb their grandparents, whose remains were buried in clay vessels on Kaami land.

An APG representative added that they regarded the TCO as one unit, a family, with all communities having a right to participate. The ministry, he said, could not be allowed to divide the people by allowing some communities to feel more affected than others. As soon as he had finished, a woman stood up to say that they would either all work together or not at all; after all, they were in *their* TCO, in their home as it were, and things were going to be done their way.

YPFB Woman responded by trying to diffuse the argument: the *comunarios*, she said, already knew what it was like to have a seismic line on their land, so it wasn't necessary to include all of them in all of the meetings. Besides, compensation was going to be paid out per *capitanía*, so no one was going to be excluded.

The debate went back and forth for a bit, until the Kaami official who had spoken before took the word again. They weren't servants of the ministry, he said. The ministry had scientists, but the Guaraní had wise people with empirical knowledge, *ipaye*, who needed to go along on the exploration to make smoke so everything would turn out well. Another man agreed: the elders needed to consult the owners of the land, the *iya*. Perhaps 'those from the state' didn't know how things were done among the Guaraní. Perhaps they didn't understand about the *iya*, and if they didn't, they likely never would; the *iya* were not from their world, and they needed to take someone who knew how to talk to them.

As the Guaraní kept talking of respect for their rights, their culture, and their land, YPFB Woman kept translating their concerns into numbers: two participants per community, four *arakuaa iya* (*ipaye*), eight local consultants. In the final meeting minutes, presented to all workshop participants after a prolonged lunch break, the *mburuvicha reta*'s impassioned speeches were summed up in one line: 'Special attention was paid to the Guaraní practises and customs.' The inclusion of the *ipaye* achieved, however, all participants declared themselves happy to sign the document in their communities' names.

Later that night, I found myself sitting in an old friend's *oka*, speaking to one of her nephews. A former YPFB consultant, he had more insight than most *comunarios* into the workings of the Bolivian hydrocarbons industry. I told him that I couldn't help wondering how much of the technical details in the YPFB's document the *comunarios* and *capitanes* had really understood before they put their names to it. He said that it could indeed happen that the *mburuvicha reta* didn't understand something properly or didn't think of something before signing off on it, and that later problems would emerge because of that, or things that other *comunarios* didn't like, and they would then accuse those who had made the agreement with the company that it was their fault. In order to avoid the participants' not understanding properly, the booklet had been written in Guaraní alongside Spanish, which was quite a novelty. Before, the consultations had used to be so exclusive that the activities of the oil companies had caused divisions among *comunarios* and also between *comunidades* because people were jealous of others receiving more money. He said this was the first time that he had seen the *ipaye* be included in the exploration deal. I asked whether he thought that there was any chance that, if the findings suggested that drilling was too risky, they would abandon the project. He said there was not: *sí o sí*, they were going to do it, because it was a 'national priority.'

The APG's trouble with CIDOB and the YPFB's urgency in pushing their new hydrocarbons project made it fairly clear that there was little the *comunidades* could do to refuse the YPFB's proposals. What they had done, however, was to put on a show of increased unity, and to insist on exerting influence over that which they *could* control; that is, the inclusion of *ipaye* in the initial exploration of the land to be tested for gas deposits. Once again, a particular aspect of 'Guaraníness' was being foregrounded to serve as an identity marker in a particular situation. In doing so, the participants of the consultation meeting also demonstrated what it meant to be progressive in Bolivia's pluricultural era. Rather than giving up on one's indigenous ways and assimilating to a mestizo lifestyle as the colonials would have had it, the new progressive meant bilingual information booklets and respect for forest owners in territories to be opened to industrial exploitation.

There is no denying that such gestures could not resolve the tensions inherent in Evo Morales's double-edged approach to indigenism and industrialisation (see Tockman and Cameron 2014). However, the fact that these negotiations were taking place at all is testament to the long way the indigenous movements have come since their coming-into-being. Since the time of my fieldwork, indigenous movements as well as individuals have also increasingly embraced the use of digital media, which has given them a much larger platform than before. I follow my old friends' Facebook posts on local scandals, environmental disasters, and cultural events, and with figures like the sociologist and anthropologist Elías Caurey, who runs his own blog and twitter account,[1] the 'young Guaraní professional' many of my acquaintances used to promote as an ideal to aspire to has finally emerged into the public consciousness (Díaz Arnau 2018). How these tensions will play out in the future, with the climate crisis threatening Guaraní *comunidades* with ever more extreme droughts and floods and resistance against hydrocarbon extraction increasing on a global level, and with Bolivia entering a new political era after the ousting of President Evo Morales in November 2019, remains to be seen.

* * *

In this book, I have explored the history of Cañón de Segura, a Guaraní *comunidad* in the southeastern lowlands of Bolivia. Both of these notions, history and *comunidad*, are contested: there is no one version of history, any more than there can ever be a definitive *communidad*. One aim of this study has been to examine the politics of specific claims on the history of *comunidad* and the uses to which the notions of 'history' and 'community' are put in the *oriente*. This cannot be a purely conceptual exercise. The *comunidad* of Cañón is home to very real people; a second aim has therefore been to describe the ways in which the lives and activities of these people constitute the *comunidad* as they see it. Taken together, these two lines of discussion make the concept of *comunidad* highly problematic: it is both created in a specific history of claims and contests, and embodied in the lives that people lead.

These multiple registers of *comunidad* are clearly evident in relation to law. My own deliberately partial version of 'Bolivian and Guaraní history,' pieced together from the works of other scholars in order to provide a narrative with a particular capacity and function, is combined with a historical account of a different order that zooms in on the issue of captive communities. This second-order narrative, while also being a product of my own assembling activity, draws on a different type of sources, that is, documents that were produced (or appropriated) by the workings of the Bolivian legal system. On one level, this narrative tells us something about the legal situation of, and complications created for, *comunidades cautivas* and their inhabitants before the passing of the INRA Act of 1996. However, on another level, it also alerts us to the high degree to which ideas about 'right' and 'wrong' relating to the legal institution of a *comunidad indígena* as they were held by the people involved in the particular case of Cañón de Segura, were informed by moral orders other than the law (such as, for example, Christian values, national and regional solidarity, and remnants of colonial attitudes about ethnic difference). These different moral orders in turn informed people's representations of the events the documents describe, and which simultaneously constituted the reason for their creation. In the representation of the case that emerges through the combination and juxtaposition of the various documents, we can see how these different moral orders intertwine in a way that makes it impossible to separate 'the legal' out from 'the rest.'

In the case of the *comunarios*, representations of their position appear in the documents mostly in a collective form (with the exception of the testimonies given by certain individuals in court). This general position is brought down to the level of personal experience by the memories of the *comunarios* presented in the second chapter. While the main tenor of these more personal representations is the same (that is, the fact that the *comunarios* were justified in their claims and the *patrones*' treatment of them was wrong, and that the move to Cañón constituted a great improvement to their situation), there is great variety in the details remembered by different people and the emphasis they put on different aspects of the occurrences: some mainly focus on the legal proceedings, whereas what is most memorable to others is their personal experience of fear or hardship. These personal perspectives could not be conveyed in this form by the generalised statements of the various representatives purporting to talk for the *comunarios* we find reproduced in the documents. Rather, the memories alert us to the fact that a *comunidad* is not only inhabited by *comunarios* (as the official and supposedly ethnically similar inhabitants of a legally recognised and defined place),[2] but also by *people* with different experiences and perspectives. Put differently, the fact that all the people living in a *comunidad* are *comunarios* should not lead us to assume that they are all the same, or that, indeed, a *comunidad* is a homogeneous and undifferentiated field of human interaction. At the same time, the shared elements of *comunarios'* experiences had created a historical tradition within Cañón that understood 'history' as a finished object with a particular use value. To the *comunarios*, 'history' was a thing of the past, both in its content and in its creation, which further qualified it as a product of the scriptural practice of powerful outsiders. In short, we can see the community as both located within a specific history and a site from which to take a perspective on that history. We might say that Cañón is both contextualised by history and the context for it. This means that the community, while it takes a particular form as a result of specific happenings and actions in the past, and is therefore 'subject to history,' also serves as a resource from which particular kinds of histories can be written, remembered, and used, and as the site of their embodiment in people's lives.

These embodied, intimate life histories, which fall outside of the objectified, textual 'history' *comunarios* used in their relations with outsiders, are to be found in the meanings the *comunarios* themselves attached to the concept of '*comunidad*,' with particular reference to the areas of work, fiestas, spatial organisation, and tensions among the *comunarios* as well as their aspirations for the future. In the case of Cañón de Segura, a rupture that produced a dramatic change in the *comunarios'* circumstances is clearly identifiable in their move from one location to another and the accompanying change in their legal position. This rupture is also discernible in the everyday activities and attitudes of its inhabitants, in that it had become one of the defining features of the ways in which *comunarios* talked about what it meant to live in a 'free *comunidad*.' This material demonstrates the dangers inherent in the continuing regurgitation of 'classic' ethnographic sources about Guaraní culture and society as it remains common in the literature produced by development agencies. Attending to *comunarios'* concepts of *comunidad* demonstrates that these sources are best used in their capacity of historical documents. Used critically in such a way, classic sources can provide useful background information to contemporary ethnographies, and indeed serve to help us identify what changes have occurred within Bolivian Guaraní culture over time. However, they cannot be taken as authoritative sources on *comunidad*, a contemporary social form in continuous flux, and the site and medium of embodied histories.

These changes do not imply a total disjuncture between *comunidad* in the present and Guaraní cultural practices of longer standing. One of the central themes that emerged from *comunarios*' discourses about living free and in peace was that of work. The opposition between the *comunidad* and the *propiedad* of the *patrones* was expressed in people's emphasis on their ability to work '*tranquilo*' (in one's own field, according to one's own timing and capacities). Working *tranquilo* was the kind of work that was performed by *comunarios* (as opposed to peons of a *patrón*), and as such a marker of their identity as 'free' people. However, while the types of work that were carried out by the *comunarios* of Cañón were often recognisable as 'classically Guaraní' (such as the strong emphasis on maize in the arrangement of *chacos* and production of food items), the larger organisational patterns of the past (*motïro*) had been largely reduced to an immediate practical function (the creation of temporary work parties for the accomplishment of larger jobs). As such, the idea of work, whilst remaining essential to people's perception of their own identity, had become removed from its former position at the centre of reciprocal inter- and intra-village relationships and taken on a new significance that better reflected the *comunarios*' lived experience.

I have suggested the communal fiesta as a more fruitful context for understanding reciprocity among contemporary Guaraní people. While again removed from the contexts we find reproduced in classical texts on Guaraní culture (that is, warfare and chiefly banquets), like these now defunct institutions, the fiesta in its contemporary form is of central importance to the reproduction and fortification of community sociality. This was expressed by the activation of kinship and friendship ties in the financing and organisation of fiestas; the positioning of *comunarios* in relation to each other in the ritualistic order of the fiesta as an event; and the cathartic resolution (or at least expression) of conflicts under the license of drunkenness. The 'active ingredient' of the fiesta was the *chicha*, a highly meaningful substance in that it was the product of the combined work of the *comunarios* (sowing, harvesting, chewing, and brewing of maize), and as such a symbol of the *comunidad* itself. In short, fiestas reinforced the *comunarios*' sense of 'belonging,' in the double sense of reminding them of their unity as a group, as well as ascribing each person their proper place within it.

The transformation of Guaraní life as embodied history is equally evident in the spatial organisation of Cañón. The positions of *comunarios*' houses in relation to each other express people's relationships and engagements in community life. However, equally notable in the makeup of Cañón as a place was its high internal mobility. Guaraní people are often represented in the literature as possessing a high tendency toward 'nomadism,' and their *comunidades* a high degree of instability. Here, a tradition of mobility clearly interacts with the legal institution of the *comunidad* and the legal titles associated with it. Many *comunidades* nowadays either possess a title to their land or are trying to obtain one. The fixity of these legal claims meant that the norm in Kaami was certainly for *comunidades* as a whole to stay put, while their internal makeup was in constant flux due to the movements of individual *comunarios* within the community territory. This internal mobility further expressed itself in the movements of animals and objects, and in the re-appropriation of objects and structures to whatever use was in demand at any one time. Cañón as a human settlement was, at the time, relatively new and therefore not yet marked with the traces of generations that could symbolise people's attachment to the place; yet, on the other hand, the very fact that these movements of people, animals, things, and purposes were possible to such a high degree within its boundaries expressed this attachment by constantly reminding people of their status as owners of their own land.

In an important sense, the transformations of Guaraní life, and the constant renegotiation of the notion of *comunidad* I documented in Cañón, are an effect of the tensions and frictions inherent in the community's connections to geographically larger and more powerful social and economic systems. This is apparent in the community's constantly changing and evolving face as its inhabitants sought to 'develop' it toward ever greater improvement. In order to illuminate this desire, I reversed the focus at this point to approach the meaning of *comunidad* from a perspective of absence rather than presence. On the one hand, the '*tranquilidad*' people liked to propose as one of the defining attributes of Cañón was often upset by expressions of jealousy between *comunarios*. This upsetting of order was closely tied up with *comunarios*' ideas about what the *comunidad* was still lacking and what, therefore, needed to be developed, in that both had to do with money: while *comunarios* often negated the fact that money formed an integral part of the *comunidad*'s economy, money was in fact often at the root of *comunarios*' jealousies of each other, and being more financially autonomous further constituted one of their main goals for the future of their *comunidad*. The importance in this lay partly in the *comunarios*' concern about outside forces wanting to turn their *comunidad* into the semblance of a town, complete with the *patrón-peón*-like relationships typical of *karai* forms of organisation. This concern was exacerbated by the sometimes involuntary outmigration of *comunarios* caused by their need to earn money that put a darker spin on their perceived freedom of movement. In short, the ways in which their *comunidad* stood in opposition, not only to the *propiedad*, but also to the town, was one of its central defining features in the eyes of the *comunarios*.

What this book shows above all is that '*comunidad*' is a complex, multidimensional reality that appears in different ways in different contexts. Rather than as an entity possessing certain specific properties, the *comunidad* is perhaps better seen as being constituted by different potentialities that can be activated at different times and by different actors (cf. Strathern 1988). However, these actors were not necessarily the *comunarios*: much as they stressed 'freedom' in their assessments of life in the *comunidad*, this freedom was not total but constituted and limited by various different factors, many of which were created by pressures that originated from outside the *comunidad*.

For one, Guaraní *comunidades* have long been the subjects of governmental and non-governmental development agencies' aims to 'develop' them according to ideas derived from the domain of international development. Within Kaami, these agencies' strong focus on 'capacity building' and the role of leaders revealed certain generalised presuppositions about the organisation of *comunidades* that often co-existed with (N)GO workers' more specific knowledge about Guaraní society and culture. I used CIPCA as an example in order to demonstrate the generic way in which issues pertaining to 'development' were approached by employees of even the most thorough organisations. This generalised notion of development was reflected in the ideas of Guaraní people themselves, who had come to see project implementation, workshop organisation, and capacity building as 'things that were provided by organisations.' Whereas the organisations' aim in providing these services was the creation of a greater degree of autonomy through the encouragement of a 'DIY' system of knowledge dissemination among the populations of the *comunidades*, the *comunarios* rather saw the training of more professionals from among their own ranks as the means to this end.

The notion and status of indigenous communities was also affected by the circulation and contestation of the idea of indigeneity in regional politics. The cultural projects of Guaraní and *karai* people in the Department of Santa Cruz, and particularly Camiri, represented different and indeed largely opposing forms of identity politics. Much of the material culture produced by Guaraní people went to fund efforts to ensure the continuation of their way of life (*ñande reko, teko*), whereby different individuals put different spins on what this way of life entailed, which could—according to their own situation—be more 'traditional' or more 'modern.' In a way, the closing-off of history as 'finished' facilitated the emergence of the latter: by leaving history behind them, the Guaraní had opened up new possibilities of forming relationships with the *karai*. It allowed them to celebrate the warriors of old, at the same time as young people reinvented themselves as 'diplomats' and professionals in the present.

To the *comunarios* of Cañón, their own ability to work constituted one of the most important aspects of their *teko*. *Karai*, on the other hand, continually sought to undermine their move toward more independence by denying the existence of this ability and only regarding work that was carried out within the margins of the established power structures as valid. The *karai* cared for the *teko* only inasmuch as it served their own interests, notably within the context of their own identity project in the service of regional politics, a role that was more easily fulfilled by the products of Guaraní material culture than their own politically questionable status as *patrones*. I have suggested that we can look at this phenomenon in terms of 'containment,' in that *karai* mainstream culture continuously sought to incorporate the products coming from the *comunidades*, at the same time as it tried to control the lives of the people who inhabited them according to colonial-style ethnic hierarchies. Ironically, then, both Guaraní and *karai* people enlisted 'Guaraní culture' in their respective struggles for liberation, even though one of the two parties saw the other one as the very oppressor from whom it sought to liberate itself.

The circulation of identities and their symbols should not be seen in isolation from the embodiment of *comunidad* by definite people, however. This is clear in the field of regional and local politics more generally. Here, too, the same colonial attitudes could be seen at work in the frequent attempts of local and departmental elites to relegate the inhabitants of *comunidades* to a subordinate position in the service of their own political projects. However, once again, the matter was complicated by the Guaraní's strong presence as political actors in their own right, which made reducing them to the position of political pawns (or perhaps 'peons') an ultimately impossible endeavour. Consequently, as the political landscape of the *karai* elites kept shifting along the lines of their connections with each other and other sectors of the population, the *comunidades*, too, changed position within these constellations according to both the manipulations of the elites and their own political strategies. The concreteness and flexibility of these political alignments mean that, rather than looking at *comunidades* as entities whose positions within any political landscape we can try to determine, it is more helpful to see their varying positionings, like the community itself, as the effect of the activation of different potentialities by different actors and/or at different points in time.

There are almost as many perspectives on what a *comunidad* is, should be, or should do as there are people with an interest in them. While I have identified certain larger trends as were present at the time of my fieldwork, the *comunidad* itself eludes us. Whether we see it as a legal entity, a physical place, a group of people, a symbol of culture, an embodiment of rural poverty, or a political unit, none of these perceptions exist independently of each other, nor are the *comunarios* themselves immune to the consequences of the actions of those who would see the *comunidad* in a different way. As a consequence, perceptions, too, are in a constant state of flux. Ultimately, the way people cannot quite agree about what a *comunidad* is tells us more about the lives of the people in it than a singular and integrated account of *comunidad* could ever do.

NOTES

1. Available at: http://eliascaurey.blogspot.com; https://twitter.com/ecaurey?lang =en (accessed 11 September 2019).

2. As illustrated by the memory of Rogelio Torres, non-Guaraní people can in some circumstances become *comunarios* of Guaraní *comunidades*.

Bibliography

Abu-Lughod, L. 1991. 'Writing Against Culture,' in *Recapturing Anthropology: Working in the Present* (ed.) R. Fox. Santa Fe: School of American Research Press.

Albó, X. 2008a. 'Bien vivir = convivir bien.' CIPCA notas 217. Available at: http://cipca.org.bo/index.php?option=com_content&view=article&id=248:zdpa&catid=78:zdpa&Itemid=114 (accessed 12 August 2011).

———. 2008b. 'The "Long Memory" of Ethnicity in Bolivia and Some Temporary Oscillations,' in *Unresolved Tensions: Bolivia Past and Present* (eds.) J. Crabtree and L. Whitehead. Pittsburgh: University of Pittsburgh Press.

———. 1990. *La Comunidad Hoy*. La Paz: CIPCA.

Albro R. 2006. 'The Culture of Democracy and Bolivia's Indigenous Movements,' in *Critique of Anthropology* 26(4):387–410.

Alconini, S. 2002. *Prehistoric Inka Frontier Structure and Dynamics in the Bolivian Chaco*. Unpublished PhD Thesis, University of Pittsburgh.

Álvarez Moreno, R. 2011. 'Propiedad y "dominium" en Castilla a finales del siglo XV: "Celestina" como "civitas non recte instituta,"' in *Celestinesca* (35): 9-42.

Anaya, S. 2004. 'International Human Rights and Indigenous Peoples: The Move Toward the Multicultural State,' in *Arizona Journal of International and Comparative Law* 21: 13–61.

Antezana, L. 1969. 'La Reforma Agraria Campesina en Bolivia (1956–1960),' in *Revista Mexicana de Sociología* 31(2): 245–321.

APG (ed.) 2007. *Ñamometei Ñande Ñemongeta: Construcción del estatuto de la autonomía de la nación guaraní*. Camiri: Ñeeñope Grupo Editorial Guaraní.

———. 2008. 'Pronunciamiento.' 8 April. Available at CIDOB: http://www.cidob-bo.org/index.php?option=com_content&task=view&id=137&Itemid=1.

Ardren, T. 2004. 'Where Are the Maya in Ancient Maya Archaeological Tourism? Advertising and the Appropriation of Culture,' in *Marketing Heritage: Archaeology and the Consumption of the Past* (eds.) Y. Rowan and U. Baram. Walnut Creek, Lanham, New York, Toronto, Oxford: Altamira Press.

Assies, W. 2011. 'Bolivia's New Constitution and Its Implications,' in *Evo Morales and the Movimiento al Socialismo in Bolivia: The First Term in Context, 2006–2010* (ed.) A. Pearce. London: Institute for the Study of the Americas.

Bacchiddu, G. 2016. '"Before We Were All Catholics": Changing Religion in Apiao, Southern Chile,' in *Native Christians: Modes and Effects of Christianity among Indigenous Peoples of the Americas* (eds.) A. Vilaça and R. Wright. London & New York: Routledge.

Belaunde, L. 2001. *Viviendo Bien: Género y fertilidad entre los Airo-Pai de la Amazonía peruana.* Lima: CAAAP/BCRP.

Binswanger-Mkhize, H., J. de Regt and S. Spector (eds.) 2009. *Scaling Up Local and Community Driven Development (LCDD): A Real World Guide to Its Theory and Practice.* E-book available at: http://siteresources.worldbank.org/ EXTSOCIALDE VELOPMENT/Resources/244362-1237844546330/5949218-1237844567860/ Scaling_Up_LCDD_Book_rfillesize.pdf.

Boas, F. 1982. *Race, Language, and Culture.* London & Chicago: University of Chicago Press.

Bonilla, H. (ed.) 1991. *Los Andes en la Encrucijada: Indios, comunidades y estado en el siglo XIX.* Quito.

Bossert, F. and D, Villar 2001. 'Tres dimensiones de la máscara ritual chané,' in *Anthropos* 96(1): 59–72.

Brown, M. 1993. 'Facing the State, Facing the World: Amazonia's Native Leaders and the New Politics of Identity,' in *L'Homme*, 126/128: 307–326.

Butler, B. 2006. *Holy Intoxication to Drunken Dissipation: Alcohol Among Quichua Speakers in Otavalo, Ecuador.* Albuquerque: University of New Mexico Press.

Byrne, D. 1996. 'Deep Nation: Australia's Acquisition of an Indigenous Past,' in *Aboriginal History* 20: 82–107.

Caballero, G., J. Ramírez Mattos, V. Villalta, M. González Lelarge, and S. Ruíz 2010. *Buenas Prácticas: Un camino hacia la autodeterminación–Distrito Indígena Guaraní Kaami, Bolivia.* Camiri: PADEP-GTZ.

Caballero Espinoza, A. 2008. *Iyambae: Gestión pública intercultural para el autogobierno.* Camiri: PADEP-GTZ.

Cabrera, J. 2003. 'Declaración.' Available at: http://www.puebloindio.org/ONU_ info/GTPI03_GuaraniBolivia.htm [accessed 05 January 2021].

Campanera Reig, M. 2012. ¿Campesina o Nativa? Derecho, política e identidad en los procesos de titulación de comunidades en la Amazonía Peruana,' in *Quaderns-e de l'Institut Català d'Antropologia* 17(1):10–24.

Canessa, A. 2014. 'Conflict, Claim and Contradiction in the New "Indigenous" State of Bolivia,' in *Critique of Anthropology* 34(2): 153–73.

———. (ed.) 2005. *Natives Making Nation: Gender, Indigeneity, and the State in the Andes.* Tucson: University of Arizona Press.

———. 1998. 'Procreation, Personhood and Ethnic Difference in Highland Bolivia,' in *Ethnos* 63(2): 227–47.

———. 2007. 'Who Is Indigenous? Self-Identification, Indigeneity, and Claims to Justice in Contemporary Bolivia,' in *Urban Anthropology and Studies of Cultural Systems and World Economic Development* 36(3): 195–237.

Capitanía Kaami 2007. *Manual de Organización*. Camiri.

Carrithers, M., M. Candea, K. Sykes, M. Holbraad and S. Venkatesan 2010. 'Ontology Is Just another Word for Culture,' in *Critique of Anthropology* 30(2): 152–200.

Castañón Pinto, P. 2011. 'Guaraní ¿Cautivos?: Espacio y auto/representaciones,, in *Anales de la Reunión Anual de Etnología n. 22, Sem. IV: Antropología Social y/o Cultural*. Available at MUSEF: http://hdl.handle.net/123456789/283.

Castellanos, D. 2015. 'The Ordinary Envy of Aguabuena People: Revisiting Universalistic Ideas from Local Entanglements', in *Anthropology and Humanism* 40(1): 20–34.

Charlton, R. and R. May 1995. 'NGOs, Politics, Projects and Probity: A Policy Implementation Perspective,' in *Third World Quarterly* 16(2): 237–55.

Chocano Mena, M. 2000. 'La comunidad entre la realidad económica y el discurso,' in *Estado-nación, Comunidad Indígena, Industria: Tres debates al final del milenio* (eds.) H. König, T. Platt and C. Lewis. Cuadernos de Historia Latinoamericana No 8. AHILA.

Clastres, H. 1995. *The Land-Without-Evil: Tupí-Guaraní Propheticism*. Chicago: University of Illinois Press.

Clastres, P. 1977. *Society Against the State*. Oxford: Blackwell.

Clifford, J. 1988. *The Predicament of Culture: Twentieth-Century Ethnography, Literature, and Art*. Cambridge, MA & London: Harvard University Press.

CNN Español 2015. 'Millonario escándalo de corrupción en Bolivia: Investigan desfalco en el Fondo Indígena.' 11 December 2015. Available at: https://cnnespanol.cnn.com/2015/12/11/millonario-escandalo-de-corrupcion-en-bolivia-investigan-desfalco-en-el-fondo-indigena/ (accessed 4 September 2019).

Coello de la Rosa, A. 2005. 'Espacios de Exclusión, Espacios de Poder: La reducción de indios de Santiago de Cercado a la Lima colonial (1568–1590),' in *Estudios sobre América: Siglos XVI-XX* (eds.) A. Gutiérrez Escudero and M. Laviana Cuetos. Seville: AEA.

Colloredo-Mansfeld, R. 1999. *The Native Leisure Class: Consumption and Cultural Creativity* in the Andes. Chicago & London: University of Chicago Press.

Colque, G., E. Tinta and E. Sanjinés 2016. *Segunda Reforma Agraria: Una historia que incomoda*. La Paz: TIERRA.

Combès, I. 2006. 'De los Candires a Kandire: La invención de un mito chiriguano,' in *Journal de la Société des Américanistes* 92(1): 137–64.

———. 2005a. *Etno-historias del Isoso—Chané y chiriguanos en el Chaco boliviano (siglos XVI a XX)*. La Paz: PIEB/IFEA.

———. 2005b. 'Las Batallas de Kuruyuki: Variaciones sobre una derrota chiriguana,' in *Bulletin del Institut Français d'Études Andines* 31(2): 221–33.

———. 1992. *La Tragédie Cannibale chez les Anciens Tupí-Guaraní*. Paris: Presses Universitaires de France.

Combès, I., N. Justiniano, I. Segundo, D. Vaca and R. Vaca 1998. 'Kaa Iya Reta: Los Dueños del Monte.' *Proyecto Kaa Iya*. Santa Cruz: CABI/WCS.

Combès, I. and K. Lowrey 2006. 'Slaves without Masters? Arawakan Dynasties among the Chiriguano (Bolivian Chaco, Sixteenth to Twentieth Centuries),' in *Ethnohistory* 53(4): 689-714.

Combès, I. and T. Saignes 1991. *Alter Ego-Naissance de l'identité chiriguano*. Paris: Cahiers de l'homme, NS XXX.

Combès, I. and D. Villar 2004. 'Aristocracias Chané: "Casas" en el Chaco argentino y boliviano,' in *Journal de la Société des Américanistes* 90(2): 63–102.

Comisión Interamericana de Derechos Humanos (CIDH) 2009. 'Comunidades Cautivas: Situación del pueblo indígena guaraní y formas contemporáneas de esclavitud en el Chaco de Bolivia.' OEA/Ser.L/V/II. Doc. 58.

Conklin, B. 1997. 'Body Paint, Feathers, and VCRs: Aesthetics and Authenticity in Amazonian Activism,' in *American Ethnologist* 24(4): 711–37.

Crabtree, J. 2008. 'A Story of Unresolved Tensions,' in *Unresolved Tensions: Bolivia Past and Present* (eds.) J. Crabtree and L. Whitehead. Pittsburgh: University of Pittsburgh Press.

Crivos, M., M. Martínez, M. Pochettino, C. Remorino, A. Sy, and L. Teves 2007. 'Pathways as "Signatures in Landscape": Towards an Ethnography of Mobility among the Mbya-Guaraní (Northeastern Argentina),' in *Journal of Ethnobiology and Ethnomedicine* 3, 2. Available at: http://www.ethnobiomed.com/content/3/1/2.

Dastagir, A. 2017. 'Is It OK for a White Kid to Dress up as Moana for Halloween? And Other Cultural Appropriation Questions,' in *USA Today*. 23 October. Available at: https://eu.usatoday.com/story/news/2017/10/23/halloween-cultural-appropriation-questions/780479001/ [accessed 04 January 2021].

Davis, S. 2002. 'Indigenous Peoples, Poverty and Participatory Development: The Experience of the World Bank in Latin America,' in *Multiculturalism in Latin America: Indigenous Rights, Diversity and Democracy* (ed.) R. Sieder. Basingstoke & New York: Palgrave MacMillan.

Deere, C. and M. Leon 2001. 'Institutional Reforms of Agriculture Under Neoliberalism: The Impact of the Women's and Indigenous Movements,' in *Latin American Research Review* 36(2): 31–63.

Defensoría del Pueblo 2016. 'Informe defensorial sobre la violación de derechos humanos de la Capitanía Takovo Mora, perteneciente al pueblo indígena Guaraní.' Estado Plurinacional de Bolivia: Canasta de Fondos Suiza-Suecia-Países Bajos. Available at: https://cedib.org/wp-content/uploads/2016/03/VIOLACION-DE-DDHH-TAKOVO-MORA.pdf (accessed 4 September 2019).

De la Cadena, M. 2010. 'Indigenous Cosmopolitics in the Andes: Conceptual Reflections beyond "Politics,"' in *Cultural Anthropology* 25(2): 334–70.

———. 2000. *Indigenous Mestizos: The Politics of Race and Culture in Cuzco, Peru, 1919–1991*. Durham & London: Duke University Press.

———. 1995. '"Women Are More Indian": Ethnicity and Gender in a Community Near Cusco,' in *Ethnicity, Markets, and Migration in the Andes: At the Crossroads of History and Anthropology* (eds.) B. Larson, O. Harris and E. Tandeter. Durham, NC & London: Duke University Press.

Delgadillo Terceros, W. 2008. *Chaco: Experiencia de descentralización intercultural en el distrito indígena guaraní de Kaami*. La Paz: PADEP/GTZ.

Díaz Arnau, O. 2018. 'Elías Caurey y el "guaraní modern,"' in *Correo del Sur*. 8 April. Available at: https://correodelsur.com/ecos/20180408_elias-caurey-y-el-guarani-moderno.html (accessed 11 September 2019).

Dietrich, W. 1986. *El idioma Chiriguano–Gramática, textos, vocabulario.* Madrid: Instituto de Cooperación Iberoamericana.

Dundes, A. 1981. *The Evil Eye: A Folklore Casebook.* New York: Garland Publishers.

Dunkerley, J. 2007. *Bolivia: Revolution and the Power of History in the Present.* London: Institute for the Study of the Americas.

Eade, D. 2007. 'Capacity Building: Who Builds Whose Capacity?,' in *Development in Practice* 17(4–5): 630–9.

Easterly, W. 2005. 'What Did Structural Adjustment Adjust? The Association of Policies and Growth with Repeated IMF and World Bank Adjustment Loans,' in *Journal of Development Economics* 76(1): 1–22.

Eaton, K. 2007. 'Backlash in Bolivia: Regional Autonomy as a Reaction against Indigenous Mobilization,' in *Politics & Society* 35(1): 71–102.

Echevarría, R. 1998. *Myth and Archive: A Theory of Latin American Narrative.* Cambridge—New York—Melbourne: Cambridge University Press.

El Deber. 1991a. 'Denuncia: Sacerdote incita a invadir propiedades ganaderas.' 13 August.

———. 1991b. 'Denuncian que sacerdote instiga a indígenas.' 1 August.

———. 2005. 'Guaraníes, esclavos del siglo XXI.' 2 May.

Equipo Nizkor. 2003. 'Pronunciamiento del Pueblo Guaraní.' Available at: www .derechos.org/nizkor/bolivia/doc/guaranibol.html.

Escobar, A. 1997. 'Anthropology and Development,' in *International Social Science Journal* 49(154): 497–515.

Escobar Córdoba, F. 2006. 'El derecho romano de la propiedad en la doctrina civil colombiana,' in *Criterio Jurídico* 1(6): 311–26.

Fabricant, N. 2009. 'Performative Politics: The Camba Countermovement in Eastern Bolivia,' in *American Ethnologist* 36(4): 768–83.

Fausto, C. and D. Rodgers 1999. 'Of Enemies and Pets: Warfare and Shamanism in Amazonia,' in *American Ethnologist* 26(4): 933–56.

Feather, C. 2010. *Elastic Selves and Fluid Cosmologies: Nahua Resilience in a Changing World.* Unpublished PhD thesis, University of St. Andrews.

Ferguson, J. 1994. *The Anti-Politics Machine: 'Development,' Depoliticization and Democratic Power in Lesotho.* Minneapolis: University of Minnesota Press.

Feris, S. 2017. 'Moana, Elsa, and Halloween,' in *Raising Race Conscious Children.* 05 September. Available at: http://www.raceconscious.org/2017/09/moana-elsa -halloween/ [accessed 04 January 2021].

Fernández García, M. 2009. 'Bolivianos en España,' in *Revista de Indias* LXIX (245): 171–98.

Ferraro, E. 2011. '*Trueque*: An Ethnographic Account of Barter, Trade and Money in Andean Ecuador,' in *The Journal of Latin and Caribbean Anthropology* 16(1): 168–84.

Field, L. 1999. 'Complicities and Collaborations: Anthropologists and the "Unacknowledged Tribes" of California,' in *Current Anthropology* 40(2): 193–210.

Fortis, P. 2015. 'Smoking Tobacco and Swinging the *Chicha*: On Different Modes of Sociality Among Guna ('Kuna') People,' in *The Master Plant: Tobacco in Lowland South America* (eds.) A. Russell and E. Rahman. London-New Delhi-New York-Sidney: Bloomsbury.

Frankland, S. 2001. 'Pygmic Tours,' in *African Study Monographs*, Supplement 26: 237–56.

Fundación TIERRA. 2007. *Los Nietos de la Reforma Agraria: Tierra y comunidad en el altiplano de Bolivia.* La Paz: Fundación TIERRA.

Garcilaso de la Vega. 1966. *Royal Commentaries of the Incas.* Austin: University of Texas Press.

Garduño, A. 2017. 'El dilema de la apropiación cultural,' in *Jóvenes Construyendo.* 27 June. Available at: https://blogjovenesconstruyendo.wordpress.com/2017/06/27/el -dilema-de-la-apropiacion-cultural/ [accessed 04 January 2021].

Geertz, C. 1973. *The Interpretation of Cultures.* New York: Basic Books, Inc.

Gell, A. 1986. 'Newcomers to the World of Goods: Consumption Among the Muria Gonds,' in *The Social Life of Things: Commodities in Cultural Perspective* (ed.) A. Appadurai. Cambridge: University Press.

Gianotten, V. 2006. *CIPCA y Poder Campesino Indígena: 35 años de historia.* La Paz: CIPCA.

Gordillo, G. 2006. 'The Crucible of Citizenship: ID-Paper Fetishism in the Argentin-ean Chaco,' in *American Ethnologist* 33(2): 162–76.

———. 2012. '"They Say We Aren't From Around Here": The Production of Culture Among a Displaced People,' in *Confronting Capital: Critique and Engagement in Anthropology* (eds.) P. Gardiner Barber, B. Leach and W. Lem. New York & London: Routledge.

Gose, P. 2008. *Invaders as Ancestors: On the Intercultural Making and Unmaking of Spanish Colonialism in the Andes.* Toronto–Buffalo–London: University of Toronto Press Inc.

Gotkowitz, L. 2007. *A Revolution for Our Rights: Indigenous Struggles for Land and Justice in Bolivia, 1880–1952.* Durham, NC & London: Duke University Press.

Gow, P. 1995. 'Land, People, and Paper in Western Amazonia,' in *The Anthropology of Landscape–Perspectives on Place and Space* (eds.) E. Hirsch and M. O'Hanlon. Oxford: Clarendon Press.

———. 2000. 'Helpless—The Affective Precondition of Piro Social Life,' in *The An-thropology of Love and Anger: The Aesthetics of Conviviality in Native Amazonia* (eds.) J. Overing and A. Passes. London & New York: Routledge.

———. 1991. *Of Mixed Blood: Kinship and History in Peruvian Amazonia.* Oxford: Clarendon Press.

Graeber, D. 2005. 'Fetishism as Social Creativity or, Fetishes Are Gods in the Process of Construction,' in *Anthropological Theory* 5(4): 407–38.

Gray, A. 1997. *Indigenous Rights and Development: Self-determination in an Ama-zonian Community.* New York & Oxford: Berghahn Books.

Green, M. 2003. 'Globalizing Development in Tanzania: Policy Franchising through Participatory Project Management,' in *Critique of Anthropology* 23(2): 123–43.

Greene, S. 2004. 'Indigenous People Incorporated? Culture as Politics, Culture as Prop-erty in Pharmaceutical Bioprospecting,' in *Current Anthropology* 45(2): 211–37.

Grindle, M. 2004. *Despite the Odds: The Contentious Politics of Education Reform.* Princeton & Oxford: Princeton University Press.

Groke, V. 2015. '*Dueños, Duendes, Bichos*: Non-Human Agents and the Politics of Place-Making in a Bolivian Guaraní Community,' in *Bulletin of Latin American Research*, 34: 184–196.

Guerrero, A. and T. Platt. 2000. 'Proyecto Antiguo, Nuevas Preguntas: La antropología histórica de las comunidades andinas cara al Nuevo siglo,' in *Estado-nación, Comunidad Indígena, Industria: Tres debates al final del milenio* (eds.) H. König, T. Platt and C. Lewis. Cuadernos de Historia Latinoamericana No 8. AHILA.

Gupta, A. and J. Ferguson. 1997. 'Discipline and Practice: "The Field" as Site, Method, and Location in Anthropology,' in *Anthropological Locations* (eds.) A. Gupta and J. Ferguson. Berkeley–Los Angeles–London: University of California Press.

Gustafson, B. 2009. *New Languages of the State: Indigenous Resurgence and the Politics of Knowledge in Bolivia*. Durham, NC & London: Duke University Press.

———. 2006. 'Spectacles of Autonomy and Crisis: Or, What Bulls and Beauty Queens Have to do with Regionalism in Eastern Bolivia,' in *Journal of Latin American Anthropology* 11(2): 351–79.

———. 2011. 'Power Necessarily Comes from Below: Guaraní Autonomies and Their Others,' in *Remapping Bolivia: Resources, Territory, and Indigeneity in a Plurinational State* (eds.) N. Fabricant and B. Gustafson. Santa Fe: School for Advanced Research Press.

———. 2010. 'When States Act Like Movements: Dismantling Local Power and Seating Sovereignty in Post Neoliberal Bolivia,' in *Latin American Perspectives* 173, 37(4): 48–66.

Gutiérrez, M. 1965. *Las lenguas de la familia tupí guaraní en Bolivia*. Cochabamba: Marcos Feliciano Gutiérrez.

Guzmán, G. 2012. *Camiri—Forjadores de Senderos. Una obra diferente escrita con el esfuerzo de sus habitantes*. Camiri: self-published.

Guzmán, I. (ed.) 2008. *Saneamiento de la Tierra en Seis Regiones de Bolivia, 1996–2007*. La Paz: CIPCA.

Harris, M. 2005. 'Riding a Wave: Embodied Skills and Colonial History on the Amazon Floodplain,' in *Ethnos* 70(2): 197–219.

Harris, O. 1995. 'The Sources and Meanings of Money: Beyond the Market Paradigm in an Ayllu of Northern Potosí,' in *Ethnicity, Markets, and Migration in the Andes: At the Crossroads of History and Anthropology* (eds.) B. Larson, O. Harris and E. Tandeter. Durham, NC & London: Duke University Press.

Harten, S. 2011. 'Towards a "Traditional Party"? Internal Organisation and Change in the MAS in Bolivia,' in *Evo Morales and the Movimiento al Socialismo in Bolivia: The First Term in Context, 2006–2010* (ed.) A. Pearce. London: Institute for the Study of the Americas.

Harvey, P. 1994. 'Domestic Violence in the Peruvian Andes,' in *Sex and Violence: Issues in Representation and Experience* (eds.) P. Harvey and P. Gow. London & New York: Routledge.

———. 1997. 'Peruvian Independence Day: Ritual, Memory, and the Erasure of Narrative,' in *Creating Context in Andean Cultures* (ed.) Rosaleen Howard-Malverde. New York & Oxford: Oxford University Press.

Healy, K. 1982. *Caciques y Patrones: Una experiencia de desarrollo rural en el sud de Bolivia*. Cochabamba: Ediciones El Buitre.

———. 1991. 'Political Ascent of Bolivia's Peasant Coca Leaf Producers,' in *Journal of Interamerican Studies and World Affairs* 33(1): 87–121.

Healy, K. and S. Paulson. 2000. 'Political Economies of Identity in Bolivia, 1952–1998,' in *The Journal of Latin American Anthropology* 5(2): 2–29

Heath, D. and M. Carballo. 1969. 'Bolivia's Law of Agrarian Reform,' in *Land Reform and Social Revolution in Bolivia* (eds.) D. Heath, C. Erasmus and H. Buechler. New York; Washington; London: Frederick A. Praeger Inc.

Henare, A., M. Holbraad and S. Wastell 2007. *Thinking through Things: Theorising Artefacts Ethnographically*. London & New York: Routledge.

Hennessy, A. 1978. *The Frontier in Latin American History*. London: Edward Arnold (Publishers) Ltd.

Hewlett, C. 2017. 'Community Capacity Building: Transforming Amerindian Sociality in Peruvian Amazonia,' in *The Cambridge Journal of Anthropology* 35(1): 114–30.

High, C. 2012. 'Between Knowing and Being: Ignorance in Anthropology and Amazonian Shamanism,' in *The Anthropology of Ignorance: An Ethnographic Approach* (eds.) C. High, A. Kelly and J. Mair. New York: Palgrave Macmillan.

———. 2006. 'Oil Development, Indigenous Organisations, and the Politics of Egalitarianism,' in *Cambridge Anthropology* 26(2): 34–46

Hirsch, S. 2003a. 'Bilingualism, Pan-Indianism and Politics in Northern Argentina: The Guaraní's Struggle for Identity and Recognition,' in *The Journal of Latin American Anthropology* 8(3): 84–103

———. 2003b. 'The Emergence of Political Organizations Among the Guaraní Indians of Bolivia and Argentina: A Comparative Perspective,' in *Contemporary Indigenous Movements in Latin America* (eds.) E. Langer and E. Muñoz. Wilmington: Scholarly Resources Inc.

Hobsbawm, E. and T. Ranger. 1983. *The Invention of Tradition*. Cambridge: University Press.

Holbraad, M., M. Pedersen and E. Viveiros de Castro 2014. 'The Politics of Ontology: Anthropological Positions,' in *Cultural Anthropology* (website). Available at: http://culanth.org/fieldsights/462-the-politics-of-ontology-anthropological-positions [accessed 18 May 2016].

Hoyos, M. and J. Blanes. 1998. *La Participación Social y Política en el Mondo Guaraní. Estudio de Caso: Los Pueblos de Izozo y de Iupaguasu. Documento Preliminar para la Discusión*. La Paz: CEBEM.

IEG. 2010. 'Ten Years of Social Fund Activities in Bolivia.' Available at World Bank: http://lnweb90.worldbank.org/oed/oeddoclib.nsf/DocUNIDViewForJavaSearch/5F548B94FB509F04852567F5005D8F5B?opendocument (accessed 23/08/2011).

ILO. 1989. *C169-Indigenous and Tribal Peoples Convention, 1989 (No. 169). Convention concerning Indigenous and Tribal Peoples in Independent Countries (Entry into force: 5 Sep 1991)*. Geneva: 76th ILC session. Available at: http://www.ilo.org/dyn/normlex/en/f?p=NORMLEXPUB:12100:0::NO::P12100_ILO_CODE:C169 (accessed 19/04/2016).

INE. 2015. *Censo de Población y Vivienda 2012 Bolivia: Características de la pobración*. La Paz: Instituto Nacional de Estadística. Available at: https://bolivia .unfpa.org/sites/default/files/pub-pdf/Caracteristicas_de_Poblacion_2012.pdf (accessed 28/01/2019).

INRA. 2002. 'Resolución de dotación y titulación de tierras comunitarias de origen nº TCO-DOT-TIT-008-2002.' La Paz 17 June.

Ingold, T. 1994. 'Introduction to Culture,' in *Companion Encyclopedia of Anthropology: Humanity, Culture and Social Life* (ed.) T. Ingold. London: Routledge.

Jackson, J. 1989. 'Is There a Way to Talk About Making Culture Without Making Enemies?' in *Dialectical Anthropology* 14: 127–43.

Julien, C. 2007. 'Kandire in Real Time and Space: Sixteenth-Century Expeditions from the Pantanal to the Andes,' in *Ethnohistory* 54(2): 245–72.

Karst, K. and K. Rosenn 1975. *Law and Development in Latin America: A Case Book*. Berkeley-Los Angeles-London: University of California Press.

Kidd, S. 2000. *Love and Hate among the People Without Things: The Social and Economic Relations of the Enxet People of Paraguay*. Unpublished PhD Thesis, University of St. Andrews.

———. 1997. 'The Working Conditions of Indigenous People in the Chaco,' in *Enslaved Peoples in the 1990s: Indigenous Peoples, Debt Bondage and Human Rights.* Copenhagen: Anti-Slavery International.

Killick, E. 2009. 'Ashéninka Amity: A Study of Social Relations in an Amazonian Society,' in *Journal of the Royal Anthropological Institute* 15(4): 701–18.

Klein, H. 1964. 'American Oil Companies in Latin America: The Bolivian Experience,' in *Inter-American Economic Affairs* 18(2): 47–72.

———. 1982. *Bolivia: The Evolution of a Multi-Ethnic Society.* Oxford: University Press.

———. 1993. *Haciendas and Ayllus: Rural Society in the Bolivian Andes in the Eighteenth and Nineteenth Centuries*. Stanford: University Press.

———. 2011. 'The Historical Background to the Rise of the MAS, 1952–2005,' in *Evo Morales and the Movimiento al Socialismo in Bolivia: The First Term in Context, 2006–2010* (ed.) A. Pearce. London: Institute for the Study of the Americas.

Kohl, B. 2003. 'Democratizing Decentralization in Bolivia: The Law of Popular Participation,' in *Journal of Planning Education and Research* 23:153–64.

———. 2002. 'Stabilizing Neoliberalism in Bolivia: Popular Participation and Privatization,' in *Political Geography* 21: 449—7–2.

Kohl, B. and L. Farthing 2012. 'Material Constraints to Popular Imaginaries: The Extractive Economy and Resource Nationalism in Bolivia,' in *Political Geography* 31(4): 225–35.

Kohl, J. 1978. 'Peasant and Revolution in Bolivia, April 9, 1952–August 2, 1953,' in *Hispanic American Historical Review* 58(2): 238–59.

Kroeber, A. L., and C. Kluckhohn 1952. *Culture: A Critical Review of Concepts and Definitions*. Papers of the Peabody Museum of Archaeology and Ethnology, Harvard University, 47(1).

LaBarre, W. 1938. 'Native American Beers,' in *American Anthropologist* 40: 224–37.

Langer, E. 2002. 'The Eastern Andean Frontier (Bolivia and Argentina) and Latin American Frontiers: Comparative Contexts (nineteenth and twentieth Centuries),' in *The Americas* 59(1): 33–63.

———. 1989. *Economic Change and Rural Resistance in Southern Bolivia, 1880–1930*. Stanford: University Press.

———. 2009. *Expecting Pears from an Elm Tree: Franciscan Missions on the Chiriguano Frontier in the Heart of South America, 1830–1949*. Durham, NC: Duke University Press.

Latton, M. 2016. 'Jedem Stamm seine Bräuche,' in *Jungle World*. 01 September. Available at: https://jungle.world/artikel/2016/35/jedem-stamm-seine-braeuche [accessed 04 January 2021].

Ledezma, J. 2007. 'Elementos y base territorial para la construcción de la propuesta de autonomía indígena,' in *Ñamometei Ñande Ñemongeta: Construcción del estatuto de la autonomía de la nación guaraní* (ed.) APG. Camiri: Ñeeñope Grupo Editorial Guaraní.

Lema, A. 2001. *De la Huella al Impacto: La Participación Popular en municipios con población indígena*. La Paz: Fundación PIEB.

Lévi-Strauss, C. 1966. *The Savage Mind*. The Nature of Human Society Series. London: Weidenfeld & Nicolson.

Li, T. 2007. *The Will to Improve: Governmentality, Development, and the Practice of Politics*. Durham, NC: Duke University Press.

Lowrey, K. 2003. *Enchanted Ecology: Magic, Science, and Nature in the Bolivian Chaco*. Unpublished PhD thesis, Department of Anthropology, University of Chicago.

———. 2007. 'Estrategias Socioeconómicas de los Guaraníes del Chaco Boliviano Comparadas con las de los Guaraníes Occidentales del Chaco Paraguayo.' Unpublished paper presented at the XXVII Encuentro de Geohistoria Regional, Asunción, Paraguay, 16, 17, and 18 August.

———. 2008. 'Incommensurability and New Economic Strategies among Indigenous and Traditional Peoples,' in *Journal of Political Ecology* 15: 61–74.

Lucero, J. 2006. 'Representing "Real Indians": The Challenges of Indigenous Authenticity and Strategic Constructivism in Ecuador and Bolivia,' in *Latin American Research Review* 41(2): 31–56.

———. 2008. *Struggles of Voice: The Politics of Political Representation in the Andes*. Pittsburgh: University of Pittsburgh Press.

Lusthaus, C., M.-H. Adrien, and M. Perstinger. 1999. 'Capacity Development: Definitions, Issues and Implications for Planning, Monitoring and Evaluation.' Universalia Occasional Paper No. 35.

MacCormack, S. 1999. 'Ethnography in South America: The First Two Hundred Years,' in *The Cambridge History of the Native Peoples of the Americas, vol. III: South America*, Part 2 (eds.) F. Salomon and S. Schwartz. Cambridge: University Press.

Mallon, F. 1992. 'Indian Communities, Political Cultures, and the State in Latin America, 1780–1990,' in *Journal of Latin American Studies* 24, Quincentenary Supplement: The Colonial and Post-Colonial Experience. Five Centuries of Spanish and Portuguese America: 35–53.

Maloney, C. (ed.) 1976. *The Evil Eye*. New York: Columbia University Press.

MASRENA. 2001. 'Plan de Ordenamiento Comunidad Cañón de Segura, Municipio de Camiri.' Camiri: Prefectura del Departamento de Santa Cruz / Cooperación Técnica Alemana (IP/GTZ).

Maybury-Lewis, D. 1999. 'Lowland Peoples of the Twentieth Century,' in *The Cambridge History of the Native Peoples of the Americas, vol. III: South America*, Part 2 (eds.) F. Salomon and S. Schwartz. Cambridge: University Press.

McNeill, W. 1986. 'Mythistory, or Truth, Myth, History, and Historians,' in *The American Historical Review* 91(1): 1–10.

Medina, J. (ed.) 2002. *Ñande Reko: La comprensión guaraní de la vida Buena*. La Paz: FAM-Bolivia/PADEP.

Melià, B. 1988. *Ñande reko, nuestro modo de ser y bibliografía general comentada*. La Paz: CIPCA.

———. 1996. 'Potirõ: Las formas del trabajo entre los Guaraní antiguos "reducidos" y modernos,' in *Revista Complutense de Historia de América*, 22. Madrid: Servicio de Publicaciones UCM.

Mercado Chávez, O. 2011. *Genocidio Camba Cruceño: Genocidio contra la nación cautiva camba cruceña*. Santa Cruz de la Sierra 450 años de fundación. Available at: http://www.orlandomercadoch.com/Genocidio%20Camba%20Cruceno.pdf.

Métraux, A. 1930. 'Etudes Sur la Civilisation des Indiens Chiriguano,' in *Revista del Instituto de Etnología de la Universidad Nacional de Tucumán* I: 295–493.

Mog, J. 2004. 'Struggling with Sustainability—A Comparative Framework for Evaluating Sustainable Development Programs,' in *World Development* 32(12): 2139–60.

Montenegro, F. 2007. 'Elementos conceptuales y antecedentes históricos organizativos para el debate sobre autonomía guaraní, in *Ñamometei Ñande Ñemongeta: Construcción del estatuto de la autonomía de la nación guaraní* (ed.) APG. Camiri: Ñeeñope Grupo Editorial Guaraní.

Mosse, D. 2005. *Cultivating Development: An Ethnography of Aid Policy and Practice*. London & Ann Arbour: Pluto Press.

———. 2003. 'The Making and Marketing of Participatory Development,' in *A Moral Critique of Development: In Search of Global Responsibilities* (eds.) P. van Ufford and A. Kumar Giri. London & New York: Routledge.

Müller, U. (ed.) 1999. *Planificando el Uso de la Tierra: Catálogo de herramientas y experiencias*. Eschborn: Deutsche Gesellschaft für Technische Zusammenarbeit (GTZ) GmbH. Available at: http://www.mpl.ird.fr/crea/taller-colombia/FAO/AGLL/pdfdocs/catalogo.pdf (accessed 17 March 2016).

Nijenhuis, G. 2002. *Decentralisation and Popular Participation in Bolivia: The Link Between Local Governance and Local Development*. Utrecht: Koninklijk Nederlands Aardrijkskundig Genootschap / Faculteit Ruimtelijke Wetenschappen Universiteit Utrecht.

Nordenskiöld, E. 1917. 'The Guaraní Invasion of the Inca Empire in the Sixteenth Century: An Historical Indian Migration,' in *Geographical Review* 4(2): 103–21.

Oliveto, G. 2010. 'Chiriguanos: La construcción de un estereotipo en la política colonizadora del sur andino,' in *Memoria Americana* 18(1): 43–69.

Ortiz, I. 2009. 'Forced Labor and Servitude of Guarani Men and Women.' United Nations Permanent Forum on Indigenous Issues. Available at SSRN: http://ssrn.com/abstract=1814261.

Ortiz García, E. 2002. *Mbarea–Invitación*. Cuadernos de Investigación de la Cultura Guaraní no. 1. Camiri: APG/Teko-Guaraní.

———. 2004. *Toponimia Guaraní del Chaco y Cordillera–Ensayo lingüístico, etnográfico y antropológico*. Camiri: Teko-Guaraní.

Ortner, S. 1995. 'Resistance and the Problem of Ethnographic Refusal,' in *Comparative Studies in Society and History* 37(1): 173–93.

Overing, J. 2008. 'The Backlash to Decolonizing Intellectuality,' in *Anthropology and Humanism* 31(1): 11–40.

Overing, J. and A. Passes (eds.). 2000. *The Anthropology of Love and Anger: The Aesthetics of Conviviality in Native Amazonia*. London: Routledge.

PADEP-GTZ. 2010. *Experiencias Destacadas para el Proceso de Cambio. Programa del apoyo a la gestíon pública descentralizada y lucha contra la pobreza de la Cooperación Técnica Alemana PADEP-GTZ 2002–2010*. La Paz.

Padwe, J. 2001. '"Development with Identity": The "Spatial Needs Identification Study" And Indigenous Land Titling in Bolivia.' Paper submitted to the workshop 'Conservation and Sustainable Development: Comparative Perspectives,' Yale Centre for Comparative Research, 30–1 August.

Pagden, A. 1982. *The Fall of Natural Man: The American Indian and the Origins of Comparative Ethnology*. Cambridge: Iberian and Latin American Studies.

Palenque, E. 1991. 'Solicitada,' in *El Deber*. 6 August.

Pärssinen, M. 1992. *Tawantinsuyu: The Inca State and Its Political Organization*. Helsinki: Suomen Historiallinen Seura.

———. 2003. 'When Did the Guaraní Expansion Towards the Andean Foothills Begin?,' in Pärssinen, M. and A. Korpisaari (eds.). *Western Amazonia—Amazônia Ocidental: Multidisciplinary Studies on Ancient Expansionistic Movements, Fortifications and Sedentary Life*. Helsinki: Renvall Institute for Area and Cultural Studies.

Pärssinen, M., A. Siiriäinen, and A. Korpisaari. 2003. 'Fortifications Related to the Inca Expansion,' in Pärssinen, M. and A. Korpisaari (eds.). *Western Amazonia–Amazônia Ocidental: Multidisciplinary Studies on Ancient Expansionistic Movements, Fortifications and Sedentary Life*. Helsinki: Renvall Institute for Area and Cultural Studies.

Peña, A. 1999. *La fundación de Camiri* (2nd ed.). Santa Cruz: El País.

Perreault, T. and G. Valdivia. 2010. 'Hydrocarbons, Popular Protest and National Imaginaries: Ecuador and Bolivia in Comparative Context,' in *Geoforum* 41: 689–99.

Pierre, B. 1997. 'Classification of Property and Conceptions of Ownership in Civil and Common Law,' in *Revue générale de droit*, 28(2): 235–74.

Pifarré, F. 1992. 'Guaranís: El derecho a ser pueblo,' in *Cuarto Intermedio* 23: 3–19.

———. 1989. *Historia de un Pueblo*. La Paz: CIPCA.

Plan Desarrollo Rural Cordillera. 1986a. *Diagnóstico-Estrategia*, vol. 1. Santa Cruz: CORDECRUZ / CIPCA.

Plan Desarrollo Rural Cordillera. 1986b. *Diagnóstico-Estrategia*, vol. 2. Santa Cruz: CORDECRUZ / CIPCA.

Plata, W. 2008. 'El Discurso Autonomista de las Élites de Santa Cruz,' in *Los Barones del Oriente: El poder en Santa Cruz ayer y hoy* (ed.) X. Soruco. Santa Cruz: Fundación TIERRA.

Platt, T. 2014a. 'Un archivo campesino como "acontecimiento de terreno,"' in *Fuentes.* Revista de la Biblioteca y Archivo Histórico de la Asamblea Legislativa Plurinacional 33: 6–18.

———. 1982. *Estado Boliviano y Ayllu Andino: Tierra y tributo en el norte de Potosí.* Lima: Instituto de Estudios Peruanos.

———. 1999. 'Imagined Frontiers: Recent Advances in the Ethnography of the Southern Andes (Review Essay),' in *Bulletin of Latin American Research* 18(1): 101–10.

———. 2014b. 'Seísmos de la mente: un duelo chamánico en el Sucre de finales del siglo XX (Bolivia),' in *Au miroir de l'anthropologie historique: Mélanges offerts à Nathan Wachtel* (eds.) J. Garavaglia, J. Poloni-Simard, and G. Rivière. Rennes: Presses Universitaires de Rennes.

———. 1992. 'Writing, Shamanism and Latin American Identity; or Voices From Abya-Yala,' in *History Workshop* 34: 132–47.

Platt, T., T. Bouysse-Cassagne, and O. Harris 2006. *Qaraqara-Charka: Mallku, Inka y Rey en la provincia de Charcas (siglos XV-XVII). Historia antropológica de una confederación aymara.* La Paz: Instituto Francés de Estudios Andinos / Plural Editores / University of St. Andrews / University of London / Inter American Foundation / Fundación Cultural del Banco Central de Bolivia.

Postero, N. 2000. 'Bolivia's *Indígena* Citizen: Multiculturalism in a Neoliberal Age.' Paper prepared for the Latin American Studies Association Meetings, Session: *Indigenismo/Mestizaje: New Views on Key Concepts,* 16 March.

———. 2017. *The Indigenous State: Race, Politics, and Performance in Plurinational Bolivia.* Oakland: University of California Press.

———. 2007. *Now We Are Citizens: Indigenous Politics in Postmulticultural Bolivia.* Stanford: University Press.

Presencia 1991. 'Guaraníes de provincia Cordillera denuncian diversos abusos.' 27 July. La Paz.

Ramos, A. 1994. 'The Hyperreal Indian,' in *Critique of Anthropology* 14(2): 153-71.

Rappaport, J. 1990. *The Politics of Memory: Historical Representation in the Colombian Andes.* Cambridge–New York–Melbourne: Cambridge University Press.

Read, J. 2002. *The Rough Guide to Bolivia.* London & New York: Rough Guides Ltd.

Reed, R. 1995. 'Household Ethnicity, Household Consumption: Commodities and the Guarani,' in *Economic Development and Cultural Change* 44, 1: 129–45.

Renard-Cassevitz, F., T. Saignes, and A. Taylor-Descola. 1986. *L'Inca, l'Espagnol et les Sauvages-Rapport Entre les Sociétés Amazoniennes et Andine du XVe au XVIIe Siécle.* Paris: Editions Recherches sur les Civilisations.

'Resolución de Autonomía de los Pueblos Indígenas de Santa Cruz.' 31 March 2008. Santa Cruz. Available at ANMCLA: http://www.medioscomunitarios.org/bolivia/pag/index. php?id=33&idn=6246.

'Resolución de Rechazo a los Estatutos Autonómicos de los Pueblos Indígenas de Santa Cruz.' 31 March 2008. Santa Cruz. Available at ANMCLA: http://www.medioscomunitarios.org/bolivia/pag/index.php?id=33&idn=6246.

Riester, J. 1984. *Textos Sagrados de los Guaraníes en Bolivia: Una cacería en el Izozog*. Santa Cruz de la Sierra: APCOB.

Rivera, J. 2005. 'Los pueblos indígenas y las comunidades campesinas en el sistema constitucional boliviano. Pasado, presente y perspectivas al future,' in *Anuario de Derecho Constitucional Latinoamericano* 11(I): 195–213.

Rivera Cusicanqui, S. 1987. *Oppressed But Not Defeated: Peasant Struggles Among the Aymara and Qhechwa in Bolivia, 1900–1980*. Geneva: United Nations Research Institute for Social Development.

Roca, J. 2008. 'Regionalism Revisited,' in *Unresolved Tensions: Bolivia Past and Present* (eds.) J. Crabtree and L. Whitehead. Pittsburgh: University of Pittsburgh Press.

Roduner, D. 2003. "Valoración Fiscal de la Contribución de Mano de Obra y Materiales Locales en Inversión y Mantenimiento de Obras Públicas Municipales," in *Documento de Trabajo: Casi-Impuestos Comunales: Una fuente de financiamiento subestimada*. Parte A: Estudios de Caso-Uncía, Caripuyo, Villamontes, Lagunillas y Macharetí. La Paz: Padep/GTZ.

Rondinelli, D. 1983. 'Projects as Instruments of Development Administration: A Qualified Defence and Suggestions for Improvement,' in *Public Administration and Development* 3: 307–27.

Roper, J. 2003. 'Bolivian Legal Reforms and Local Indigenous Organizations: Opportunities and Obstacles in a Lowland Municipality,' in *Latin American Perspectives* 30(1): 139–61.

Rubenstein, S. 2007. 'Circulation, Accumulation, and the Power of Shuar Shrunken Heads,' in *Cultural Anthropology* 22 (3): 357–399.

Sahlins, M. 1985. *Islands of History*. Chicago: University of Chicago Press.

Saignes, T. 1990. *Ava y Karai: ensayos sobre la frontera chiriguano, siglos XVI–XX*. La Paz: Hisbol.

———. 1982. 'Guerres indiennes dans L'Amérique pionnière: le dilemme de la résistance chiriguano à la colonisation européenne. (XVIe-XIXe siècles),' in *Histoire, Economie, Société* I: 77–103.

Salles, E. and H. Noejovich 2008. 'Las Lecciones de la Historia: Repensando la política económica del Virrey Toledo,' in *Economía* 31, 61: 27–50.

Sanabria, H. 1972. *Apiaguaiqui-Tumpa. Biografía del pueblo chiriguano y de su último caudillo*. La Paz & Cochabamba: Los Amigos del Libro.

———. 1999. 'Consolidating States, Restructuring Economies, and Confronting Workers and Peasants: The Antinomies of Bolivian Neoliberalism,' in *Comparative Studies in Society and History* 41, 3: 535–62.

Sánchez, W. 1998. 'La Plaza Tomada: Proceso histórico y etnogénesis musical entre los Chiriguano de Bolivia,' in *Latin American Music Review* 19, 2: 218–43.

Sarmiento Barletti, J. 2011. *Kametsa Asaiki: The Pursuit of the 'Good Life' in an Ashaninka Village (Peruvian Amazonia)*. Unpublished PhD Thesis, University of St. Andrews.

Saunders, N. (ed.) 1998. *Icons of Power: Feline Symbolism in the Americas*. London & New York: Routledge.

Schwartz, S. and F. Salomon. 1999. 'New Peoples and New Kinds of People: Adaptation, Readjustment, and Ethnogenesis in South American Indigenous Societies

(Colonial Era),' in *The Cambridge History of the Native Peoples of the Americas, vol. III: South America*, Part 2 (eds.) F. Salomon and S. Schwartz. Cambridge: University Press.

Siiriäinen, A. and M. Pärssinen. 1997. 'Eighty Years After Erland Nordenskiöld: The Question of the Eastern Frontier of the Inca Empire,' in *Revista Xaman* 4/97 (The web based newsletter of the Iberoamerican Centre of the University of Helsinki, http://www.helsinki.fi/hum/ibero/).

Smits, K. 2014. 'The Neoliberal State and the Uses of Indigenous Culture,' in *Nationalism and Ethnic Politics* 20(1): 43–62.

Soruco Sologuren, X. 2011. 'El Porvenir, the Future That Is No Longer Possible: Conquest and Autonomy in the Bolivian Oriente,' in *Remapping Bolivia: Resources, Territory, and Indigeneity in a Plurinational State* (eds.) N. Fabricant and B. Gustafson. Santa Fe: School for Advanced Research Press.

Spalding, K. 1975. 'Hacienda-Village Relations in Andean Society to 1830,' in *Latin American Perspectives* 2, 1: 'Confronting Theory and Practice': 107–21.

Stocking, G. 1968. *Race, Culture and Evolution: Essays in the History of Anthropology*. New York: The Free Press.

Strathern, M. 1988. *The Gender of the Gift*. Berkeley–Los Angeles–London: University of California Press.

Taussig, M. 1987. *Shamanism, Colonialism and the Wild Man: A Study in Terror and Healing*. Chicago: University Press.

Taylor, A.-C. 2007. 'Sick of History: Contrasting Regimes of Historicity in the Upper Amazon,' in *Time and Memory in Indigenous Amazonia* (eds.) C. Fausto and M. Heckenberger. Gainesville: University Press of Florida.

Theodossopoulos, D. 2010. 'Tourists and Indigenous Culture as Resources: Lessons from Embera Cultural Tourism in Panama,' in *Tourism, Power and Culture: Anthropological Insights* (eds.) D. Macleod and J. Carrier. Bristol-Buffalo-Toronto: Channel View Publications.

Tilley, C., W. Keane, S. Kuechler, M. Rowlands and P. Spyer (eds.) 2006. *Handbook of Material Culture*. London-Thousand Oaks-New Delhi: Sage Publications.

Tockman, J. and J. Cameron 2014. 'Indigenous Autonomy and the Contradictions of Plurinationalism in Bolivia,' in *Latin American Politics and Society* 56 (3): 46–69.

Todd, Z. 2016. 'An Indigenous Feminist's Take On The Ontological Turn: "Ontology" Is Just Another Word For Colonialism,' in *Journal of Historical Sociology* 29(1): 4–22.

Toranzo Roca, C. 2008. 'Let the Mestizos Stand Up and Be Counted,' in *Unresolved Tensions: Bolivia Past and Present* (eds.) J. Crabtree and L. Whitehead. Pittsburgh: University of Pittsburgh Press.

Turner, T. 1991. 'Representing, Resisting, Rethinking: Historical Transformations of Kayapo Culture and Anthropological Consciousness,' in *Colonial Situations: Essays on the Contextualization of Ethnographic Knowledge* (ed.) G. Stocking. *History of Anthropology*, vol. 7. Madison & London: University of Wisconsin Press.

Tylor, E.B. 1871. *Primitive Culture: Research into the Development of Mythology, Philosophy, Religion, Art, and Custom*, vol I. London: John Murray.

Urioste, M. 2003. 'International Land Coalition–News–The Abandoned Agrarian Reform: Valleys and High Plains.' 3 August. Available at Fundación TIERRA: www.landcoalition.or/ne_Aug03_abagriform.htm.

Uvin, P. 1998. *Aiding Violence: The Development Enterprise in Rwanda*. West Hartford: Kumarian Press.

Valle Mandepora, R. 13 March 2008. 'Proceso de Saneamiento TCO Alto Parapetí.' Available at CIPCA: http://www.cipca.org.bo/index.php?option=com_content&view= article&id=1367:zdpa&catid=85:zdpa&Itemid=124 (accessed 2 March 2016).

Varese, S. 1996. 'The Ethnopolitics of Indian Resistance in Latin America,' in *Latin American Perspectives* 89, 23(2): 58–71.

Vargas, N. 2015. 'Guaraníes dejan la CIDOB y exigen su inclusión en el fondo,' in *Página Siete,* 31 August. Available at: https://www.paginasiete.bo/nacional/2015/8/31/guaranies-dejan-cidob-exigen-inclusion-fondo-68451.html (accessed 4 September 2019).

Viceministerio de Tierras. 2008a. 'Ganaderos de la "Media Luna" Crean un Comité de la Defensa de las Haciendas del Chaco Integrado.' Bulletin no. 45. La Paz. 20 May.

———. 2008b. 'Guaraníes Cautivos: No tiene valor legal la investigación de diputados opositores en haciendas del chaco cruceño.' Bulletin no. 37. La Paz. 28 April.

Wachtel, N. 1977. *The Vision of the Vanquished: The Spanish Conquest of Peru through Indian Eyes, 1530–70*. London: The Harvester Press Limited.

Walker, H. 2009. 'Baby Hammocks and Stone Bowls: Urarina Technologies of Companionship and Subjection,' in *The Occult Life of Things: Native Amazonian Theories of Materiality and Personhood* (ed.) F. Santos Granero. Tucson: University of Arizona Press.

Warburton, D. 2009. *Community and Sustainable Development: Participation in the Future*. London: Earthscan.

Webber, J. 2008a. 'Rebellion to Reform in Bolivia. Part II: Revolutionary Epoch, Combined Liberation and the December 2005 Elections,' in *Historical Materialism* 16, 3: 55—7–6.

———. 2008b. 'Rebellion to Reform in Bolivia. Part III: Neoliberal Continuities, the Autonomist Right, and the Political Economy of Indigenous Struggle,' in *Historical Materialism* 16, 4: 67–109.

Weber, M. 2004. 'Politics as a Vocation,' in *The Vocation Lectures* (eds.) D. Owen and T. Strong. Indianapolis & London: Hackett Publishing Company.

Weismantel, M. 1991. 'Maize Beer and Andean Social Transformations: Drunken Indians, Bread Babies, and Chosen Women,' in *MLN* 106(4): 861–79.

Zavaleta Reyles, D. 2008. 'Oversimplifying Identities: The Debate over What Is *Indígena* and What Is Mestizo,' in *Unresolved Tensions: Bolivia Past and Present* (eds.) J. Crabtree and L. Whitehead. Pittsburgh: University of Pittsburgh Press.

Ziff, B. and P. Rao (eds.) 1997. *Borrowed Power: Essays on Cultural Appropriation*. New Brunswick: Rutgers University Press.

Documents from the archive at IDAC (Camiri, Bolivia):

APG 1991. 'Acta N°.' 20 July.

Avilés, G. 1994. 'Dr. Guido Avilés Cueto: Asesor Juridico Agrario de la Presidencia de la República.' 18 March. La Paz.

Bruno, P. and family. 1991. 'Señor Leonidas Chilo y Señora Vilma Guzman.' 10 November. Itacua.

Centellas, E. 1992. 'Al Señor Juez Agrario Móvil del Departamento.' 11 May. Camiri.

Chilo, L. 1992. 'Declaración Informativa Prestada por Leonidas Chilo Bonilla.' 12 June. Camiri.

Claure, V. 1992. 'Testimonio.' 25 March. Camiri.

Córdova, J. 1994. Señor Dr. Roderich Von Owen.' 10 June. Camiri.

Cuéllar, E., A. Vaca, and A. Antenor. 1994. 'Señor: Rodrigo Von Owen.' 10 June. Camiri.

Gómez, P. 1997. 'Registro de la Propiedad Inmueble Rural.' 13 August.

Guzman, V. 1992. 'Declaración Informativa Prestada por Wilma Guzman García de Chilo'. 11 June. Camiri.

Justiniano, H. 1992. 'Camiri, 17 de Noviembre de 1.992.' 17 November. Camiri.

Justiniano, M. and V. Torrez 1992. 'Informe en Conclusiones de Diligencias de Policía Judicial'. 23 July. Camiri.

Martinez, S. 1994. 'Ref: Informe de Inspección Ocular por Parte de Intervención Concejo Nacional de Reforma Agraria y el Departamento Recursos Naturales CORDECRUZ Consorcio IP/CES/KWC.' 2 July. Camiri.

Medrano, L. 1994. 'Recibo.' 28 April. Camiri.

Medrano, L., and A. Verazain. 1994. 'A la Opinión Pública de la Provincia de Cordillera.' 9 May. Camiri.

Michel, F. 1992. 'Itakua: Investigación histórica jurídica.' 22 September. Camiri.

———. 1994a. 'Ref.: Su conocimiento.' 23 May. Camiri.

———. 1994b. 'Señores Delmar Artunduaga, Armando del Río.' 6 June. Camiri.

———. 1994c. 'Señores Armando del Río, Arturo Pinto.' 10 June. Camiri.

———. 1994d. 'Señor Dr. Rodrigo Von Owen.' 11 June. Camiri.

———. 1994e. 'Señores Comité Ejecutivo A.P.G.'. 8 November. Camiri

———. 1994f. 'Señor Delgar Artunduaga, Armando del Río.' 8 November. Camiri.

Michel, F. and Comunarios 1992. 'Señor Juez de Partido: Amparo Constitucional.' 9 November. Camiri.

Michel, F., I. Nassini, and H. Leyton. 1991. 'Señora Fiscal de Partido'. 17 February. Camiri.

Montalvo, A. 1992. 'Sentencia.' 15 May. Camiri.

Montero, J. 1991a. 'Comisión Instruida.' 8 August. Santa Cruz.

———. 1991b. 'Dr. Franz Michel.' 13 August. Santa Cruz.

Montero, R. 1899. 'En Lagunillas . . .' 12 August. Lagunillas.

Nasini, I. 1991a. 'Estimada Señora.' 6 May. Camiri.

———. 1991b. 'Ref.: Testimonio de los Comunarios de Itacua y del Párroco de la zona acerca del conflict con la señora Olga Vannucci y el señor Eloy Palenque.' 17 June. Camiri.

Palenque, E. 1992. 'Solicitada: A la Opinión Pública.' 8 June. Camiri.

Palenque, S. 1992. 'Demanda dotación de tierras fiscales.' 7 April. Camiri.

Paredes and Bruno. 1991. 'En la ciudad de Camiri . . .' 3 October. Camiri.

Paredes and F. Gómez. 1991. 'En la ciudad de Camiri . . .' 3 October. Camiri.

Paredes and M. Gómez. 1991. 'En la ciudad de Camiri . . .' 3 October. Camiri.

Paredes, M. Romero, and A. Romero. 1991. 'En la ciudad de Camiri . . .' 3 October. Camiri.

Paredes and Segundo. 1991. 'En la ciudad de Camiri . . .' 3 October. Camiri.

Peñaranda, M. 1991. 'Señor Jefe de la Guardia Provincial.' 15 June. Camiri

Pinto, A. and A. Del Río. 1994. 'Señor Franz Michel Torrico.' 7 June. Camiri.

Plata, S. 1992. 'Declaración Informativa Prestada por Silvia Plata de Guerra.' 18 July. Camiri.

Pozo Vedia, A. 1991. 'Ref: Abstención de amenazas y libre transitabilidad.' 20 May. Camiri.

Rengel, C. 1997. 'Señor Director Departamental del Instituto Nacional de Reforma [Agraria].' 13 May. Santa Cruz.

Rioja, E. 1992. 'Señor: Sadoc Palenque'. 18 February. Camiri.

Romero, M., V. Demetrio, and J. Altamirano et al. 1994. 'Convenio Transaccional entre las Comunidades Itakua-Cañón de Segura y Urundaiti'. 12 March. Camiri.

Rueda, T. 1992. 'Declaración Informativa Prestada por Telesforo Rueda Alpiri.' 27 June. Camiri.

Suárez, A. 1994. 'Orden Instruida.' 14 May. Camiri.

Vannucci, C., and O. Vannucci 1992. 'Señor Jefe de la Policía Provincial.' 8 June. Camiri.

Vannucci, O. 1991. 'Ref.: Respuesta Avuestra de Fecha 6/05/91.' 31 July. Itacua.

Vannucci, O., C. Vannucci, and E. Palenque. 1992. 'Desmentido Público.' 23 September. Camiri.

Vannucci, O., C. Vannucci, and A. Vannucci. 1991. 'Señor: R.P. Ivan, Parroco del Servicio Religioso en el Campo, Presente.' 24 April. Camiri.

Von Oven, R. and A. Zarzycki. 1994. 'Señores Asamblea del Pueblo Guarani–APG.' 17 June. Santa Cruz.

Index

About the Author

Veronika Groke is an anthropologist and writer based in London. She holds a PhD degree from the University of St. Andrews, Scotland.

www.ingramcontent.com/pod-product-compliance
Lightning Source LLC
Chambersburg PA
CBHW050635280326
41932CB00015B/2650